SOMEONE ELSE'S
COUN[TRY]

*We meet our new neighbour. She takes us into her house.
There is a security-screen door.*

Gotta lock up. There's Nyungars around.

Really?

*We step through the front door and right in front of
us, on a stained occasional table, is a framed photo of an
Old Nyungar Fulla. I suddenly feel like I'm in the
middle of a Monty Python script.*

Oh, who's this? An uncle of yours?

The woman looks mortified.

No. We bought it in a shop.

They're probly looking for their uncle's photo.

Who?

The Nyungars.

What Nyungars?

The Nyungars who are around.

*The woman gives me a look. Doesn't know how to
respond. So she pretends it didn't happen. This is what
us wadjulas do. What we're really good at. Pretend I
didn't speak. Pretend nothing happened. None of it.*

Peter Docker was born in Wiilman Country at Narrogin, Western Australia, and is of Irish, Cornish and English heritage. He grew up on a station in Wudjari Country at Coomalbidgup, near Esperance. He has worked as a dairy-hand, hay-carter, wheat-bogger, window-washer, bank teller, lift driver, barman, been an infantry officer in the army reserve, sung in a rock band, and has been a professional actor for fifteen years.

He lives with his family in Walyalup (Fremantle), the place where his great-great-grandfather was transported in chains a hundred and fifty years ago.

He has had short stories published in Australian literary journals and has written for stage and radio. *Someone Else's Country* is his first book.

SOMEONE ELSE'S
COUNTRY

PETER DOCKER

Fremantle Arts Centre Press

Australia's finest small publisher

First published 2005 by
FREMANTLE ARTS CENTRE PRESS
25 Quarry Street, Fremantle
(PO Box 158, North Fremantle 6159)
Western Australia.
www.facp.iinet.net.au

Consultant Editors Ray Coffey and Lesley Zampatti
Production Vanessa Bradley
Cover Designer Marion Duke
Cover photographs courtesy Frances Andrijich and Marion Duke

Typeset by Fremantle Arts Centre Press
and printed by Griffin Press.

National Library of Australia
Cataloguing-in-publication data

Docker, Peter, 1964– .
Someone else's country.

ISBN 1 920731 57 1.

1. Docker, Peter, 1964– . 2. Aboriginal Australians —
Biography. 3. Aboriginal Australians — Social conditions.
4. Actors — Australia — Biography. I. Title.

305.89915092

Publication of this title was assisted by the Commonwealth Government
through the Australia Council, its arts funding and advisory body.

Without love, support,
encouragement and patience
from Jane, Cleo and Jack
this book could never
have been completed.

This is a work of non-fiction. Whilst the individual people appearing in this story are real, identities have been fictionalised to protect their privacy, and that of innocent bystanders. Except where obvious, the author has only retold those aspects of the story which belong to him.

Singing Country

Sitting on the balcony of a fourth-storey apartment in Toorak Road, Melbourne. Wurundjeri Country, south of Woiwurung Country, just north-west of Boonwurrung Country. To be honest, I'm not sure how I got here.

Uncle James the Cowboy is talking to me. Sometimes he hits his clap-sticks together to emphasise a point. Hits his sticks in time with his heartbeat. Speaking to me in English to begin with. The hair on my arms and the back of my neck stands up when I realise he's slipped from English to Kriol, and now to Language. And I'm still sitting with my head down, eyes lowered, nodding my understanding.

Aawu. Aawu (Yes).

I get a cold feeling in the pit of my stomach when I realise that his lips are no longer moving and his voice is still in my head. Deep in my head.

I look to Ned. He smiles knowingly. Looks away.

I don't look into Uncle's eyes. Partly out of respect. Partly common sense. Partly fear.

They've been sitting on the balcony for a long time now — Uncle and Ned — talking, singing, clap-sticks going.

The voice in my head has stopped.

Uncle needs a cigarette. As I go inside to get it Uncle starts up a new song.

You know what he's doing? the Rat says.

I shake my head.

He's singing his Country.

He's what?

I'm not sure if I speak this question or just think it.

He's singing his Country closer.

I look at the Rat as though I suddenly don't understand English. I look out of the window to see the city crowding in. The lights, the noises, seem to blur for a moment. Like they're not really there. An illusion. Where are we really? We're in a land where an old Arrernte man can sing his Country. Can make his beloved desert move closer to him by singing. Time doesn't exist. Distance doesn't exist. Songs exist. Uncle starts up high and spirals down vocally. Repeating his sacred Dreaming word over and over. It buzzes like a bullroarer in his head. The building vibrates with the song. The very air around us hums and crackles.

But Uncle had disrespected Mum earlier on in the evening. Or it seemed that way, anyway. I didn't witness the incident. Uncle had asked Mum to sit on his knee, or something like that. So there is tension. Tension all around. Even for me. My first thought is, disrespect Mum and there's gunna be real trouble, no matter who the fuck you are!

But I wait for a sign from Mum. She can take care of herself. This is a Gunditjmara matriarch from a matrilineal coastal people. Fierce warrior people who bore the brunt of the Invasion. Never stopped fighting. Never will. A woman who can stand back-to-back with her son in a country pub, smacking rednecks down. A woman who can take on multi-billion-dollar mining companies and send them packing with their tails between their legs.

Tension. Especially for the Rat. This is his place. Ned and Uncle James are Countrymen. Ned is Pitjantjatjara. The Rat is Arrernte. All desert men. Ned and Uncle James are Lawmen and the Rat hasn't been through Law.

He's had Ned at his place for a week or so now. Feeding him. Nyandi. Beer.

The Rat is stuck in the middle. Caught between the two worlds.

The Lawmen call him to the balcony and shut the glass door behind him. They drill him. His head is down. He goes to look up. Uncle hits him on the top of the head. A swift sharp blow. The Rat looks down. Has to. This is Old Way. Desert way. Not a Man yet. In Uncle's eyes.

Mum isn't happy about this. She knows the Rat has come up from the dirty streets of a red-dust desert town, Nbandwe (Alice Springs). He supports his brothers and sister and mother with his wages. Always has. Never had a childhood. Had to be the man for his family. The Rat is a warrior who has stood up his whole life — fighting The War of attitude, sometimes the fist war, for his mob. The Rat is a real man.

So the Rat tried to calm Mum down.

Mum is not my blood mum. She is Spirit Mum. Skin Mum. She's Henry's mum and Henry is my djaambi (brother). So my mum too. Has played my mum in a movie. In real life. I am honoured to call her Mum. Once, I mistakenly called her Auntie, but she quickly corrected me.

She's been there when I've needed her.

Ned is dancing now. Uncle James is playing slow sticks and singing. I see the firelight jumping and flickering in Ned's eyes. My mind tells me there is no fire. I've learnt not to rely on my mind. The mind can lie. I can't tear my eyes away from Ned.

Then Mum is telling Ned I am a good one. They share this look of deep openness.

When Ned speaks his voice is light but strong like his touch.

I look into his eyes — I see him. Not his skin, err … colour.

Mum listens. Patiently waiting in case Ned has something more to say. It'd be years before I'd realise how important the silences are. How much is said with them.

I am honoured but shamed to overhear this, even though I had to be expecting it.

Earlier in the night I had stood with Little Big Man's woman. Little Big Man was close by, that tight bundle of Wiradjuri energy. I was telling her she had a good man. Made a big show of praising him up. She smiled her love to him. He to her and me. A family look. A brother to a brother, standing with his woman.

I'm away from my family. I feel homesick.

Uncle James tells me I am his nephew now. He hugs my head to his chest. He sings a song to confirm my nephewdom. Ned hugs me.

I keep the cigarettes and VBs coming when they want them.

I've lost track of time. I've lost track of me.

Ned tells me he is my brother.

You got grey in your beard? Ned asks me suddenly. How old are you? You got grey? Is your grandfather older than my grandfather?

My grandfather was born in 1896, I offer.

Ned nods sagely to himself. His big woolly Pitjantjatjara head computing my status.

Elder brother, he says, so quietly that a whisper would be a scream. I nod.

Aawu.

The Rat will always be my brother too. I sit next to my mum. I'm surrounded by family and definitions of family that I never expected but now must accept. I must accept them because they resonate deep within me, all around me, like Uncle's song. The other men are outside now.

Mum begins to speak. I listen.

The Nothingness. Mum talks about the vast Nothingness.

Culture and family are endless.

Individuals are Nothing. Feelings are Nothing. In the Nothing there is endless sadness and endless joy. Nothing.

Bigger than anything we could ever express. In any language.

Mum is annoyed with the Lawmen, at their treatment of the Rat. She is the only person here they don't outrank in Culture way. Seniority way. Any way. We are all grateful for her presence. Her balance. Even the Rat, caught in the middle. Mum doesn't think what they're doing to the Rat — pulling rank — is appropriate.

It's bigger than that, Mum says into the fire. Bigger than that.

But the Rat knows he has to go home. Any disrespect to Uncle will cost him dearly in his own Country.

Bigger than that, Mum repeats.

The bush sings around us. The fire crackles. We are so completely insignificant. Nothing. The tenuous grasp I thought I had on Culture is gone. Into nothing.

Behind us Cheree seems upset. Seeing her man in this situation is new to her too. She is a Murri from Cherbourg way, up there in Waka Waka Country in Queensland. Different Culture again. For Europeans, it'd be like comparing Sicilian Culture to Norwegian Culture. All Europeans — but completely different.

The Rat is with the men. I'm called to be with them. Even though Mum doesn't like it, I get up to go to the balcony. I got responsibilities too. I kiss Mum. It's not just Uncle. It's the Rat.

There are many ways to become a Man, I think.

Many rituals. Many ceremonies. Many paths. Nothing.

Uncle is different now from the shy old man bird I met hours earlier, shielding his power and playing Jacky Jacky. I was in the laneway outside the theatre. Uncle was introduced to a young gubbah next to me. The young gub squares off, squeezes Uncle's hand hard and looks him in the eye.

G'day, Mate.

Uncle looks off into the distance to hide his power. Big smile on his face, he goes into his cowboy-rave.

I'm Cowboy James. Me, I'm stockman. Drover. I bin riding bulls all over. I bin top boss cowboy, me.

Cowboy James reminds me of Bart Billon. Bart is Wangkathaa man. A stockman. A rainmaker. I wasn't even going to school the last time I saw Bart.

It's my turn. I drop my head and offer my hand. Just put it there. Cowboy James reaches out and his pink palm barely touches mine. His skin feels cool. When I speak my voice is quiet, just for him.

Hello, Uncle, I whisper.

Uncle flashes me a look I feel to my boots but I don't dare look up.

My boy, Uncle whispers back, and touches me on the upper arm with hardened old fingertips.

Now, hours later on this balcony, Uncle is strong. A rock. A tree. A lizard. Clap-sticks beat out his heart. He looks bigger. Older. Country must be getting closer. We talk for a long while, in the quiet way of the bush. The quiet way of family.

And then I must go. My own family pulling on a string attached to my lower belly from across the Nullarbor. I came over for this work. For my brothers. My sisters. Uncles. Aunties. Nephews. Nieces. Mum. Came to fight The War of attitude.

I drag my six huge pieces of luggage down the stairs. I go across the road to the taxi rank. I have kissed and hugged everyone. The Rat comes down to make sure I'm alright. Mum's words are all around me. Fuelling me. My feelings are Nothing. My doubt is Nothing. Uncle's parting ghost of a grip still feels like it has me. His cool strong hands. Ned's eyes with the firelight still dancing in them. Mum. Sister Cheree. These are my family too.

Kele mwerre anthurre (Go really good way), the Rat says.

Kele mwerre anthurre, I say back.

I'm gone. In the cab to the airport the Rat rings me twice. My brother. And I'm getting out. It's cold. The luggage is hard to manoeuvre. The line is long, my brain is tired. These things are Nothing. I get checked in. I stand out in front of the terminal and smoke a huge joint. Past caring. Caring is nothing. And suddenly I'm dozing on a plane.

Henry, my djaambi, has described his Gunditjmara coastline for me many times. As we cross the southern coast to leave Victoria, I'm looking out the window, looking out for his sacred Country. Then I see it swim into view, the bay, the three-pronged headland, like some marsupial crouched on the coastline. I watch it until it slides away, under the belly of the plane. I keep this close to my heart.

And I always look out for Wudjari Country when we cross the coast back over Western Australia. Where I grew up on Lort River Station at Coomalbidgup. Where I learned to love my Country. East of Munglinup, west of Dalyup. All Nyungar names. All Nyungar Country.

I can pick Yonda Quagi from the air, the beach closest to Red Island. The last island close to the shoreline on the western end of the Recherche Archipelago. I doze.

And then I'm sat up in my seat as though slapped — Uncle's song is in my ears. In my head. It's like he's sitting in the seat next to me, the sticks and song making the whole plane vibrate. I look around. No-one else seems to hear it. Uncle singing me home. I am Nothing. I doze off.

Look at me when I'm talking to you

How did I get there? On that balcony in Toorak Road? To explain that, I've gotta go back. Way back.

I'm an unemployed actor. Living in St Kilda. Boonwurrung Country. Finished a job a couple of months ago. I heard about this play set in the travelling boxing tents, written by this Arrernte fulla, Uncle Kumanjai Dempster. (Kumanjai means Spirit, used for people who've passed away. Some mobs say Pringhael. Same thing.)

I'd done some boxing training with Brett, this tough gubbah fulla on the periphery of the Melbourne acting world. Sparred a few times in Kelly's Gym. But I rarely shone in the ring.

I auditioned for the director by shadow-boxing in my singlet. Every boy spends a lot of time shadow-boxing. I was terrible. But got the job. Pointy nose. Pale skin. Thin top lip. Tough-guy eyes. I can do that.

A week later, I'm walking into the Fitzroy All-Stars Gym to meet Robby.

By then I'd also done a few training sessions there, with Old Don. Old Don had fought Uncle Kumanjai Dempster's father. Old Don lost the fight and an eye. Had to have it replaced with a glass eye after the fight. Old Don grew up in South Africa. Could only do one thing well in his life. Fight. Box.

An artist with the gloves. Obi-Wan Kenobi with a shrill nasally voice. Old Don gets me to move my feet. To drill it. To get power in my punches. To jab like a bastard. Keep him off me and hurt him every time he gets close.

So I walk into the gym and there are two Koori lads sitting there. My hair is shoulder length. Robby's head is shaved. A shining cannonball.

He doesn't get up to greet me. I sit. We shake hands flat gub way. We're both pretty tentative.

G'day.

G'day.

Stephen Motor.

Robby Clarke.

Hey, Robby.

Hey, Pete.

Steve.

… Yeah, Steve.

I'm aware of Robby's physique. Chest, arms, shoulders pushing at the sweatshirt material. Eyes bright. Pumped and ripped as a bastard. A Yorta Yorta warrior. I'm happy for my training. The skip-rope rhythm pounding through my head. Robby is in the Olympic squad. A hurdler. I still hold the record at my high school for 110-yard hurdles: 13.8 seconds. Robby and I understand each other.

So we're rehearsing. A play about the old-time boxing tents. The play is set in and around the violence that the Koori men generate inside the ring for the entertainment of the crowd.

But, the real violence is psychological and spiritual and is acted upon the Koori men outside the ring. Even the successful Australian lightweight champion wasn't allowed to keep his earnings — under this Act passed by parliament, it all goes into a government account and is then doled out a bit at a time. It's an old story. Two hundred years old in this country. Control everything. That's the government position. Give them fuck all.

So we're getting notes on the second or third day, and the director appears to be very nervous. She gives a note to George. George is probably the best thing in the show. His wit is razor sharp and fast as anything. He is a huge man but dances around the stage as light as a fairy. One of the Little People.

Us Irish have got to stick together, I say to him late at night in a bar.

George gives me a look like he might knock me out. I'm sure he could. Then laughs. His laugh is as big and gentle as a lake. George is a Ngarrindjeri man. Lived by lake and sea for six hundred generations (but got an Irish surname).

George is looking away and down when the director gives him the note. Maybe he doesn't respect her. Maybe he does. Maybe he's bored. Maybe the notes are shit. Maybe he's just looking away and down.

Blah blah blah blah, she says. Scribbles something quickly and then suddenly blurts out: And look at me when I'm talking to you!

Her comment goes off like a pistol shot.

I look down. Don't want to look at the brother now. There is a collective sigh in the room. George doesn't respond.

My whole fucken life, everyone in the room is thinking. The clap-sticks bringing our hearts together. Talking. Talking. No-one listening now. We sit in our own bubbles. Our own universes. We're adults. In a workplace. We're patient. After a while the talking peters out. Runs out of steam. She looks around for a moment, then takes a breath like she's going to continue.

Might get a cuppa tea, Uncle Backy announces loudly as he gets up and leaves the room.

Smooth as a ballet, everyone is up and gone. The talker is left all alone. She has a look on her face like she doesn't get what just happened. It's a wadjula look that I will come to get used to.

We like our tea with milk and plenty of sugar. We all grab biscuits, too.

Tap! Tap! Ow!

We get to dress rehearsal. Three weeks later. Dragged ourselves there.

The play culminates in a huge boxing match between the hero and me. I've come to symbolise everything the hero has to combat to make it in the new world. Robby and I have worked hard on the stunt, but are hampered by the fact that Robby hasn't been there much. His commitments to his training for the Olympic squad have eaten into rehearsal time quite severely.

In a normal fight scene there might be three or four moves. In the boxing-match scene there are dozens and dozens of moves, choreographed so the actor playing the commentator can follow them and construct the story for the audience.

Robby and I have a chat and decide that we'll still do the stunt at about seventy-five per cent speed, for safety's sake.

The dress rehearsal is going well. We get to the big fight scene. The theatre company has invited a bunch of board members and friends to watch. They start barracking. The director starts yelling at Robby to go harder and faster. I can still hear the writer, Uncle Kumanjai Dempster in my head.

During rehearsals and during actual performances he was the only one barracking for me.

Knock im out, Iceman!

Carn, Iceman! Hit im!

I got the feeling that Uncle could probably still flog all of us young fullas put together.

Robby and I come together for about the third time. Exchanging punches in our worked-out combinations, when Pow! A leather steam-train cracks me on the nose. My knees buckle and I slowly begin to sink towards the mat. The air around me pops and crackles like multi-coloured Rice Bubbles in coca-cola. My knees hit the mat.

I hear this little old lady who is part of the invited audience turn to her friend: Oh, that blood looks so real!

And now blood is pissing out of me and everything is in slow motion. I have to sit. An icepack arrives eventually to try to stem the blood.

Robby is distraught. Annoyed for allowing himself to feel pushed, for not being as prepared as he felt he should've been. Punching accurately takes a lot of training.

But it's just one of those things: do stunts for long enough and something will go wrong. Everything happens for a reason. This bruising will feel symbolic much later on. (The bruising on the way in.)

So we're sitting in the emergency department of the big city hospital. I keep getting sent to the back of the line because all I've got is a broken nose. There are two car crashes, a stabbing and an old gunshot wound before me.

The bloke with the old gunshot wound comes over to show me. He's got this homemade bandage on it. Bedsheets, I'd say.

He lifts it up so I can see the blue green purple hole in his guts. It's swollen a lot too. He says he can feel the slug if he pushes his little finger into the hole.

I sit there with my nose bleeding and head thumping. I touch my nose. The gunshot wound is giving me ideas. I can move my nose. It's agony as the bone grinds on bone. This is pain I'll get to know well.

After three hours I see a young doctor who is rushed off his feet. He tells me he can't do anything.

What if it heals crooked?

We can always break it again to straighten it.

So I get the idea. Now I'm not sure why we bothered coming down here.

Ah, yes. Insurance.

Each night for the next six weeks I find myself in front of the mirror tapping the side of my nose with my index finger until it looks straight.

Tap! Tap!

Ow!

Tap! Tap!

Ooow!

I don't wanna get it broken again. And now I have to perform the show with my nose broken. I can't afford another whack there or I'm out of the play.

The original mistake is never repeated. On opening night I accidentally push my face into Robby in one of the clinches and nearly faint from the shock of pain that floods my head. Someone gives me a line after the show and the pain is gone. The magic of drugs.

All the while I'm getting close with Robby and George and Uncle Backy. Things long forgotten from my childhood in remote Wudjari Country are coming back to me.

My loud mouth and tight moom

Wudjari Country, mid-1970s. I'm at the agricultural show in Esperance. The show is the biggest thing to happen all year. The Country and Western Festival in summer was only small then.

The talk at school for weeks leading up to and weeks after the show is always the sideshow rides. I never gave a shit about the rides. Rode them if I could, didn't care if I didn't.

When I was younger I used to work at the church stall, Lucky Envelopes. Father Gleen saw no conflict of interest in running a rigged soft-gambling racket. The money went to the church. Not working there this year.

This year I'm there with Pringhael Gil and Pringhael Harry. We'd had a drink out of Pringhael Harry's mum's liquor cabinet. So I'm pissed. And sixteen. And got a mouth. You get the picture.

I get separated from my mates in the light-and-sound assault of sideshow alley. I go around behind the tents to have a rest from the blaring light and glaring sound and I see these other blokes near the back of the wild-west-round-up. I get stuck right into them with the mouth. Can't remember what set me off. Nothin, probably.

There are four of them. All a year older than me. Ports lads. Hard working-class boys. And suddenly I'm in a bit of trouble. Outnumbered and outgunned. Not in the public view. Probably gunna get a real hiding here. These Ports lads step up. Their mouths are going now.

Wha'd you say you little cunt?

I'm gunna hurt you!

Smack you in the fucken head!

I hold my ground as they move up. Oh, shit.

Suddenly all around me there are other lads in the semi-darkness. They come up fast and stand by me. I don't look around. I'm still watching these lads in front of me for signs of impending sudden movement.

Who you fucken talkin to?

I know Jackson's soft Wongi voice from hundreds of footy training runs and games. The Ports lads have this stupid where-did-youse-come-from-and-what-are-youse-buttin-in-for? look on their faces as they look at Jackson and his two cousins. They stop in their tracks. Jackson's cuz standing to my left speaks.

Well … fuck off then!

Yeah, fuck off.

The Ports boys turn as one and fuck off. Jackson and his cousins laugh. They slap me on the back. They laugh more.

Your moom was goin like that!

Jackson holds up his left hand in imitation of my sphincter muscles spasming out of fear.

They all laugh, and then all do it and laugh again.

I'm laughing now.

You got any more charge, Brother?

Got a bottle hidden. Follow me.

All we've thought about

As we rehearse and perform the boxing-tent play we live in each other's pockets. Robby and I and George and even Uncle Backy are inseparable.

Wherever I go with the Mob we get stared at. Talked about. Approached by an endless stream of twenty-something girls who want to get laid and twenty-something boys who want to fight. This is the way things are. Everyone puts up walls in their own way to protect themselves. Ignore it. Pretend it's not there. Do what you have to do.

One night I'm out drinking with Robby and George. We get separated from each other near the McDonald's in South Melbourne. It's about three in the morning. We need some shit food to soak up the grog. I'm on the footpath searching the passing traffic for a cab. I'm always the cab monitor. We don't have to take a vote or draw straws. They won't stop for anyone else.

I look back to the bizarre golden fluorescent light to see Robby surrounded by rednecks. Not real rednecks; these are the outer-suburban-well-fed-but-still-plenty-angry-for-no-apparent-reason variety. They're in verbal land. I read it from where I am. Robby doesn't look too worried. If I were those boys I'd be starting to get worried about that furrowing Yorta Yorta brow. I'm not gunna miss out.

As I'm turning and stepping off I feel a presence beside me. A car has pulled up, a door opens and out steps George. And George is a big presence. We step off with the same mind, the same heartbeat. As though there were clap-sticks, marking it for us. All we've thought about is injustice and boxing for two months. We've trained to fight in the gym every day. And now we get this. Thank you, God.

No-one from the circle has the guts to take the first swing at Robby. The first swinger is obviously gunna get hit. They circle like hyenas with each one from the pack waiting for the others to hit.

Robby doesn't have to look around. He knows we'll be coming. George and I stride. Covering ground but not rushing.

One of the pack gets that hunted feeling and turns to see us. The same feeling I'd got one time in the East Perth lock-up in cell number three. There are six or eight of them. We stride. As one they turn and cross the road against the lights. Moving like a school of fish who've seen the sharks coming. Walking just a little too quickly for comfort. And George and I are there, next to Robby. Watching them go. One of them sneaks a look back. We look evenly.

Come back and play. Pleeease.

But they can't. Bravery all gone now. We look at each other and smile our disappointed smiles.

Let's go and get a fucken drink.

You know how to talk to them

When Uncle Elmore joins the cast to be the Spirit Dancer who helps our hero overcome all, I am happy. Uncle Elmore is more my eldest brother but I call him Uncle out of respect and because he is real uncle to my stepson Stewart. (I'm not attached to this label and bring Stewie up as though he is mine.)

Uncle Elmore lives in a flat in the same block as my partner, Liz, and me. Elmore is a Ngan'giwumirra man. Uncle Elmore never walks past the window without coming in to share a joke, or to help Stewart with his recorder or guitar.

Elmore is a songsmith. A muso. The main actor in the best film ever made in this country about this country. Elmore was discovered at a railway station by the film director's wife.

He never dropped in when he was charged up. Well, once; he was just so happy and wanted to share it. That's what Elmore is like, strong and warm.

When I first met Elmore he was charged up.

I was a new young actor with one of the big old establishment actors' agents. The agency used to put on a little gathering every now and then for them and all the actors to get together for a drink and a social chat. Of course, once the actors had all had a drink all they wanted to do was harass the agent about their lack of work, and slag off those actors getting all the work. Loads of fun.

I get there late for some reason. I think I'd been doing my lift-boy job at Myer: 'First Floor — Miss Shop, Ladies' Shoes. Going Up!' The drinks were in full swing by the time I arrived. Advanced state of swing. I get caught in several boring conversations with pretty attractive people.

After a while someone comes running out to me. I'm standing in the paved Victorian garden.

Can you come in? Elmore's out of control! You know how to talk to them! Can you come?

I was catapulted back to being the shy young bank teller at a busy inner-city branch in Wajuk Country, Perth. I'd only done one half-day a week at the inquiry counter. I didn't know much about how to do anything at this stage, so I was always worried I'd get asked to do something I didn't know how to do. And I always did. The older hands all seemed to hate teaching or telling you anything, so it wasn't easy to learn.

This day, well the first time, I was standing at the big adding machine. The manager's secretary was having a turn at the inquiry counter. She came to me with a strange look on her face. Like she just got poked with a sharp stick in a soft spot.

Can you help me?

What?

I couldn't believe my ears. The boot was suddenly on the other foot.

I need your help?

Yeah?

There's this old man at the counter …

Yeah?

Well, you grew up on a station.

I suddenly recognise her emotion. Fear.

I lean out and look past her to see this Old Nyungar Fulla leaning against the counter. I didn't even look back at her. I'd already seen him. It'd be rude not to move straight away. I march up to the counter.

Turns out to be this lovely Old Fulla. Lost his passbook. Doesn't know his number. I write down his name. Find out what branch. This is the days before the full computer link-up. I phone the branch. I get the savings bank manager who is really pissed off to have to do something so menial, but the rest of his team are busy. I'm hanging on, waiting for the answer.

Eh, Boy, wha'd e reckon?

Talkin to the boss. Says his boys all busy.

Tell him to do it himself.

He is.

We both laugh.

You know what boss means?

… Bag of sheep shit!

We laugh some more.

I get the details and generate a passbook on the computer. Get the Old Fulla to sign it.

Thank you, my boy.

And that was it. From then on, whenever anyone from the Mob came into the branch they'd ask for me. Many of the aunties would just walk up to the counter and if anyone else went to come over they'd just point at me. Once I passed a message from a mother to her daughter up in Jukun Country, Broome, via a contact at the branch there.

After that first time, the manager's secretary comes over and thanks me. I shrug. She steps in close to me.

It's just the smell I can't deal with, she confesses.

Which is pretty funny to me. Bart Billon would've had a laugh. The only stockman who no-one wanted to ride with in the front of a ute was a pommy bloke who'd immigrated ten years earlier but had rigidly stuck to his once-a-week bath regime as though he was still in the old country. Stunk like a bastard. The manager's secretary wouldn't've lasted five minutes out there.

So here I am, sidling up to Uncle Elmore at my agent's house. He's leaning over a young blond actress whose breasts are spilling out of her lacy top. He has a bottle of wine in one hand and a cigarette in the other. He turns and looks at me. I've seen him turn it on in a movie. I can see he's not acting. Even now I can see it. Angry Elmore is fucken scary. But I can see this other man in his eyes. Strong Man waiting. It is to this man that I will be talking.

Whadda you fucken want?

People are scared of you.

That's their fucken problem!

He's got me there, I think. What can I say? It *is* their problem.

The blond actress sees he is distracted by me and makes a quick exit. Elmore looks after her.

Where you goin?

She doesn't look back. Doesn't reply. They're all really keen until they get in over their heads. She runs out quickly. Vainly trying to hoist her top up over her escaping bosom.

You're too charged up, Uncle.

Ya wanna fucken go?

I'm not here to fight you. I'm here to help you leave.

I'm not fucken goin anywhere!

Take the bottle if you want. People are scared. You have to go.

Fuck you!

Elmore turns and stumbles down the stairs towards the front door. I follow. He gets out on to the street and stands there. Swaying. Eyes blazing at me. He suddenly throws the wine bottle on to the road. It explodes. He looks at me.

Goodnight, Uncle.

Fucken cunt!

Elmore stalks off up the road. Stagger stagger. Roll roll. Fuck, it was a rush to meet him, those blazing eyes.

I go back into the party. I go back to a different room so I don't have to deal with the conversation. But it doesn't matter. I don't last much longer.

There's some fucken factory that makes those TV actors. The blokes workin on the brain part of the assembly line went on strike for higher pay, cause they reckoned they were doing the most important work, but the owners called their bluff and just kept making them with perfect bodies anyway. Realised they didn't need the brain. Just gets in the way, pushes up production costs. Fucken unions.

See, I couldn't last any longer.

The next time I meet Elmore, it's 2.00 am on Fitzroy Street, St Kilda. We're both near the end of a long hard night. I shit myself when I see Elmore.

Hey! My boy! Peter Mopoke!

Stephen, Stephen Motor.

Yeah, Stevey Boy!

Elmore embraces me warmly. We look at each other and laugh. We're connected now. Even under the spell of the grog, Elmore had seen that I didn't belong at the party either.

You want one last charge?

Just one, eh, Uncle?

No-one can refuse Uncle Elmore's smile. I give him mine back.

We go into this bar full of gangsters and pimps and prostitutes. We get some vodka. There is a piano. Uncle Elmore starts to play. He plays classical, he plays the blues, he sings Frank Sinatra. The late-night drinkers applaud and yell out requests. The drinks are now free. Uncle gets me singing. A woman with red hair and red lipstick tries to get Uncle to go out to the carpark with her. Uncle Elmore is playing music and won't go.

At about five-thirty we go back to my place for a smoke. Uncle sees my boomerangs, gifts from my Wongi brothers, grabs them up and sings Language songs using them as clapsticks. Owl Dreaming. Uncle dances around my flat. The firelight flickers in his eyes. I wish I had a fire. Outside the sun is coming up over Boonwurrung Country.

At seven-thirty we go for breakfast. Sitting in Greasy Joe's in St Kilda and Uncle's mobile phone rings. Uncle answers it and has a rattling conversation in Language. He rings off.

My mother, he grins at me.

I drink my coffee. Feel it and the sun begin to warm my bones. My buzzing head is slowly cleared by the warmth and light and caffeine. We go back to my place and Uncle gives me a two-hour guitar lesson.

Owl Dreaming
and goin to the fucken pub

Uncle Elmore gets in to the theatre early every night. He brings his flute. His clarinet. His didj. He walks around the dressing room playing. Plays didj patterns through his clarinet. Everyone who can play anything joins in.

Uncle Elmore and Uncle Backy have a big laugh together. They smoke nyandi out the back lane and laugh with their eyes. But Elmore doesn't have much to do in the actual show. He wonders to me why he didn't get considered for Uncle Backy's role. But if the gubbah director seems wary of Uncle Backy, she'd be terrified of Uncle Elmore. I don't mention this. Not my place to say.

It is on stage where Uncle Elmore comes alive. He plays with the audience. Holds them in the palm of his hand. The didj he plays seems to get inside you. Hums along your bones until your whole body is vibrating with it. And then Uncle is dancing his Owl Dreaming. Special dance. Transforming himself with music and rhythm.

One night he comes in fully charged up. Tense. Upset about something. He hangs around the dressing room for a bit. We're all getting ready to go on. No-one has time to listen to his gripe.

I'm goin to the fucken pub, he announces and stalks off.

After a while, Uncle Kumanjai Dempster comes in. His Arrernte brow is deeply furrowed.

Where's Elmore?

He asks the room full of people. Everyone looks down. Lucky Uncle Backy is there. Not much fazes Backy.

Said he was goin to the pub.

Uncle Kumanjai Dempster looks to Uncle Backy. They look at each other for a long time. Uncle Kumanjai Dempster storms out. We hear him yelling out as he's leaving the building. He's wild as hell!

Who the fuck does he think he is? If I find him, I'll drag the useless cunt out and fucken flog im! Then I'll drag his sorry arse back here!

Uncle is closer to seventy than sixty but at that moment we are all hoping he doesn't find Elmore. Uncle's father was a boxing-tent man and him too. Me or George or Robby probably wouldn't have a chance. We do the show without Elmore. Robby just fudges the scene where the Spirit is meant to appear to him. They play a recorded sound effect. We don't see Uncle Elmore on this show again.

Next night, Stephen turns up to play the Spirit Dancer. Nyawaygi man, North Queensland coastal Country. Quiet and keeps to himself in the dressing room. Has another fulla with him for support. They speak Language quietly in the corner as Stephen paints up and attaches feathers to his arms, legs and hair. Everyone gives them space.

Stephen gives the audience a fright with his grunting and his shake-a-leg. Stephen carries a spear and woomera on with him. He looks like he knows how to use it. The spear makes the audience nervous. Gets us excited. Robby is pumped by it. Make more spear.

Uncle Kumanjai Dempster is happy. He still says he's gunna flog Elmore if he sees him. Elmore stays away.

After the show each night I stand in front of the mirror and tap my broken nose straight.

Tap!

Ow!

Tap!

Oow!

Tap!

Ooow!

Looking straight now.

And then the season of the play is finished. And the world around me, and within me, appears changed forever. As if I can suddenly see invisible things (or they can see me).

Would you mind keeping it down?

A year or so passes, and Australia wins the right to host the Olympic Games. As part of the Olympic build-up the host nation has certain cultural responsibilities, and so a large festival of indigenous performance art is cooked up for Eora Country — Sydney. The Festival of Dreaming.

So we get to do Uncle's boxing-tent play again. There'll be a new cast to take the show to Sydney because some of the original performers are working on other shows at the Festival of Dreaming. And a new co-director, Bill Wiseman. Noonuccal man on a mission.

I know it's King coming over to do the show. Doing Robby's part. When I first met King, he burst into my house like a willy-willy. A big strong Nyungar who'd done a reading of a play at the same theatre I'd worked at that day. King embraced me like a long lost brother, called me his Coorda (brother), reversed the joint in his mouth, placed his lips against mine to blow smoke into my mouth. That was a year or so ago now. I've wanted to work with him ever since. He's got a bit of a rep, you know? So I'm getting fit, training like a bastard, morning, noon and night.

King comes over to my place the night before the first day of rehearsal. He's got a sparkle in his eye. Fire in his belly. He's pretty edgy. Trouble at home with his kids and trouble here with his woman.

We have a smoke. Tell each other fight stories. King's got heaps. I'm really looking forward to it now, despite the snake coiling in my belly.

The first day goes pretty well. The new cast and new co-director inject new energy. We're all pretty excited.

Uncle Kumanjai Presto is down from Sydney to rehearse with us in Melbourne. Footscray. Wurundjeri Country. That Old Man, that Indinji/Komet man has us all laughing in the first five minutes. And Uncle always has something to follow the joke. Wicked and wise.

The reading is pretty stilted. No-one is very fluent. No English in our hearts. It doesn't matter. It's the chemistry. Uncle Kumanjai Dempster's words are a skeleton.

Uncle tells us that he wrote the play for King after meeting him in Kaurna Country, Adelaide. Been waiting for King to bring his energy to the role.

At lunchtime King and I decide to go for a drive. He has his woman's BMW. King only knows one way to drive. Fucken flat out.

We have to go to the theatre company office first. King's mobile phone won't work and he has a message to ring WA. We go into the office. The bloke we talk to, this gubbah fulla called Paul, is pretty unhappy about King calling long distance. And he seems nervous. King gets on the phone after talking his way past Paul.

The phone conversation quickly becomes heated. King finds

out that his ex-Mrs's fulla has smacked his kids around. King is ropeable. Finally the conversation finishes. It's been pretty hard for all of us to listen to. Harder for King. He's shaking and visibly upset.

Look, would you mind keeping it down when you're on the phone?

All eyes in the room turn to Paul. Then to King. Like some weird tennis match. When King's voice comes it comes up from some strangled place. Strangled in boiling lava.

I was talkin to my fucken kids!

But Paul is still going to play PC serve and volley.

This is our workspace and …

King is across the room in a flash of lightning. He grabs PC Paul by the scruff of the neck and slams him against the wall. There is a sharp intake of breath from a woman standing behind me. King puts his face very close to PC Paul's. Really looks at him.

Leave it, Coorda.

I'm talking quiet. Trying to calm a bucking stock horse.

Not worth it, Coorda. Not worth it.

PC Paul is frozen with fear. Stepped into The War Zone with his university educated letter-to-the-editor zeal. King's face is dangerously close to his. His balga-sap Nyungar eyes burning into him.

Leave it, Coorda. Don't worry about it.

King pushes PC Paul away and heads for the door. I follow him. PC Paul goes to speak to me. He's still got righteous indignation written all over him. I glare at him. I wish King had knocked him out now.

And we're both gone. Leaving the theatre company mob to

talk about how unpredictable and violent King is. They're all worried about the show. King does a huge burn-out in the carpark.

We go to the boxing gym and give the heavy bag a hiding.

Lunch with Uncle

Uncle Kumanjai Presto tells me that he's s'posed to have a nurse with him for his health condition. His wife organised one for him from this big home care agency. Uncle says it was going pretty well until his wife came home one day and met the allocated nurse. Uncle smiles conspiratorially and looks around as if we might be overheard. He laughs suddenly at the memory. A quick downpour in the desert.

The nurse was young and blond and …

Uncle chuckles to himself, his hands subtly stroke large invisible bosoms, and I giggle like a little boy overhearing a man's conversation for the first time.

Uncle brings this wickedness to his character, the old boxing trainer, says he learned it from these old Murri fullas who could intimate the filthiest things without really saying anything at all. All the while appearing to be having a very innocent conversation.

Ron Waddell, the young Yorta Yorta boxer, and I take it in turns driving Uncle around; to and from work, wherever he wants to go.

Let's go get some lunch, he says to me on the second day of rehearsal.

I follow Uncle's directions in Liz's old Ford until we get to a little backstreet in Footscray. The Country that William Buckley roamed across with the Boonwurrung, Wurundjeri and Woiwurung over a hundred and seventy years ago, trapping fish and spearing the occasional wallaby.

I park the car and we walk to this little cafe. As we go up the street I notice that it is exclusively a north African hang-out. No-one here looks like me. I'm fine. I'm with Uncle. We get a few curious looks. We go in and sit down and I'm still not quite sure where we are or why we're here. Lunch. There are no menus.

A large bosomy north African woman comes over to us to take our order. Now I know why we're here. She is beautiful with brightly coloured cloth swathing her ample curves and her poise and her rich velvety skin. Uncle orders for me. I get a coke and he has a yoghurt drink. Then, a few moments later, our food arrives.

To serve, three women, all big and sexy come out. I'm pretty overwhelmed but they aren't that interested in me. They put out the food and Uncle manages to engage the whole three of them in conversation. They smile, laugh, sway their voluptuous bodies in time with the African music streaming from little tinny speakers suspended above the kitchen doorway by strands of copper wire.

Uncle tastes the spicy meat and okra stew and gives them a big smile. I eat. The food is incredible. The view magnificent. The three women eventually return to the kitchen. Uncle gives me a big smile.

Good tucker, eh, my boy?

Uncle makes me feel like I'm twelve years old. I giggle.

Every time we go for lunch, Uncle brings me here. Uncle's joy of flirting with the beautiful African women never abates. They're all old enough to be my mum but their up-front physical and sexual power starts to affect me. I look forward to taking Uncle to lunch. My love of the food increases each time I come.

Wars ya can't win

Each morning on the way to rehearsal I pick up Lucy from her flat in East St Kilda. Lucy is Yamatji, a legendary beauty. She lives with Mark, this Murri fulla.

I always have to wait for Lucy. Mark is troubled. Lucy is pregnant with their second child. For breakfast she's already into a cask of Coolabah. Mark pleads with me with his eyes.

One morning he is outside having a cigarette when I arrive. They've been fighting. I'm not smoking. Training too hard in the gym.

I dunno what to do, Bruz.

She drinkin?

Mark sucks on his Winnie Blue and looks up the street.

Gotta stop her, Bruz. Whatever it takes.

Mark nods and stubs out his cigarette.

It's for the child, I hear myself saying.

I'm not a counsellor. I drink. I smoke. I've been addicted to whatever is going. Who the fuck do I think I am?

Lucy and I drive to work in silence. She stinks of booze. She is just starting to show. The alcohol makes her feel really sick. She puts up with the feeling. I don't know what to say. It's her thing. Their thing. Some wars ya can't win. Fills my guts with a sad angry feeling.

War and peace

The biggest town in Wudjari Country is named after a French ship which sheltered in the heart-shaped bay nearly two hundred years ago. Esperance. Hope.

A short time after this the coastal areas were overrun with foreign whalers and sealers. The same virulent and ruthless viral strain infecting the Boonwurrung and Gunditjmara coastline thousands of kilometres to the east. Soon after this came the inland settlers with their livestock and their fences and their diseases and their industrial-age weapons. As the original population was decimated, the town grew quickly.

In the late 1960s, early 1970s, it was still a pretty remote place, not connected to Adelaide or the eastern states by two-wheel-drive road, and ten hours' drive from Perth.

The main street in those days led down to the ocean. There is a drop in elevation too, so that the street flows into the sea like a river. In actual fact, separating the end of the street and the beach is a big bituminised carpark (to accommodate patrons from the nearby hotel) and some small sand dunes with low vegetation.

Situated in the carpark, right at the end of the main street, is an old public toilet block. No-one seems to know when it was built. The street focuses your eye squarely on the brick and cement toilet block, an island in a river-mouth.

This particular day I'm busting to go to the toilet. Mum is doing the fortnightly shopping in the town's only supermarket in the main street. I'm in about Grade Two. I come out of the supermarket and hurry down to the toilet block. I can see this mob hanging around. These are the fringe-dweller mob from Bandy Creek, about three hours walk, east along the beach. Everyone looks really pissed.

As a station kid, used to stockmen, jackaroos and shearers, I know what pissed is. Adults in this state are usually to be avoided. But I'm really busting, so I hurry on.

This one fulla starts to weave his way over like he's going to intercept my progress. But as he gets close, he suddenly trips and falls face down in front of me. His head hits the concrete with a whack that reverberates up through my school shoes.

For a moment, I'm scared, don't know what to do. Still busting for a piss. This fulla on the ground suddenly growls something and rolls over. Well, least he's alive.

I step past him and rush in to the toilet. I pull the top of my shorts straight down, no time for fancy zip work now, pull out my lil pipi and piss as hard and fast as I can — my head and eyes turned over my right shoulder at the doorway.

I'm just finishing when that fulla comes careening around the corner and slams into the facing wall. My pipi goes away by itself and I turn to face him, backed up against the urinal. Blood is streaming from a deep cut in his forehead. He shuffles towards me. I'm frozen. He stops in front of me. I'm looking him fair in the eye to show that I'm not afraid. That's what my brother does in these situations, and he's not afraid.

This bloody fulla puts out his hand. He just wants to shake my hand. I smile. He slumps back against the wall. I move like I'm going to help. But I know he's way too heavy for a lil fulla like me. I watch him. He slumps a little more. He seems to be falling asleep. His blood is still flowing freely. I walk out. Uncertain.

Just outside there is a group of men sitting down. They have flagons of McWilliam's port and they're all shouting and gesticulating. Just out from the men there are two women stripped to the waist and hitting each other with sticks. I stare at their huge bare breasts. One of them fullas sitting on the ground growls at me. A guttural rumbling noise like the lions in the circus. I take off and run straight across the road. When I'm almost across, I look back to see one of the women fall heavily on the concrete.

I get across. I'm back in the main street. Wadjulas are moving here and there. Getting out of cars. Packing shopping bags in boots. Standing in front of shop windows. I start walking. I look back again. Across the road, the toilet block is a war zone. I know. I've just been there. It is bloody hell. Here it is a peace zone.

My brother who is not afraid is waiting for me outside the supermarket. We walk together to the bakery to buy bread.

There are these two little Nyungar kids in the shop. They buy a loaf of bread each. As soon as the baker hands them the brown paper bags, they tear them open and start ripping into the bread, while turning and running out of the shop. Bare feet.

Probly all they get for a week, my brother observes.

I have no idea what is going on. No-one seems to notice. No adults, anyway. No-one seems to know anything. To care. Like the People are invisible.

After that, whenever I'd come to town, I'd look for them and see them there. Hanging around the toilet block, drinkin. I was worried about that fulla who hit his head. So much blood. And those women. Something's not right here. That's obvious.

That toilet block figures in my nightmares to this very day.

Here is the situation

When we head up to Eora Country we find out that Uncle
Kumanjai Presto can't do the show. His sickness won't allow
him to go on. So Uncle Elmore steps in.

On the first day in Sydney we have TV cameras watching us
rehearse. Watching Uncle Elmore stepping up to the batter's
mound. Cameras seem to change everything. Uncle is funny.
He loves to improvise, which is lucky because he's only had the
script two days before we open.

I'm billeted with a mate of mine in Redfern. King is just
round the corner, staying with a theatre director friend.

I find a gym in the university nearby where I can pump
weights. Every day before the show I do the stairway in the
carpark next to our performance space. Up and down three
times, my body buzzing with my own positive chemicals.

From the moment we arrive, some of the officials from
Sydney Organising Committee for the Olympic Games
(SOCOG) seem to go out of their way to treat us with scorn
and disdain. There was a terrible accident on one of the other
shows where part of the audience seating collapsed. The
SOCOG boys are shitting themselves.

We're performing in a tent set up on a lawn in the grounds of the university. It rains very heavily for the first few days we're there. Our playing space gets wet and our dressing rooms are flooded.

Because of the stunts in the show we can't afford any slips on the sports mat. I don't wanna break my nose again.

In our dressing room there is twenty-five centimetres of water on the floor. There are electrical cables sitting in the water. King and I decide we aren't getting changed in there. We're old-fashioned about standing in water with powered-up cables in it.

We bring these concerns to the administration through our stage management. They get passed up the line. Some SOCOG fulla gets on the phone and tells us not to worry about it. He's not the one who has to stand in the water to get changed.

We have a team meeting and decide that we can't go on under these circumstances. So they send out a little delegation to deal with the troublesome artistes. We have a sit-down meeting. I'm voted the Equity rep by the cast, which is funny, me being the only gub.

So this fulla, with his fake-leather briefcase and his two-hundred-dollar-off-the-rack suit, sits down to talk with us. He lists each of our concerns and says that he'll make sure it gets attended to in due course.

This is pretty unacceptable to us and the argument rages back and forth for twenty minutes. I don't know what to say. It's the Festival of Dreaming. And this group of gubbahs sitting here talking through issues that affect The Mob. This reminds me of other councils, meetings, government organisations.

Finally Mr Fake-leather-briefcase speaks.

Here is the situation: you'll open your show as advertised and we'll endeavour to work on the problems. You people have got to realise that we're doing our best and we'll do it when we can.

Bill Wiseman, that Noonuccal man, finally speaks up.

Here is the situation: you'll get an electrician out today to fix the wiring and someone to fix the leaks in the tent. You people have got to realise that this is a safety issue and if it doesn't happen we won't go on.

There is an awkward silence. Everyone looks to Bill. Bill is a quietly spoken fulla. Full of gentle compassion. Here, he is just talking straight-up. Big deal. Bill shrugs. What else is there to be said. This is the position. We aren't here to negotiate.

This is what Mr Fake-leather-briefcase fears the most. Talking to them. He thought we were just whingeing. Prima donnas. He didn't realise we were just being straight-up. He's come out with his fake-leather briefcase full of bandaids and glass beads and blankets and nobody wants them. I don't think he has a Land Rights sticker on his car. He storms off in a huff.

I want to say that if it needs further discussion, we've got King and Craig out the back murdering a boxing bag. Where we come from, arguing is what you do just before the punching starts.

An electrician and a team of blokes to work on the tent turn up in an hour or so. The gubs from the theatre company spend several hours trying to untwist their knickers. Bill is calm as a cucumber. Seems like just another day at the office to him.

George and Robby, who are working on a Shakespeare play directed by Arrernte man Neil Bosun, drop in to have a look at rehearsals. They're both happy and full of beans. They say they'll meet us later on at Baba Du.

Baba Du

The director of the festival is Joanna Johns, a Bundjalung woman. She realised that we'd all need a place to hang out after our shows, for social and other business, and so Baba Du is born. The Sydney Theatre Company bar and balcony at the end of a pier just below the Sydney Harbour Bridge is the space. All of us who had anything to do with it will remember it all our lives.

Baba Du is taken from the Language of this Country, meaning a good place to meet.

This Mob, the Eora People, with Kuring-gai to the north, Dharug to the west and Tharawal to the south, were the first to face the pale invaders from across the sea. There is a story that Manly is so named because as Cook's ship rode at anchor there, an Eora fulla paddled out in his canoe to inspect the ship. This Eora warrior was taken all over the ship to satisfy his curiosity. Cook was amazed at this fulla's lack of fear — at how *manly* his conduct was.

Cook had had little contact with the People at this stage. Earlier, when he put in to shore in Kurnai Country way to the south, he saw this Kurnai fulla fishing in a flat canoe with his woman tending an on-board fire. So Cook rows up in a boat full of armed marines to attempt some discourse with this fulla.

When Cook arrived in Tahiti he was greeted by naked women draped in flowers, when he landed in New Zealand he was greeted by four hundred Maori warriors doing the Haka on the beach, but when he had his marines row up to this Kurnai fulla he got nothing. This fulla wouldn't look at him, wouldn't speak to him, would not acknowledge his existence in any way. After a frustrating half-hour of trying to communicate, Cook gives up and gets his marines to row him back to his ship and they sail away northward, towards Botany Bay.

With the Harbour as the backdrop to Baba Du, the Festival of Dreaming seems well named. Looking out across the water, it is easy to dream the bridge away, the lights, the roads, the buildings, to picture the odd cooking fire, to smell that fish cooking.

As with all festival clubs, Babu Du is where we have our festival. A good place to meet, and dream.

We have our opening night and everything goes pretty well. Uncle Elmore excels as the old trainer despite not having rehearsed. Has the audience in stitches. It's a long way from the night he walked out on us in Boonwurrung Country, in Melbourne, to go to the fucken pub. Uncle is light of spirit — we all hope for a chance to atone for the shit we do, to rebuild those burnt bridges.

King has a hire car. Not his favoured Commodore, but a nippy little city car. And he knows instinctively how to push it to the limit.

King is feeling really good. His uncle who taught him to

dance and who was a tent fighter to boot, came to see our show tonight. King's uncle loved the show.

We race through the city in the hire car, tyres squealing on every corner, no pausing for troublesome orange or just-red lights. We get down to the wharf. There is a thin strip of concrete running along the pier next to the theatre buildings.

King fangs the car down this wafer of road over the water. I mean, really fucken fangs it. The end of the pier races up towards us. I'm gripping the console. Knuckles drained of colour and straining. I'm noticing that the windows work electrically. If we go in the drink we'll have to get the whole door open. Wait till the car sinks down a bit. I hope King doesn't get trapped behind the wheel. Duck-diving was never my forte. And now King is braking hard. The tyres screech. The bonnet dips and bucks this way and that as King fights to keep it straight.

Oh, fuck.

We're going in for sure. The water floats up to us. The car stops dead. The tyres centimetres from the edge of the jetty. King is laughing at me.

How ya goin, Coord? he laughs at me.

Just park the fucken car.

King parks the car. We go up the back stairs.

Just inside the door we run into Uncle Charlie. Uncle Charlie is an Eora man. This is a good omen for us. Uncle Charlie welcomes us to his Country.

Uncle Charlie is in charge of security and any other business that requires the attention of a man from this Country. He asks us about the water problems. Neither of us are surprised that he knows about it.

I tell him about Mr Fake-leather-briefcase telling us, 'Here is the situation …' I tell him Bill Wiseman's response. Uncle Charlie has a huge laugh. It booms out of him suddenly like happy thunder. King and I laugh with him.

Ya shouda seen this wadjula's face …

And we laugh. Uncle is a huge man. Huge belly. Huge handlebar moustache. He wears a suit and tie. He knows about the true nature of being a host. Uncle Charlie shakes our hands. Slaps our backs. Touches us on the upper arms. We're smiling and feeling at home. He gets called away and we start to walk into Baba Du. As I move through, eyes start to turn and look at me. Curious.

Shit, a wadjula. What's he doin here? Jeez, they're funny looking fullas.

I look across a sea of faces. The biggest mob of people. I don't see any faces like mine. Shit. This is weird.

King runs into someone he knows. I know this fulla's face, even though I've never met him before.

Years ago I stood, curious, as his father cut deep lines into his chest with a knife-sharp rock in a ceremony at the Western Australian Institute of Technology. I didn't know what it was at the time. This Old Fulla with grey hair and beard, chanting under his breath and steadily running the rock-point across his torso, the blood running down his skin, protesting about the British government refusing to give back bones and skulls of the People taken during the war for land a hundred years before.

Anyway, I find myself standing in a circle of fullas. This fulla is doing the introductions. He goes around the circle and says who everyone is. Everyone except me. I'm not sure what to feel.

I'm standing in a row boat trying to talk to a man with a long fishing spear in his hand. He ignores me completely. He's not afraid of my marines with their muskets, he doesn't know what they are. Doesn't give a fuck. I don't speak his Language, I don't know his Country, I'm not his Blood, I'm not his Skin, I don't exist, so how can he talk to me? He just keeps on fishing.

I'm experiencing what Robby and Freddy and George, Henry and King deal with twenty times a day, every fucken day. I'm not like everyone else here. I stand out. People have mixed feelings about me. Everyone's life is full of bad experiences with people who look like me. I've got short hair for the play. Looking like a jungai (police officer) doesn't help. Fear. Hatred. (I was told the jungai is a Wiradjuri word describing a type of squid. Once the police get their suckers into you, they never leave you alone your whole life: jungai.)

King looks across and notices what has happened.

What about Stevey?

He points at me with his chin. The circle of fullas all look at me. Like they're seeing me for the first time. They scrutinise me. Look right through to my heart and soul. Suddenly their laughter crackles all around me like gunfire. There is no fear. No hatred. Just didn't notice me.

Oh, shit, we forgot the skinny little wadjula!

King and I move away and they're still laughing about it. I touch him on the arm. Nod and little smile. King is still laughing about it himself.

We run into Robby and George and Uncle Backy and Craig and Dylan.

Robby takes me over and introduces me to his mother. Robby and I are both from matrilineal cultures. Robby's mum is sitting at a table with some aunties. She smiles up at me and offers me her hand. I take it. She pulls me gently but firmly in closer so she can look at me. There's nothing quite like a mother's touch. Robby and I understand this.

Hello, Stephen.

Hello, Aunt.

She is still holding my hand. Still smiling at me. Looking into my eyes. She gives a little nod and releases me.

I turn and smile at Robby. He gently nods. Then inclines his head slightly — up and over. I nod. We go out to the balcony to join the others for a smoke.

My good-luck boy

I'm staying with this good mate from acting school days in Redfern. I can walk to work and to the gym at the uni. I enjoy the walk. It takes me through The Block. King had taken me for a drive down there before we opened. After all I'd heard I didn't know whether to be scared or not. No-one came near me. I spent ten years living in St Kilda. I could see shit going on but no-one worried me.

After about my third walk through The Block, a couple of fullas started nodding to me. It wasn't cause they thought I was a tough guy, even I couldn't kid myself that much. They knew who I was. The grapevine. Anyway, on this day I was just on the street near my mate's place when I hear this voice yelling out.

Eh!

I start looking around.

Eh! Eh!

I look across the road to see Uncle Charlie from Baba Du with this other fulla outside the TAB.

Eh! Stevey Boy!

He waves me over.

Come in here with me.

He grabs me by the arm and drags me into the TAB.

I'm putting on a bet. You gunna bring me good luck.

Uncle is very excited. He rubs me with his hands as though I really am his good-luck talisman, his lucky silver coin. I'm smiling wide and stupid. But warm wide and stupid. Uncle fills out his ticket, goes to the window and puts on his bet. He drags me along with him. Then back over to the TV.

You wanna beer?

Nah. Workin.

This is my nephew Des.

Des gives me the full handshake. Uncle gets him and Des a beer. The race starts on TV. It's an eleven-hundred-metre sprint. Over in a minute. Uncle wins. He slaps me on the back. Rubs my arms again like I'm his 1880 shilling. Slaps my back. He's giving me more of a hiding than King every night in the stunt fight in the play. I'm giggling.

See! Told ya! You're my good luck!

I gotta go to work, Uncle.

You go, my boy. See you later.

See ya, Des.

Yeah, Bruz.

That night after the show we're at Baba Du when Uncle Charlie calls me over to where he's standing at the end of the bar, next to Mr Fake-leather-briefcase, the arsehole from SOCOG. His suit is rumpled. He is way charged up. Uncle hands me a drink.

Here, my boy. Any you fullas hungry?

Yeah.

Uncle leans over the bar and lifts out a huge tray of pastries and sandwiches and hands it to me. I walk back to where I'm standing with a big mob and put the food on the table. Everyone dives into it. I turn and go back to Uncle. He's talking to the barman.

Yep, all of them on the same docket with the food.

Uncle hands me a whole tray of vodka and bourbon drinks. Fake-briefcase stumbles against me. He turns around to apologise. He is drunk and paranoid. He sees me and his face lights up.

Oh! Another wadjula!

Then he realises who I am and instantly becomes very unsure again. I might as well be one of them. He sways on his feet.

Sign here, says Uncle.

Uncle puts the pen in the SOCOG official's hand and he signs for the grog and food. He's got no idea what he's signing. Uncle holds up a beer glass to me.

Cheers! My good-luck boy!

Uncle gives me a warm smile. He is teaching me. Them Uncles always teaching. I nod. I'm taking the lesson. A huge mob of us drink for free that night. And we drink well.

You're right, Uncle

I'm standing on the streets of Redfern with Uncle Charlie and Cousin Des. Uncle is telling me a story. He acts it out with gusto.

These fullas burst into this bank in Redfern, wearing overalls, boots, ski-masks, they point shotguns at everyone in the branch.

On the fucken floor you cunts! Get down! All of you! Fucken hurry up!

But there is this Old Uncle, see, he's sittin on a chair in the branch, he's waiting for the bank staff to do something for him, he's gotta sit down, you know, he's an Old Fulla. But these young fullas with the guns are saying get down, but for him to get to the floor is slow, you know, he's got full grey beard, this Old Fulla, he's gotta stand up first. So he's putting all his effort into standing up and he's so slow, he's like slow motion, and everyone else is getting down so the young lads really notice him. Quick as a flash, the first fulla with the shottie goes over to him.

Not you, Uncle!

Uncle looks up, half-way through tryin ta stand up.

You're right, Uncle.

This young fulla motions for Uncle to stay seated and he does.

The other fulla is already over the counter. They get sixty thousand dollars and piss off. The fucken jungais arrest em an hour later just a few streets from The Block. And they are wondering, How'd you know it was us? Eh? How'd yas know?

You're right, Uncle, Uncle repeats, waving his air shotgun around in the street, and we all laugh.

Uncle shakes my hand. He rubs me as if I'm a lamp and he wants to make the genie come out.

Coming to the tent tonight, he says.

Uncle shapes up to me. Throws a couple of slow soft punches.

I'm ducking and weaving. Play counter-punch.

I'll see you there, Uncle. I'll be the wadjula.

Take us to Baba Du

The boxing-tent show goes well this night. The audience are mainly Kooris, Nyungars, Gooris and Murris and are raucous as hell. King is on fire. Uncle Elmore is a riot. Uncle Charlie and Des come to the show.

They all head off to Baba Du — we tell them we'll meet them there. I go off to the dressing room. Put an icebag on each elbow and smoke a big nyar-ha. How do you get tennis elbow from boxing?

Anyway, this big mob of us are goin to Baba Du. We get cleaned up and go down to the main road to get a cab. King doesn't have his car tonight. We need two cabs. We stand near the road to hail. Twenty minutes later we're still standing there and nine cabs for hire, nine empty cabs, have gone by. Don't stop, won't stop. They see us there trying to hail — slow down — see everyone's skin, and quickly speed away. They kind of look away with funny little expressions on their faces, like they're on holiday in Bali and they meant to do a fart and now they're sitting in a warm sticky wet mess; trying to pretend to themselves and the world that they've done nothing wrong. Done nothing. Done nothin fucken right, that's for sure.

Well, we're all getting a bit tense here. Half the drivers going by are north Africans. Maybe their aunties in Melbourne served spicy meat and rice to Uncle Kumanjai Presto and myself. You'd think they'd fucken stop. But they don't.

Joline, our Yorta Yorta sister, is over it.

This is bullshit! Why won't they stop? What century do they think it is?

Maybe I should tell me cousins to stop bashing taxidrivers.

We all turn to look at the voice.

King laughs back at us: What?

We all laugh. Uncle Elmore isn't fazed.

Right. Everyone behind the bus stop.

We all start to move back.

Not you.

He points at me with his chin. I'm looking back. Who me? What?

You out the front.

Gestures with his lips for me to move forward.

So everyone goes and hides behind the bus shelter, leaving the skinny wadjula with the nice haircut, wearing the trackie top fringed with colours of the flag that he got in a trade with a Pinjarup man, to hail a cab.

About forty-two seconds go by before a cab slides into the kerb to pick me up. I hate this fucken country. Not Eora Country. This fucken country. You know what I mean.

Going to Sydney Theatre Company. The wharf. Pier four.

Sure.

I open the back door and four people run out from behind the bus shelter and jump in. The Turkish cabbie is giving me the evil eye.

What the …?

I shrug. Just fucken deal with it.

There's nothing he can do apart from take them where they wanna go. I slap the roof when the doors are closed. Station-way.

Uncle Elmore roars with laughter as the cab takes off.

I assume the position. Another forty-two seconds go by and another bloke stops for me. I open the front door and give the driver a big smile. King and the others run out and jump in. I love this fucken country. You can be anything.

The driver is looking at me like I just fucked his sister.

Take us to Baba Du.

Laughter.

What?

Take us to Baba Du.

Laughter.

Where do you want to go?

Baba Du, fuck ya, King chimes in, all smiles.

Laughter.

The driver considers King through his rear-view mirror.

There's no need to swear.

There's no need to care.

Assorted giggling. We drive off.

Dooligahs in Paradise

Stewie and Liz come to see the show in the boxing tent. They fly up from Melbourne. We treat ourselves and stay at the Novotel in Darling Harbour.

After the performance I'm talking to Paulie Softbell. Paulie is a Ku-ku/Meriman man from Darnley Island, in the Torres Strait. Brilliant writer, actor and animator. He's telling me how much he loved the show.

I was yellin so much when you and King were going for it. The only person yellin more than me was this lil Koori kid next to me!

Laughter.

Paulie keeps moving.

See ya at Baba Du!

Laughter.

See ya there, Bruz.

I meet up with Liz. The Koori kid Paulie was talking about is our son, Stewie. It's not hard to see. Tanned complexion, dark hair, big brown eyes, soft nose, split watermelon smile. We jump in a cab for Baba Du.

We talk about Liz's family history. Out on the First Fleet.

The first gubbah ever hanged out here was Liz's direct ancestor. Settled in Gundungurra Country, Goulburn. Arrived in Eora Country. Travelled through Kuring-gai and Dharug Country to get there. Got supplies up on the road through Tharawal Country. Ran a dairy and became famous for making cheese. Blessed are the cheese-makers.

In the seven or so generations that have felt the sun on their backs in the great south land, did someone have a relationship with one of the Gundungurra Mob? A conversation echoing through the gubbah landscape like a lone cockatoo turning cartwheels and screaming in an empty blue sky. We covet what we see. Let's face it — didn't have to be a relationship — just had to produce a child. In those early years of the penal colony gubbah women were so scarce. Goulburn was remote then.

The cab drops us off. It's a long walk up the steps. Liz and I grab one hand each and lift Stewie every second or third step. Stewie is excited. Seen a play with lots of fighting, out with Mum and Dad, out way past bedtime. It's exciting stuff. But tired too. Been a long day. Flying in a jet plane. Staying at a big hotel.

We get inside Baba Du. George and Robby make us real welcome. We get drinks. Robby takes Stewie to the bio box. Robby's cousin is the DJ. DJ who flows with the room. Big room. Big mob. Mellow. Mellow. But can party up at any moment. Funk out. Rock up. Stewie loves this. Even though he is fading fast, he still loves it. I get called out to the balcony for a smoke. Dylan is telling me that this country is the place described in the Bible.

Garden of Eden, Bruz.

Paradise.

Laughter.

Food grows on trees. Seeds on the ground. Don't have to work. Just live. No shame bout bein naked. No hoofed animals. God spoke directly to the People.

Paulie takes the smoke.

But ya know Adam wasn't my mob. Snake come up offerin apple — we eat the snake! Yaaah!

Laughter.

Uncle Backy is talking about the seating collapse at one show and the water in our boxing tent.

It's the Dooligahs, says Uncle Backy.

Spirits from the land. They aren't happy. Pissed off, in fact.

We smoke in silence for a long time. Looking out over the water.

The Dooligahs, he says quietly.

I go back inside to see how Stewie is going.

You right, Stewie?

I'm hungry.

I'm standing in the Garden of Eden. I turn around and on the bar behind me, the exact length of my arm away, are some cakes and rolls in a basket. I reach out and hand Stewie down some food. Stewie beams at me. An oh-my-God-you-didn't-pay kind of beam. I tousle his hair. His smile is a mile wide.

And then everyone around is asking where the food came from. I'm grabbing and handing forever. The little basket always seems full. Loaves and fishes. Good tucker. Happy.

Stewie eats up and gets his second wind. After playing with him for a while in the bio box, Robby helps put him to sleep in the Green Room. On a couch there.

Liz and I have a rage. She's got a big mob of friends here too.

It's good to be in Uncle Charlie's Country. We stay way late. Stewie sleeps through in the Green Room. It's comfy and warm. Sometimes it's full of people. Talkin. Laffin. Smokin. Stewie sleeps on through.

Finally Baba Du is closing. Each night is an adventure that takes years and years and always ends too soon. We wake Stewie up. He's not too big to carry but there is a ladder and plenty of stairs. We walk the long walk with our tired boy.

At the bottom of the stairs is the biggest mob of people all waiting for cabs. There aren't that many cabs. All a bit reluctant. But we're all fares. Business wins out eventually.

Most of the Mob are going to the Bourbon 'n' Beefsteak in The Cross. We're going back to our hotel. We wait. We settle Stewie onto a bench with a jacket for a blanket. It's a clear cold night in Eora Country. Stewie isn't happy. He can't sleep. Too hard. Too cold. The waiting going on forever.

For us it's pleasant to wait. Yarnin up and smokin cigarettes. So much laughter it could fill the harbour. We're still two cabfulls from the top of the line when Stewie starts to lose it. He's so tired now he's all stressed. Starts sobbing. All the Mob are noticing. People who love their children. Love their cousins, nephews, nieces. People who are missing their kids. A cab pulls up.

Eh! You mob take this cab!

This Murri woman gestures us to the cab with her lips and chin.

Eh?

Yeah, you go. You go home. We're going on.

Everyone helps us to get the distressed Stewie into the cab for the short ride to the Novotel.

Thanks, you mob.

Liz kisses and hugs the woman who called out. We get in and go.

The driver is relieved to have us gubbahs instead of the Mob waiting but disappointed we aren't going very far. We pretend we don't notice. We tell the driver to come back. There's plenty of people still to come. Plenty of fares.

Soon we're in Darling Harbour and carrying Stewie up to our room. In a few moments he is sleeping peacefully.

You alright, my brother?

I come in to work. It's a beautiful afternoon, but when I walk in there is a certain heavy feeling in the air. Small groups of people huddle in corners of the tent. Talk is quiet and sombre. I see King.

How are ya, Bruz?

King just keeps walking. His eyes low and heavy like rain clouds. A dark dust cloud swirls around his heart. I see Joline, my Yorta Yorta sister.

Hey, Sis.

Hey, Bruz.

Joline hugs me.

You alright, Sis?

I'm okay.

I just hold her and wait for it. She takes a breath. Here it comes.

We just heard bout Dylan's brother.

What about him?

Joline shakes her head. Hugs me again.

Oh, shit.

I gather myself.

Anyone seen Dylan?

He's got people with him. Flying back to WA. Show cancelled.

King close to him?

Think so.

I nod my thanks and respect to Joline. I go off to find King. He's in the dressing room. The skipping-rope whizzes like angry bees, King's feet dancing over the rope as though he's not attached to the earth. I stretch and warm up. King is focused short. His eyes clouded. After a long time the rope falls silent.

Alright, Bruz?

King just nods. What's he gunna say to me? Course he's not fucken alright! The audience are arriving and we're in costume and out in front of the tent and spruiking and playing with them. Getting them in the mood. I'm doing my pea-in-the-cup trick. Get them to bet on which cup the pea is under when I stop moving them. Give away Minties when I lose. Give em away when I win. Then the drum starts. We come to the first fight scene. Classic boxing-tent set-up. Get a local drunk loudmouth to fight the smallest Koori fighter in the troupe. Me, I'm pissed and a total arsehole (didn't need to research this role).

Fight that little bastard? This'll be easy money!

That little bastard is The Phantom. Played by ex-fighter Ron Waddell. Ron is a diminutive Yorta Yorta man with a heart as big as Phar Lap. We don't have any real worked-out choreography. Just know that certain moves really make the joke work. Me going for a king hit and hitting air. Once. Twice. Ow! What was that? Someone's horse just kicked me in the guts. I look up and Ron is grinning at me.

How ya goin, Bruz?

Tonight I'm gunna try and really hit him. I make the decision then and there. Just one good hit. I shape up. Take a swing. Hit air. Swing again. Nothing. Bloody hell, I can't! Not even close. He's here, he's there, he's gone, he's over there, ow! It's a riot. The show is going well. Just before the last fight, where King fights me for the title, I'm backstage, Ron is helping me on with my gloves.

Keep your eye out, Brother.

Eh?

Watch King tonight, Brother.

Ron's voice is a light caress in my ear. His eyes tell me. And I'm out there and the audience is cheering and I'm shadow-boxing and posturing for the crowd.

I glance at King. Don't normally look. He's not moving. Not at all. Nothing. Shit. And we're getting called in for the ref's instructions. King is focused short. He can see his demon. Right there. Right here … bout where I'm standing. We touch gloves. We turn and go to our corners.

Ding! Out we come. King burls across the ring and slams a combination into me. Shit. This ain't the choreography. I'm pushing him off. Hitting him to keep him away. Jeez, I can be a slow learner. It's murder in here. The actor doing the commentary is lost. His script isn't working. King needs this. I'm there. Ding! Round two. Fight. Fight. The commentator makes a recovery and is calling the new fight well, getting a few laughs.

It comes to the end and I know I've gotta go down. I fucken don't want to.

We go into the set-up for the final stunt and I get confused for a split second and the glove that I take the knock-down punch on drifts too low. Even in that moment I know King's gotta follow through anyway. Everything has built to this. It goes to slow motion for me. He's gotta. Jesus, maybe I forced this. Needed this. After this fight, a staged ending would be piss-weak anyway.

Thump! Down I go. I lie there breathing. It seems dark. I'm swimming in a soup of tiny yellow and red glowing dots. I listen to the count.

… seven … eight …!

Shit. What happened to one to six? I try to get up. My legs go one way and I go the other, swaying then toppling sideways across the arena. Crunch. The crowd go wild, as they say. King helps me up. We bow. Go off.

King comes over to me in the dressing room.

You alright, my brother?

I'm good, Brother. Fucken good, I reply.

I laugh. King gives a tiny smile.

You alright, my brother?

I'm good, Brother. Fucken good, King replies.

We laugh. But he isn't really. At least the life is back in his eyes. That demon gone for now. We shower and change and smoke in silence. I'm thinkin bout the Dooligahs in the Garden of Eden.

Someone else's Country

I'm backstage in the boxing tent before the show sorting out the bandages for my fists when Uncle Elmore trundles in. Singing.

By the time I get to Phoenix ...

She'll be ... laaaaffin!

He laughs. He staggers. He stinks of grog.

Oh, Uncle.

Stevey, my boy!

He pulls me into an embrace.

I'm sorry, Steve.

Shoulda rung me, Unc. I woulda come and sat with ya.

I'm sorry, Steve.

Shoulda rung me.

Uncle steps back and shakes himself down. Trying to loosen that demon on his back. In his brain. His liver.

I'll be right.

You right to do the show?

Laughter.

I'll be right.

We hear female voices and Uncle spins on his heel to go and

flirt with them. Naughty Uncle. Any worry is for nothin. Show is fine. Uncle does add in a whole new routine which is pretty funny. Ya gotta expect that.

Later on we're all at Baba Du. Uncle Elmore has picked up the pace again and is making his presence felt. It's late in the night now. There's gunna be some speeches and singing. They set up a stage and a mic. Before anyone can stop him, Uncle Elmore rushes the stage and grabs the mic. Does a little Elvis to get everyone's attention.

Since my baby left me …
I've found a new place to dwell …
It's down the end of a lonely pier.
At Baba Du!

People are about to laugh when Elmore launches into his angry speech. It's not pretty. No-one moves. Uncle Elmore is a Senior Man here. He opened up pathways for many here to follow. He is a grandfather. The young men look away. The young women shift on their feet. Uncle barrels along his highway. Getting worked up, too.

Finally, Auntie Nolene Cinders disengages herself from her group and steps up onto the stage. She goes up to Uncle, clamps both arms around his thick shoulders, speaking gently to him the whole time, prises the mic from his fingers, puts it back on its stand, and leads him off the stage.

The women are the backbone, my djaambi Henry always says.

Aunt leads Uncle over to me and George and Robby and Uncle Backy. The fight has gone from Uncle as quickly as it came. He is near to weeping.

I'm sorry.

Get him some water, says Uncle Backy.

Elmore gulps down a glass of water. People are looking in our direction. Uncle Backy leads us to the balcony for a cigarette. We move as one, forming a circle around Uncle Elmore that no eyes can penetrate. No-one looks now. Behind us, Auntie starts up the speeches on the stage. The whole room is cheering and clapping. Clear out the merde with love. We stand at the rail. Light our cigarettes. Look out over the water. Uncle Backy comes to me.

You see him home.

I nod.

You see him home, he repeats, looking deep into my eyes.

I nod again.

I've been here before. Years ago when I was a soldier. I spent almost five years as an officer in the army reserve before I went fully professional as an actor. I guess I craved the experience, especially after growing up in a country town. We had two VC winners from New Guinea in our district. We knew their stories, drank them in greedily as little boys, played them out in our backyard war games.

Most of the men who trained and instructed me in the ways of war were Vietnam veterans. In army circles these men were venerated for their valour and commitment, regardless, or perhaps in spite of the political baggage surrounding the conflict.

Of course, many of them were in an almost constant struggle with their inner demons arising from their time in combat.

One particular night in the officer's mess of the Western

Australian University Regiment, Major McCourt really lost it.

Maybe I'm reminded of him because he and Elmore could be brothers, both short solid fullas with cannonball heads. And because my love and respect for Major McCourt are immense.

The good Major smashed up a bunch of stuff and let fly with a monologue so dripping in blood that Macbeth would be proud. Then he rocked back and forward on his feet, then fell straight backwards, still at attention, to land unconscious on the floor.

We young subalterns picked him up and gently carried him down to a camp stretcher we had ready. Our high regard for him only matched by our fear of manhandling him, we all knew what he'd done in Vietnam, he was a legend for it. Like Uncle Elmore, a good soldier and a good man, and we had to preserve his honour in that moment. No shame to him.

I eventually resigned my commission and left the army reserve after visiting Gallipoli.

It's a while later and I'm helping Uncle down the stairs out the front. It's been a long journey from the balcony. Plenty of stops and songs and speeches along the way. Uncle falls several times on the stairs. I grab him. Pull him up. He finally falls on the last step. He sits there and doesn't move. Stiff as a board. I sit.

Gotta go home, Steve.

I'm looking up the street for a taxi.

Gotta be in my own Country.

I stand up. One will come. Gotta be on our feet. Got no chance with these cabbies otherwise. I haul Uncle to his feet.

Come on.

I'm always in someone else's Country.

A cab slides up. I open the back door and push Uncle in.

Tell the driver where ya goin.

Eh?

Where you goin?

Newtown.

You got bunta?

Uncle fishes in his pocket and holds up a banana (fifty dollar note) so that the cabbie can see he has the fare.

See ya tomorrow, Uncle.

Yes, my boy. Tomorrow.

I shut the door carefully. Pat the roof twice. The car drives off. I go back and look at the water for a long time.

Ding! Come out fighting!

Last night. After this we'll be taking the boxing-tent show south, to tour Victoria, much the same as the original touring shows. We'll be playing in sheds. Playing to country people. Last night in the big city for us.

Show goes really well. Another full house. People yelling for their stories. People so full of joy to see their stories up on stage. Telling stories is the best way to combat the ignorance that has prevailed in this nation. When people who've been marginalised suddenly feel celebrated for who they are, there is a particular type of relief and outpouring of joy.

Last night of Baba Du too, so we decide to get all dressed up. I've been acting like it's everyone else who wants to get styled up but I got this suit I bin dyin to wear.

After the show I borrow King's car. He's gunna meet us there. I have to go round to pick up Ron from his hotel.

It's a flash big-city hotel. I park out the front and go to the concierge's desk.

Unbeknown to me, there's been this ongoing bullshit at the hotel. Staff won't clean Ron's room, room service had to be paid for in cash — the usual suspects. They have some big problem with my Yorta Yorta brother. If they'd ever been on the receiving end of one of his rips to the body they might be more polite.

Anyway, the desk staff are just in the middle of being indignant about Ron's latest request, for an iron. I march up in my flash suit, shiny shoes and short hair. I throw back my shoulders. I can smell these wankers from before the flashy fountain in the lobby.

Good evening. My name is Steve. I'm here for Mr Waddell.

What?

I glare at this tall skinny gubbah pimple factory.

I'm here to pick up Mr Waddell.

They're looking me up and down. This doesn't fit their assumptions. It's like they're stunned. How unbelievable is it that I could work for Ron? I lean in, give them my best Clint Eastwood.

Mr Waddell is a very busy man. Any time in the next three seconds would be fine.

Pimple Factory can't move. There is a tiny bubble of spit forming in the corner of his mouth. The other kid dives for the phone.

Mr Waddell? Your … driver is …

Bodyguard.

He looks to me.

I … I beg your pardon?

Actually, I'm Mr Waddell's bodyguard. His driver is sick tonight.

Oh … your … bodyguard is here to pick you up … Yes, Steve … Thank you, sir.

He puts the phone down.

He's on his way down.

Good.

They look at me. Expecting this information to give them some relief. I don't move. I stand there. Looking at these pompous gubbah wankers for a long time without blinking. It's like flight attendants who don't like getting you drinks. What the fuck else are they there for? They fidget and pretend to do shit. Move pads around. Put pens in a jar. I stare.

The lift comes down and the bell rings behind me.

Ding!

Come out fighting, I say to the desk boys with a smile.

I turn and Ron comes out of the lift all styled up.

Good evening, Mr Waddell.

Ron doesn't even look at me.

Evening, Steve.

He strides past me full of purpose, past the flashy fountain, out the hotel entrance to the hire car and stands at the front door. Oh, this lad is good. I'm moving quickly but not rushed to be at his heel. I'm looking both ways out the door and up and down like I'm guarding Malcolm X. I open the door for him. The hotel staff are craning their necks to watch us, their jaws dropping like inbred retards.

Lovely night for it, Mr Waddell.

Indeed, Steve. Indeed.

Ron gets in. I shut the door. Don't look back to the hotel boys but I can feel their eyes still on us. I get in the driver's seat. We drive off. We get around the corner and piss ourselves.

Got it from cunts like you

King pulls into this town in Jardwadjali Country. Just south of
Wergaia Country. Been on the road for a while. Sydney seems
like a dream now. Right out here in north-western Victoria.
King's like me: loves to tour; loves this audience. He's in his
woman's car. Drove straight up from Melbourne. From
Boonwurrung Country through Woiwurung, Wathaurong and
Djabwurung Country.

Drives down the main street, eyes peeled for our hotel.
These munarch (police) go past, in the opposite direction.
They see this big Nyungar behind the wheel of the BMW and
throw the patrol car into a 180, sirens and lights on full blast.
King does a U-turn and pulls up out the front of our hotel.
The munarch nearly overshoot and then scream in behind,
their car blocking King's reverse. King watches them in his rear-
view mirror. He laughs.

I'd be up and over that kerb in a fucken second if I wanted
to get away. Those fullas wouldn't last in WA, he says later.

The munarch are out of the patrol car now. One each side of
the car. King winds down his window. His beanie is pulled
down low. He doesn't look at the munarch. Stares ahead as if

the conversation is really just happening in his head. Keeps his voice low and controlled.

Is there a problem orrificer?

Why didn't you pull over?

I did.

No. You did a U-turn.

Is a U-turn illegal in this street?

When indicated by a police officer, you must pull directly over to the side of the road.

I'd already started my turn when I saw you.

Bullshit.

You were goin the other way weren't you?

Licence?

Why did you pull me over?

Licence?

King, still staring straight ahead, puts out his open hand to his woman in the passenger seat. She places the licence in his palm. King hands it out to the munarch.

This your car?

Hers.

The munarch look in at her. She's not afraid of these dumb fucks. They go back to their car to check King's details on their radio. After a while they come back. Hand King back his licence.

Whaddaya doin here?

Workin.

You got a bad attitude, you know that?

Got it from cunts like you.

What?

I said, I got it from cunts like you.

The munarch hesitate.

Why did you say you pulled me over?

They suddenly look a little bit lost. Like they're little boys just pretending to be officers of the law because they found these blue hats and big guns in an abandoned tin shack down by the river. They go back to their patrol car. They turn off their flashing blue lights and drive off.

Lloyd and I are watching all this from our upstairs hotel window. We laugh. Then we go back to shooting each other with our dart guns.

What you do

Liz had found Lloyd playing in the street outside our St Kilda house a year or so ago. It was late at night. His latest stepdad had just OD'd. His mum, Libby, was in Collingwood trying to cope. We took Lloyd in and fed him.

Liz and I both grew up in the country where that's what you do.

A few days later Libby sat in our kitchen and wept and asked us to look after her son. She was due in court in a couple of days and expected to get a custodial sentence. Some stupid woman had tried to bash Libby on Fitzroy Street but woke up in hospital herself, with two stab wounds.

When I was a kid on the station we had Ed live with us for years. Ed's dad was a drinker and Ed copped it big time. So Ed came to live with us. To escape the senseless beatings. This is the way things are.

Ed was wild. I remember him sitting up the back of the school bus. The driver, Mr Martin, asked Ed to get his feet off the seat. Ed didn't move his feet and yelled back, Behave yourself, Jack! All of us little kids gasped with shock. Ed wasn't gunna do as he was told and wasn't afraid. Called Mr Martin by his first name. Wild.

We also had young Jeffrey Singlet with us for a while, too. Jeffrey's dad had built the extension on to our house on the station and he and Dad had become good mates. Then one day a disaster. Jeffrey's Dad was fishing off some rocks at a remote beach and was swept into the sea by a freak wave. I don't think his body was ever found. Mum and Dad offered to have Jeffrey for a while to take the pressure off his grieving mother.

There's one episode that lives strongly in our family memory because it was so nearly a double disaster. A moment that made us all question the intentions of our guiding spirits.

It was a hot day. The summer of 1970 or thereabouts. Dad loaded the ute up with all of us Motor boys and Jeffrey and drove us to the swimming spot down at the Lort River.

There is this deep hole carved out of the rock that was always full and always deep no matter how much rain there had been. In fact, the level of the river had risen considerably since the adjacent land had been cleared and burnt, ready to be cropped.

Our favourite thing was to ride on Dad's back. It made you feel so secure to be moving across the water riding on Dad's broad back, his muscles moving under his skin to propel us forward effortlessly.

Dad is ferrying us kids across the river so we can sunbake on the otherwise inaccessible rock.

Kingsley, my eldest brother, has already swum there himself and I am halfway across the river on Dad's back when we hear a terrific commotion coming from the other bank. We look back to see that Jeffrey Singlet has fallen into the water. Will, my next eldest brother, is there and in a panic. Jeffrey is screaming, gasping and sinking.

Dad is always so cool in a crisis. My eldest brother, too.

Dad, I've got Stephen! Kingsley dives in to get me.

Dad yells back to the other bank.

Will! Stay there! Don't go in!

He's too little. Can't swim, but he's looking like he'll give it a try. Jeffrey will drag him down. We'll lose them both. And Kingsley is grabbing me, and we're moving to the bank. And Dad is tearing back across the water to where Jeffrey has just disappeared below the surface. Stops twice to check on Kingsley's and my progress. His mind is racing, a runaway train heading for a cliff. Am I gunna lose one child or two? Or three?

My brother gets me to the shore and pulls me up onto the rock.

Dad is gone when we look back. Under. Us Motor boys all holding our collective breaths. Valuing that air. And whoosh! There's Dad with Jeffrey. Scrambles up the rock with the child. Places him down. On his side. Clears his airway. Jeffrey suddenly vomits a huge amount of water. Dad holds him. Encourages him. More spew. Brown river water. Jeffrey coughs. We still got him.

I think I started crying. I think my elder brother comforted me. I felt his warm love through his wet brown embrace.

So Lloyd lived with us, whenever he needed to. When he wanted to go back with his mum for a while, he'd just go off and be with her.

Lil Wemba Wemba/Kurnai boy with Celtic parents. We must look a real sight on the streets of St Kilda.

Lloyd opened up our world.

His extended family visit us. We visit them. A family devastated by assimilation policies which left them vulnerable to drugs and alcohol. Even though Libby lives most of her life on the street, she is a good woman. A good mother. The bond between mother and son unbreakable, unbendable, despite all circumstances.

Libby has LLOYD tattooed across her ample cleavage. A tough woman. Could flog you or me. Both of us at once.

Car's on fire

We're in this hotel room in Kurnai Country, at Bairnsdale. We've done our show for tonight. Home tomorrow for the weekend. A week or so more and the tour will be finished.

The Mob here made us pretty welcome. I know this is Lloyd's father's Country. I searched the audience fruitlessly for faces I can connect to his.

Even a few gubs in the audience. A good show.

The river flows just behind the hotel. Lloyd's cuz, Pringhael Lenny, was born on the banks of this river. We're on the second floor. We can glimpse it through the trees. Seeing the water flow. Carrying all before it.

We're smokin up big. King and I. Don't know why. We're really pumped.

King's got a hire car. New Commodore. Keys burning a hole in his pocket. Get so hot in there they start to burn his leg. He quickly rips them out and flicks them onto the bed. Plunges his fingers into the bucket to cool them down. Makes a noise through his teeth of a hot poker going into the bucket. Gives me the smile. That crazy Nyungar smile.

You see that. Car's on fire, he says through his eyes.

I shake my head. Big stagey shakes. My face is like I'm smiling through a dried clay mask and my smile is cracking the clay.

King's hand flicks open underhanded way — a question? He's smiling like the cat who's got the cream. Can be home tonight. Tonight, eh — why wait? His eyebrows are up with the question.

I shake my head. I'll get my bag, I say out loud and turn to go.

Yaaaaaah!

King punches my arm.

Laughter.

We shape up.

Laughter.

I go a few doors down and get my bag. Hadn't unpacked a thing when we'd arrived that morning. Didn't look at the room. I meet King in the hall.

The Commodore *is* on fire too. Eats up the highway as we track the coast out of Kurnai Country into Boonwurrung Country. King is a machine behind the wheel. Like he's dreamed himself into it. Become part of the car itself. I'm cocooned in a fog of fear and nyandi.

An hour or so in we nearly miss a turn-off. I'm nursing a road map on my lap. No interior light on. Heavy mist. We're travelling. Really travelling. We swerve across at the last moment. The mist rushes in behind us to fill the hole we make.

Jeez, Brother. What about the co-driver, eh?

Eh?

You gotta keep up with it, Brother.

Yeah. Rightio.

My arms are folded in terror. My moom is clamped in my seat like a vice.

We come round a sweeping left-hander and over a rise and there is a tiny glimpse of a bonnet in the trees halfway up the far hill. King sees it first and we rapidly lose speed. Sitting on the speed limit feels like we're standing still. We go past the patrol car in slow motion.

Dunno how I got this far.

King is just loving it.

Co-driver asleep! I gotta do fucken everything!

We stop for a burger and petrol and top-up.

We're home safe in bed by about quarter to two. We fucken flew.

Cuppa tea at my place

Lloyd and Stewart and Liz in a motel room in Victoria. Morwell. Right near the border: Boonwurrung, Woiwurung and Kurnai. Lloyd and Stewart are both born Boonwurrung Country.

I've been fighting with the boys. They gang up on me and we roll around on the bed and throw mock-punches. They're so excited to be away and in a motel room and gunna see the play with lots of fighting in it again.

The room is probably the worst I've ever had to stay in on tour. Old everything. Dingy. Not overly clean. Seventies dark brown and purple decor. But I'm here with Liz and my sons. My heart is so full. Stewie and Lloyd don't even notice the shabbiness of the room. They're excited cause it's a motel room.

Since Lloyd had become part of our family it hadn't been completely easy for Stewie. Before Lloyd came in Stewie was our only son, our only joy. We all have to make adjustments, and for Stewie that meant having to share his room for the first time, and all those other little boy issues.

But that weekend it all clicked. We really felt like a family. We'd passed through some new level of acceptance with Lloyd, too. This family can work if we all commit to it.

Family is what you make it.

Some moments in life live with you forever.

Earlier on we'd been welcomed by local Elders and were given gifts as part of the ceremony. For weeks, as the theatre company had travelled around Victoria to do the play, each town was new Country to us. Welcome to Boonwurrung Country. Welcome to Yorta Yorta Country. Welcome to Wathaurong Country. Welcome to Kurnai Country. We'd been welcomed everywhere we went.

In the afternoon we drove Lloyd to a nearby town to visit his grandmother and grandfather. His grandmother is a remarkable woman. Could just about reach out and touch her love and respect for Grandfather, it is such a tangible thing. Feel the light they're giving off touching our faces.

Grandmother takes a long time to settle Grandfather back into his chair after him getting up to greet us. His voice high and soft, his hand light as baby's breath, his eyes strong as a gum tree and warm as toast.

Grandmother fusses over his slippers until they are just right. He gives her his secret smile.

We sit down like we're in our own Nana's house. Same knick-knacks on the same sideboards. Same colour schemes. On the mantel above the fireplace there are a number of family photographs. More on the wall.

Lloyd is gentle with them. Respectful.

Grandmother offers us all tea. Invites Liz into the kitchen. They talk quietly in there. Grandfather and I can't hear what they're saying. Grandfather asks me about Lloyd. How things are with him.

The house is pretty bare. No TV. No phone. No electrical appliances of any kind. Except in the kitchen Grandmother has an urn. An urn! If fifty people turned up out of the blue, they'd all get a cup of tea. No worries.

We've brought milk and some biscuits for the kids. Never turn up empty-handed. Our Boonwurrung sister taught us that.

Liz and Grandmother bring the tea into us. Lloyd and Stewie go outside to muck around. We yarn up. Drink tea. It's hard to leave when the time comes. We could talk all night.

Freddy always says that the best way to break down barriers is to invite someone into your home for a cuppa tea.

Freddy cracked me up one time with this comment. We were driving through the centre of Melbourne on our way to work. This young cop sees us, a Yamatji and a wadjula driving in Liz's old Falcon. He pulls us over. No reason. Just the fucken obvious. He checks my licence and everything. All the time looking at Freddy. Freddy has gone blank. Just simple defence. Freddy was getting arrested when this cop was still in primary school. I see the young cop looking.

Wha'd ya pull us over for?

Licence and registration check.

Bullshit.

What?

I said, bullshit.

Now I've got his attention.

Well, what's the problem, ossifer?

Your front numberplate is unreadable.

Is that it?

You'll have to get it fixed.

Is that it?

Yeah.

Then he can't think of anything else to say. I get back into the car. Drive off.

Gubbah cunt, I suddenly spit out.

Freddy looks at me. He laughs. Crazy gubbahs. He didn't realise I was getting steamed up. Just another day at the office to Freddy.

I don't think he's comin round my place for a cuppa tea, Freddy says, flat as a tack.

The way he says it, deadpan, just cracks me up. I lose it. We laugh all the way to work.

Downtown earlier that day — we'd been putting on a boxing display to encourage people to come to the show that night — Uncle Backy sees me mucking around with my sons. Uncle knows that neither of them have sprung from my loins.

See, you understand Skin, Uncle says quietly.

He's referring to a conversation weeks before on the balcony at Baba Du. I was asking Uncle about the nature of skin relationships. In indigenous societies there are two types of families, blood, going up and down like a tree, and skin, going sideways like many tributaries from a river. There'd been this talk about the nature of skin families and blood families binding the community together. I was inquiring not so much the about structure, but the feelings inside the relationships.

All of you, he adds, taking in my family with a sweep of his beard.

All of these things were buzzing in my head and singing in my heart in that moment of play-fighting in the motel room that evening with my family.

Later on that night, an old auntie at the play tells me that some families are there tonight who wouldn't have been in the same room as each other for a couple of generations, because of some old feud.

The head of security

Back in Waveroo Country, Albury–Wodonga. Just south of Wiradjuri and just west of Jaitmatang Country.

Our last show of the tour is fittingly played at the showgrounds. Just near the saleyards. We perform on a sawdust floor, the smell of livestock ever present. Good show to finish with.

After the show we all go back to someone's place right by the river. Build a big fire. Have a smoke and drink and watch the fire dance and the water flow. Both unstoppable forces. Sitting on the bank in the light of the full moon — the water seems to be above the land, flowing as a body up and above the Country. The fire is good.

Us mob from the show mainly hang together at the gathering. It's mainly gubbahs there and none of us are really used to them. We've been in another country. The Country inside our Country. And outside and all around at the same time.

Uncle Elmore's words come back to me on a waft of the warm breeze across the river. Been inside this other country for so long. Can't tell you where the border is.

In each Country we've travelled the show to, the People have welcomed us with open hearts. With Dance. With Language. With Song. With Gift-Exchange.

The evening passes and we eventually return to our motel.

The next morning I'm up at five. It's my dad's sixtieth birthday; I've gotta fly to Perth. It's a bright clear morning. The motel and town haven't stirred yet. I bundle everything into my bag and open the door of my room to let the day in. I feel tired but good.

I hear a tiny noise outside. I step out and there is Uncle Backy. Gumaa: Doer-in-the-Dawn. He does it in the dawn, alright.

Hey, Uncle.

Hello, my boy.

Uncle holds out a huge joint to me. It's pretty early. Even for me. But all I've got to do today is travel. Party at Mum and Dad's in Wajuk Country tonight. Why the hell not?

Uncle Backy's Country is just to the north of where we are standing. Uncle paces slowly back and forth. His eyes occasionally flick to the north.

I smoke. Hand it back to him.

Going home for your dad's birthday?

Yes, Uncle.

Uncle nods. Does a little dance.

Feelin good.

We smoke in silence. Uncle occasionally hums a phrase to himself.

By the time we finish his morning go, my powers of speech are greatly reduced anyway. Uncle just seems to get livelier.

My cab rolls up. Uncle Backy gives me a big hug.

Take care, my boy.

Thanks, Uncle.

See you when you get back.

And I'm driving through this sleepy country town. And I'm on the plane and flying south over Taungurong and Woiwurung Country to change planes at Melbourne for Perth.

It's a long day of terminal lounges and airline food and then I'm home in WA.

All my brothers have gathered. We go out to dinner. My younger brother reads a poem he wrote about Dad. We have a big cake. Sing Happy Birthday. Dad seems happy. We go back home. Everyone is drinking now. Me too. Haven't been drinking much doing the show. Got no tolerance. Two-pot screamer.

The phone rings. Liz in Melbourne. Wishes Dad happy birthday then talks to me. Things ain't goin so good in St Kilda. Too cold for the Parkies in Boonwurrung Country. Liz has got them all sleeping over. Libby and Lloyd and Lisa and half a dozen people she doesn't really know.

The Parkie Mob isn't a fixed group, with people constantly coming and going.

People Liz doesn't know are settling down for the night. Whole lotta charging up goin on. Needles too. Liz is worried for Stewie and for her own peace of mind. Feels like she's under siege.

Behind her it sounds like a wild party. Behind me it is a wild party. Can't hear the telephone conversation too clearly. My brothers going in hard now.

I put down the phone.

Fuck.

What's wrong?

My mum and dad try very hard to understand our position. They've always supported us even when they don't totally comprehend. I never totally comprehend. This situation is what my mum fears the most. Me too. Libby can't keep everyone in line because she's too gone herself. Liz doesn't feel completely safe. I'm a couple of thousand clicks away.

I gotta go back tomorrow.

I ring the airlines. Change my ticket. Upgrade. Can't stay for the weekend now. There's nothin worse than being away from your family when you think they might be vulnerable.

By the time I get into Boonwurrung Country the storm has blown over. I re-stack the spare mattresses, put a couple of syringes in the bin, put the spare blankets away.

I feel a bit useless. What did I think I was gunna have to do? How was I gunna do it? But the fulla is always the head of security. Just the way it is. Maybe I wasn't thinkin right because of charging up with my brothers. But, better safe than sorry.

Libby had woken up and realised that Liz's space had been disrespected and got rid of everyone. Liz and Libby are now sitting in our sunny garden drinking cups of tea and nibbling on milk arrowroot biscuits.

Without our women we're nothin. We're nothing anyway.

St Kilda gubbahs

Ring ring. Ring ring. Ring ring. Ring ring. Ring ring. Ring
ring. Ring ring. Ring ring. Ring ring. Ring ring. Ring ring.
Ring ring. Ring ring. Ring ring.

Hullo.

G'day. It's Stephen Motor here, I was wondering if …

Who?

Stephen Motor.

Who?

Steee — phen.

Peter Boathook?

Stephen Motor.

Who?

Stephen. Stephen from St Kilda.

St Kilda?

Yeah, Stephen. Stephen from St Kilda.

The gubbahs?

Yeah. The St Kilda gubbahs. I'm lookin for Lloyd.

Eeeeh. The gubbahs. Hey, Peter, my nephew.

Stephen. Who's this?

Yeah, Stephen. Charlene.

Oh, Auntie. How are you, Auntie? You good, Aunt?

Oh, yeah. I'm good.

Oh, good. Oh, Aunt, is Lloyd …

How's all your mob?

Yeah, good, Aunt.

Stewie good?

Yeah, Stewie's good. Loving his basketball.

Oh, true. Liz good?

Yeah, she's good, Thank you, Auntie.

Oh, lovely.

Is Lloyd around?

Pause.

Who?

Lloyd?

Oh, dunno. Maybe he's asleep.

Oh, Aunt, can you have a look for me, please?

Hang on.

Clunk. Walk walk. Walk walk. Walk walk. Walk walk.

Hey, Lloyd! Phone!

What?

Phone.

Who phone?

Gubbahs. St Kilda gubbahs.

Shuffle shuffle. Sniffle. Fart. Scratch. Burp. Yawn. Shuffle shuffle.

Hullo.

Eeeh! Lloyd! How are ya, lil fulla?

Good.

Wanna go for a drive?

Can my cuzzins come?

Yeah.

Sings (P Diddy): I'll see you when ya git here.

Clunk.

Fairhaven footballers

Wudjari Country, Esperance, early 1970s. The referendum which meant the original inhabitants all became citizens in their own Country is less than ten years old. I'm less than ten years old myself.

I'm watching my eldest brother play footy. Kingsley was and is my hero. Always brilliant without seeming to try very hard. He has a particular habit of standing on the footy field with his hands on his head, waiting for the ball to come to him. Sometimes he would only be a few feet away from the action, still the hands would be on the head, totally relaxed until the moment of springing into devastating action.

Every Saturday morning the football manager would drive down to Fairhaven to pick up anyone who wanted to play. Fairhaven is a big old mansion in town where all the Stolen Mob live. This is Church of England business, so us Micks never really know much about it. Except that we are jealous of the trampoline they have in the huge backyard. None of us wadjulas really knows what happens there. So there is plenty of speculation.

Fairhaven is a strange name for the place. No-one there is

fair, and it's closer to being a prison than a haven. Some might argue that a prison can be a haven. A haven from what? And for whom?

Fairhaven is known as an orphanage, except that none of the kids living there are really orphans. They were taken from their parents by police. No-one ever mentions the word 'stolen'. The parents of these kids are alive and living in the dim, distant hope that one day their children, their joys, will be returned to them by the gubment.

What would you do if the gubment passed a law and the police came to take your children? My mum says she'd fight, fight anyone for her kids. I know she would. But, I've fought the police. Hard to win.

I go into the change rooms at half-time. Just an old tin shed in those days. Pretty exciting for a little boy, to watch these young men going about their football business.

My brother is in quiet conference with the coach. This big Wongi fulla from Fairhaven is getting a rub-down by the team trainer. I wander over to the rub-down table. This big fulla smiles at me and sits up.

I'm watching the trainer's hands on his skin. Skin so different from mine. I feel strange. Kind of uncomfortable. In unknown territory. I don't know this fulla. He smiles down at me. Nods at his leg. Before I can think about it, my hand is reaching out to touch his thigh. It's warm and hairy, thick knotty muscles just beneath. Same as my big brother. He looks at me.

I suddenly feel like I've done the wrong thing. Maybe he didn't mean for me to touch him. I back away. Go and stand just near where my brother is still talking with the coach.

I've got your number

I've come into The Gatwick (Hotel) to find Libby.
Boonwurrung Country, St Kilda.

This place was built nearly a hundred years ago as a haven
for rich squatters and miners to stay in when they were in
town. Now it's ninety years later and the place has never been
touched. Nothing changed. Nothing fixed. Nothing cleaned. A
building in the autumn of its life. Weighed down by half a
century of people on the down and out staying there for a
night or two. I hear the gangsters used to work out of here.
Run a brothel too. Weighed down by all the stupid ugly
pointless dramas and deaths. Deaths from violence, from drugs,
from old age. The whole place smells like my grandfather's
dressing gown. It's like a prison in here. Or a mental asylum.
Dark. Damp. Dusty.

Ahead in the corridor there are some people talking. I go
around to the left to the front room on the ground floor. It's a
favoured room because you can hang out the window and talk
to people on the street. I knock on the wooden door.

Who is it?

Steve.

Pete?

No, Steve.

Steve? Steve who?

Yeah, who Steve?

Gubbah Steve.

Aaaaaaa!

The door is opened by Lisa. Lisa hugs and kisses me. Auntie Pringhael Esmae gives me a kiss.

Ullo, Bub, she says. Only Auntie looks me in the eye.

There is a young Wiradjuri couple sitting on the bed. I don't know them. I nod at them. The fulla nods back but doesn't look at me. She doesn't look up, either. They are both looking down at their baby, who is asleep in the pusher. Everyone is looking down now. The women's voices are very soft.

Who you lookin? Libby?

She here?

Djillawah (toilet).

I'll wait outside.

You sure?

Yeah. Nice to see ya, Aunt.

I go outside and pull the door shut behind me. The djillawah is another wooden door across the hall. I don't want to stand too close.

There are some residents talking to two people from the Legal Service.

These two young cops suddenly come in. This young copper with red hair sees this Koori woman dressed nicely.

You working, love?

The cops leer at her and nudge each other.

How much?

The cops laugh.

What did you say?

How much?

They laugh.

I'm a lawyer, you little wanker. And I've got your number.

Oooo. I'm scared.

Are you working yourself? Piss off.

The cops both adjust their gun belts. Walk on past.

Libby comes out of the djillawah.

Hey, Bruz. How are you?

Good, Lib. You alright?

I'm good.

What are you up to?

We gotta go way. Funeral.

Oh.

Yeah. Sorry. You know.

Alright, Sis. I'll see ya when ya get back.

Yeah, Bruz.

Watch out for the landlords

I met Freddy through King. King introduced me to this shy and polite Yamatji, six feet two in his socks, skin like buffed chocolate. It was in our St Kilda house. We reckon that place must've had this coming together energy there. We get the feeling people been gathering here for thousands of years.

It seems like moments later we're all working on this film together.

Freddy has come over from WA and is camping with King, but it doesn't work out. Freddy is tonguing for a drink. For a woman. King's woman is stressed about Freddy being in their house. Worried about Freddy pulling King down. King is on the wagon. I speak to the producers. Freddy comes to stay with us. Give them both some relief.

The first night we go out with George and his woman. Her auntie owns a flash restaurant on the beach. We go to buy some VB. Dario the liquor store shopkeeper calls Freddy Jacky Jacky. Watches him like a hawk. We go somewhere else for the VB. Vote with your feet.

Fucken racist wanker.

Freddy looks straight ahead. He refuses to let it get to him.

He's worked overseas. He's won huge awards for his work. He's touched people's hearts. But to Dario he is still Jacky Jacky.

Dario thinks life is about working hard. Making money. He is from a European peasant culture. He doesn't think about the blood shed to build this city. This street. He doesn't think about the Boonwurrung People whose land his shop stands on.

Maybe he actually believes that Land can be bought and sold in this Country. Maybe we should offer him some glass beads for some beer? Or some poisoned blankets?

We go to the flash restaurant. The waitress is rude to us. Frightened by the large Yamatji man, the even larger Ngarrindjeri man next to him. George keeps his cool. His woman's auntie owns the restaurant.

Freddy has had more than his quota of VB. Freddy is over it now. He eats everything with his fingers.

Traditional way, he quips to us.

We laugh. Freddy falls asleep at the table. We carry on as though all is normal. All is normal. Freddy wakes suddenly and yells out at the top of his voice, inviting the waitress to suck his cock. She declines. Everyone looks. Freddy eats his cheesecake with his fingers.

We go. Stunned that we have to pay. We had expected to be treated like family. You don't get to own big flash restaurants on the beach by giving free meals to extended family.

We walk home through the streets of St Kilda. Freddy sees a bus coming and steps straight in front of it, throws his hands up.

Yaaaaa! Watch out for the landlords!

Freddy screams at the bus driver who jumps on his anchors,

sending most of his passengers sprawling. I haul Freddy off the road. The bus takes off.

Gotta keep up my profile, Coorda.

And we laugh. Method in his madness.

We go home. I've promised the film producers a low profile.

Next day I'm called to a meeting with the producer. Told off like a naughty schoolboy. Some fuckwit has told the producer Freddy was running wild on the piss through the streets of St Kilda. A hatchet job on me. I didn't know I was already in The War Zone. In war zones there are enemies.

These people have had sheltered childhoods, I think. One trip down the street to a restaurant and then straight home is not what any of us would term 'running wild'.

I deny everything. The producer's decision is that Freddy can stay with us until we go on location in Broken Hill. Then back with King. Just the movie. I tell the producer this is a silly mistake. I know Freddy is hanging by a thread. I've got eyes in my head. There is tension between Freddy and King.

Rehearsals go on. The next day Freddy asks to borrow my guitar to go busking. They won't give him his pay at the movie and he wants some money. He asks if he can borrow my hat to collect walung. It's all I have left from my grandfather. I am reluctant. Freddy swears to look after it. I agree. A silly decision. He takes it and goes.

We are woken at two in the morning by Freddy coming home. He has Jilly in tow. A tough hippy girl. Dreads, piercings, no bra, multicoloured clothes. My grandfather's hat is gone. My guitar pick-up is smashed. The shoulder strap gone. Jilly sits cross-legged on our lounge room floor. Freddy swears he is going to marry Jilly. Tomorrow if he has time.

They go to bed. They fuck very loudly. We're sitting up now. Having a sip ourselves. A nyandi. If ya can't beat em …

Freddy and Jilly come back out. They describe to us their respective orgasms. We already knew. We heard. Freddy swears again he will marry Jilly.

Half a cup

The next day the Italian movie director comes to my house to take Lloyd shopping. She needed a lil Koori fulla in the film. When I was auditioning for the role of the sociopath outback cop I told her about Lloyd. I thought it'd be good for him. He could get some putta (money). See some of the outside world. Like Freddy, Lloyd is a natural actor (just a lot more shy).

So we can bond, the director had told me on the phone.

I can get a skateboard, Lloyd says over the noise of the TV.

Fuck, he loves that TV loud.

A couple of days later I would see the skateboard, broken clean in half at Pringhael Lenny's house.

Lloyd's cousin then still happy and laughing all the time. His ringlet curls bouncing and laughing at every step. He'd dive off the top dive-board at the Wantirna pool where we'd go with Lloyd and all his cousins. Pringhael Lenny would laugh all the way down until he hit the water.

Weeks before the skateboard bonding this woman from the government department came to interview Lloyd and us about the living arrangements. The government department has the shits with us because it had no say in the arrangement. Still trying to keep the Kurnai in check after all these years.

Liz and I are reluctant — but the gubment woman assures us the interview is only to ensure Lloyd's welfare.

The young woman is a uni graduate. Child psych or something. In her twenties. No children of her own. Doesn't know shit. Her second question to Lloyd is about Libby.

How much does your mother drink?

Lloyd flicks me a look. She misses it. I give him a tiny nod. I'm thinking the same as Lloyd. Fuck you, you never said you were gunna ask about his mother. Don't let anyone outside the Family know what you are thinking.

She asks again.

How much?

Half a cup.

The young woman looks up from her notes. There is a silence while she thinks.

How many half a cups?

Just … half a cup.

Are you sure?

Yep.

And that's it for Lloyd as well as for us. We all know she is a moron now. It's Them and Us. Who cares what you say to morons?

Do you like school?

Yep.

I'm thinking about my first day of trying to get Lloyd up the street to school. We're on the street. I'm trying to convince Lloyd of why it's a good idea. He's not convinced.

Finally a car stops. A Koori fulla in a Commodore wearing a

suit and tie. He works for the Koori Legal Service. Asks Lloyd if he's okay. Asks me if I'm okay. Gives me his card. Tells Lloyd he should go to school and give it a go. After a long time that fulla drives off.

Lloyd agrees to go to school if we can visit his cousin at the Gatwick first. I finally get him to school by lunchtime. Seemed like a good compromise at the time.

The government worker sitting at our kitchen table tries to get all in-depth.

What is your favourite subject?

Maths.

The government worker takes notes. Liz goes to make a cup of tea to hide her giggles. I watch Lloyd turn the uni graduate inside out. Effortlessly.

The day after the director's skateboard bonding session is my first day of shooting. It's my character's final moment. Being led away in shame and disgrace. King is my archrival. He glares at me from the comfort of his expensive suit. I'm led away in chains. The same as my great-great-grandfather. I play the scene.

The director is all over King between takes. Touching him. Cuddling. King's eyes are on the ground. He is married-up. A lot of directors and producers would think this is the right way to treat an actor of King's calibre.

King taught me how to put my eyes down and to misunderstand everything the advancing woman says, when you are married-up.

King looks a bit uncomfortable, but manages a laugh, anyway.

We're all trying to work together. Lloyd always looks up to King. King is sober. Nyandi but no alcohol.

The first time Lloyd met King was in a hall in the country. We were playing in Kumanjai Dempster's boxing-tent play. We were doing a tech rehearsal to perform that night. I had Lloyd with me on tour. He loved the hotel-room pampering.

Lloyd walked around the old hall decorated like a boxing tent, looking at all the people working. He became quiet. He came over to me with a strange look on his face.

Eh, Steve. No-one here charged up, eh?

Lloyd had never been around so many sober adults before. Ten years old.

I nod. No-one charged up, my son.

Lloyd was surprised. Maybe shocked. His smile lit up the hall.

He looked up at King warming up in dressing gown and boxing gloves.

Make a list

Going to the shops on Fitzroy Street. This is St Kilda. Boonwurrung Country for countless generations. I see Libby sitting on the bench near the Park Street corner. She is just sitting. She is a statue. A clay statue. She hunches against the cold. Staring ahead. So alone.

I walk up and sit next to her. I don't speak. Libby is down low. I'm trying to pull her up with my presence. She rocks gently every now and then. As though weeping. Although she isn't. Her spirit is sad. Tired.

Ngumary (cigarette)?

Libby nods slowly. I take out my tobacco and roll two smokes. It takes a long time. I'm crap at rolling. Specially in a wind. I give her the ciggie. She puts it to her lips. I light hers and then my own. She gently nods her appreciation. We inhale. Exhale smoke.

Cars fly up Fitzroy Street. The drivers don't really see us. Like we're invisible. They've taught themselves not to see us.

I watch my cigarette smoke be sucked into the air of the suburb. I'm thinking about gum leaves and Smoking Ceremony.

Lloyd's birthday tomorrow.

Libby suddenly brightens. Her eyes spark back up.

We could have a barbie. In the park.

Which barbie?

Down by the shed near the water.

Alright. I'll go shopping for some snags and that.

I'll be in the park. Come and see me tomorrow.

I nod. Finish my smoke and go. Libby sits staring at the road between her and the bottle shop.

Next day I go to the park after lunch. Libby is nowhere to be seen. No-one knows where she is. I find her sister, Lisa.

We still havin a barbie for Lloyd's birthday?

Yeah. I'll come shopping with you.

So we go to Safeway and buy a big mob of sausages, onions, bread and tomato sauce and then head back to the park. I get some lemonade and coke as well.

Back at the park it's turned cold and windy. Libby and Lloyd have turned up. Been in the city takin care of some business.

I fire up the barbie and start cooking snags. Lloyd and lil Paulie and BJ run around in the park doing little boy business.

I sit with Libby and Lisa and Auntie Pringhael Esmae, Uncle Bim and Cousin Jed. We eat snags and onion wrapped in bread and smothered with tomato sauce. The wind blows straight off the bay and cuts through us like the Native Police on horseback, galloping through our camp. Everyone is drinkin hard. I have a VB.

Where's Uncle Elton? someone asks.

Not back from Lenny's funeral yet?

What?

I hear myself asking. Everyone looks at me.

Who Lenny?

Libby looks down.

You didn't know, Bruz?

The tears brim to my eyes without warning. I look around. Into the wind. As if I'll see him again, his curls bouncing as he walks towards me. There is only the cold wind blowing up from Bass Strait.

He didn't know, I hear Libby explaining to the others.

Everyone has gone quiet. Just me and the wind in the trees. Everyone is gone. I blink my eyes and I'm all alone. Sitting in this stupid fucking park with it's stupid fucking European grass and fucking trees and they've taken Pringhael Lenny and I'm all alone. And it's not fair. He never had a fucken chance. I watch a leaf picked up by the wind go roaring across the open grass to the busy road where it is sucked under the wheels of a passing truck. A removalist's truck. Full of beautiful furniture for a beautiful bayside home. Out in Bass Strait are the islands where they took the Boonwurrung, Wurundjeri, Gunditjmara and Palawa women to keep in the rape camps for the whalers and sealers. I can't see them. I can smell the islands on this cold wind. Pain and suffering have a smell. A hundred and fifty years hasn't dulled the aroma for me.

I blink my eyes and turn back. Libby and Auntie Pringhael Esmae are comforting me. Everyone is back. I'm ashamed of my sudden grief. What right do I have to this grief? I'm like a middle-class English kid listening to gangsta rap and thinking it's all about me.

It's still a harpoon in my heart.

Pringhael Lenny and his sister. Both gone. OD. A flat in Collingwood.

Oh for fuck's sake. And sitting here in this park where everyone can disappear and leave me alone with this wind. We're all hanging by a thread. The drinkers, the heroin addicts, the dope smokers, speed users, all edging closer to the void from which we were born. The big nothing, not the Big Nothing — the vastness of Family, of Culture, Henry's mum tells me about. Just nothing.

Pringhael Lenny and his sister were drinkin and someone came around with some smack and they'd never had it before and no-one ever told them ya can't mix grog and smack and now they're both dead and never gunna see twenty.

Make a list. Get all the drinkers and drug users on it and tick them off as they go. Libby and Lloyd go to a funeral every other week.

In a war you've gotta expect people to die.

I finish my VB. Hug and kiss everyone. Go home to my heated house and my cable television.

The art of making yourself invisible

Wudjari Country, WA, early seventies. The MacArthurs were a farming family whose property backed on to the station that Dad worked on, we lived on. A few kilometres closer to Coomalbidgup (proper) from our place. We were closer to the Lort River. We used to ride horses with the MacArthurs all the time. Their kids were all about the same age as us.

They were also long-time friends of Chaz Campbell, the head stockman from the station. Them MacArthur kids always referred to Chaz as Uncle Chaz. They were the first wadjulas I ever heard use that term for someone who wasn't a blood relative. I wondered if it came from Chaz or from the MacArthurs. Chaz certainly had a lot to do with the Wongi stockmen. And the MacArthurs used to have Nyungar and Wongi servant girls. Did housework and shit for the family.

This is the 'better life' these girls were stolen from their families by wadjulas for: to be servants for the wadjulas.

I remember this one girl. Emily. Proud young Ngatjumay woman. I admired Emily for her ability to turn herself invisible. She had perfected it. Emily could come into a room full of us wadjulas — bring in a pot of soup, or something —

and then just disappear in front of our eyes.

You could stand in that laundry for minutes and not even notice her there in the corner behind the ironing board, meticulously folding up work clothes and school uniforms. If you looked carefully, after a long time you might notice her leave, a shadow flitting through the light of the doorway. Emily found the shadow in a room instinctively, effortlessly.

Years later, when I'd moved to Melbourne to become an actor, to try my hand in the big world beyond Coomalbidgup and Yonda Quagi, I would practise this technique while trying to avoid fares on the trams. Sometimes I could make myself into such a blank space that the conductor really wouldn't see me.

One day I meet Libby at the St Kilda tram stop. My Wemba Wemba sister whom I'd come to know and love and learn from. Despite being wracked with drug addiction, Libby is a good woman. But lives on the street. Street ways.

Hey, Sis.

Hey, Bruz.

We hug and kiss.

Whacha upta, my sis?

There is a big Mob waiting quietly with my Wemba Wemba sister on the platform.

One of our Mob got chucked off the tram, before. There's this new conductor. Little gubbah cunt. No offence, Bruz. We gotta retrain him. I guess he just forgot …

At that moment the tram pulls up. Libby and her Mob suddenly turn their volume up to eleven. Someone in the Mob turns on a ghetto blaster and they lurch on to the tram as though they're really pissed. Even before the tram takes off they are arcing up. Fighting and swearing, dancing and laughing.

No-one from the St Kilda Parkie Mob will have any trouble with fares for a while.

I hear my parents talking about the MacArthurs' servant, Emily. I'm in my room, which I share with my little brother. Across the dining room, Mum and Dad are doing the dishes in the kitchen. Mum washing, plastic gloves on. Dad drying and putting away. We all had our household chores but Mum and Dad did the dishes. Probably appreciated the time to talk.

I can't quite make out everything they say. Bits and pieces. Sad Emily can't be with her family. At least she has a job. And the MacArthurs are lovely people.

One day I'm mucking around in the MacArthurs' machinery shed with Grant and Thomas. An oxyacetylene bottle falls on Thomas's leg. Grant and I are pretty sure it's broken. We can't move the bottle off Thomas. We're too little. Thomas is howling. All this other stuff has collapsed as well. We've got no chance of moving anything. Grant and I shit ourselves. We don't know what to do. Mr and Mrs MacArthur are in the top paddock doing some lamb marking. Five miles away. We've got no vehicle. Grant and I stand outside the house, trying to decide what to do.

One of us will have to go. I'm the eldest …

Just then Emily comes out of the house to see what is going on. We didn't call out to her. She looks across to the machinery shed where Thomas can be seen to the right of the tractor on blocks, lying under the huge metal gas bottle. Emily turns and takes off at a full run. We watch her until she disappears around the corner. Her bare feet raised a tiny cloud of dust each time one of them touched the earth.

Grant goes for a blanket and I get a water bottle. For the shock.

Emily runs all the way to the top paddock. She hardly seems to have been gone when we hear the engine noise of the approaching vehicle. The ute pulls up and Emily is in the back. Mr and Mrs MacArthur quickly free their son. Mr MacArthur carries him to the house and Mrs MacArthur gets the ute ready for the inevitable trip to town and the hospital.

Grant and I feel guilty. We shouldn't've have been mucking around over here. Emily gives us a look, and goes inside. It was the only time I ever saw her eyes.

Fly like a fucken eagle

Five days go by before I get the call from the movie people on location in Broken Hill. It's late. The line producer calls me. Story I'm told is that King has gone crazy. Got pissed and bashed Freddy. They've been sharing a room in Broken Hill.

The truth is that I'm their second choice of troubleshooter. They called Paddy first. A crazy Celt of the old blood. It isn't until Paddy's got there that they realise he is a heavy drinker himself. In the grog grip. That old choke-hold.

They realise it when the cast and crew are treated to the Paddy and Freddy Show in the hotel that night. Paddy and Freddy get blind. Sing and dance. Entertain. They're funny. Compelling. Next day on set Freddy is hung-over. All over the shop like a madwoman's piss.

So the film people want another option. Me. I give my list of conditions. The pay. Our own place away from everyone else. Our own phone. Our own car. They reluctantly agree. And I'm at the airport too early the next day. Three planes. Changing at country airports.

For company I have two stuntmen and a bloke who specialises in purifying water supplies.

And finally I'm touching down at Broken Hill. Wiljali Country — near the border with Danggali Mob. It's still only 9.00 or 10.00 am. I've been up since fourish.

I get driven to our new digs. Freddy and Paddy are drinking port. Talking about their exploits. Freddy has a swollen face and is still sore all over from his beating. Extra work for make-up.

I lift my shirt and rip off the nyandi taped to my belly.

Paddy says his goodbyes. Begs me to try to get him back in a few days or so. I say goodbye.

Freddy and I have a smoke. I tell him what I know. My secret to surviving on tour. Do whatever you need to do to get you through the night. But don't let anyone see you do it.

Low profile.

Low profile, Freddy repeats with a big nod of resignation in his head and shoulders.

Thanks, Bro, I say.

He grabs my hand. We sit there holding hands for a long time. Release on a sigh and a smile.

We pick up our car. We drive to the Bronx. Meet Slacker.

When the Mob there see it is Freddy they all come out of their asbestos, fibro and tin houses to shake his hand. They'd have their photos taken if anyone had a camera. No-one does. No-one has anyfuckenthing. They run up to Freddy and make pistols with their fingers, quick-drawing them from inside their shirts.

Fly like a fucken eagle, they call out to Freddy.

Fly like a fucken eagle!

From his movie. His award-winning movie.

We get in the hire car. Slacker directs us to a spot way out in the bush. I'm thinking we should've asked for a four-wheel drive. We've already pushed our luck. Slacker is Wiljali man. Slacker tells us this is his grandmother's country. We smoke. We drop Slacker home.

We drive way out the other side of town. Park the car on the side of the highway. Get out and walk. The land is hard and dry. We find dead eagles. They've been zapped by the huge electricity cables. Stupid fucking gubbahs. We collect feathers. Bones. Freddy grabs a freshly dead eagle, two metre wingspan, and puts him in the boot. We get back in the car and drive.

Eventually Freddy begins to tell me his side. The dispute with King. He tells me because I have not asked. This is the way it is with men. But what Freddy is talking about is years ago. Under the bridge, surely. Freddy says he couldn't defend himself. Never wants to punch a man, to hurt anyone with his fists ever again.

Me, I've punched King — and King's punched me. I let it go. I don't care too much for explanations. What is this to do with now?

We drive home. The dead eagle stinks the car out.

Strong spirit, says Freddy.

We smile through gritted teeth. I wind down the car windows. His strong spirit is ready to make me spew.

By the time we get home with our six-pack of VB, our nightly ration for both of us, I'm the one hanging for a smoke.

Freddy puts the huge dead bird out the back door of our little place. That night I dream of huge eagles flying around our unit.

Freddy puts the TV on full blast. The TV is always on full blast. I roll. We smoke. Roll. Smoke. Freddy paces the flat continually. His eyes flick this way and that. Can't be still for a moment. I keep rolling. Gunna roll him into bed. Minimum alcohol. Don't go out. This is my strategy.

At two or three we go to bed. We'll be up at five. Sleep is elusive. I know Freddy is in bed. I can hear him snoring. Someone else is still pacing all night in the dark. Maybe moorroop (spirit). I roll on to my stomach. Pull my doona up high. Clutch my pillow. Tomorrow there is acting to be done. Maybe it's acting. Not so sure anymore. It's a film to those on the other side. But not to us. Not really.

Two dead men

Dressed as a cop. The khaki ones. Not the blue. I am a cop. All the doors through which I live are now bricked up in my mind. And these other sluicegates are open now, this filthy purple liquid soaking through my psyche, staining everything, filling me with cop thoughts. Cop being. Fear. Hatred. Know that I'm right.

I'm standing on a rocky outcrop. A significant feature. I don't know its name. Push back my hat. Raise my high-powered hunting rifle. Lean against the rock and look through the scope.

Fuck! There he is!

I look up over the scope. Whisper sweet nothings under my breath. Work the bolt on the weapon. It is well oiled and smooth. Chamber a round. Like breathing to me. All on the rhythm of my breath. I never take my eyes from the hill a hundred metres or so to my front. The artist looks at the subject, not his canvas.

Coming up over the hill is Freddy. The big Yamatji man holds a spear. There is a feather attached to the spear. His chest is bare.

This is where I aim. The body mass. I breathe in. Squeeze the trigger.

Crack!

Freddy is flung backwards and falls in a heap. I breathe out.

Cut!

The crew are spread out. Freddy hasn't moved. Up high in the vast blue of the sky, directly above where the dead man lies, an eagle circles. Tight circles. Looking down on his Coorda. I swear it wasn't there a moment ago. Jeff the gun-man flashes me his shooter's smile.

Good shot, Mate.

Jeff takes the rifle from me. I climb down from the rock. I don't know its name. There is no-one here from this Country.

Someone asks me if I want a drink. I drink a cup of cold cordial and hand back the cup. It's hot.

The gate is clear! I hear the camera assistant call out. This is the signal that we'll move on from this shot. The camera is being moved.

I move away, the shame creeping up my throat. Just walk a bit. Finally I look back. I know they can't see my tears from this distance. I wave. I smile. I turn away and a silent scream surprises me, ripping out of my throat like a cavalry charge against women and children.

The movie director is cuddling the near-naked Freddy. They sway gently as if slow dancing to music I can't hear.

It's forty degrees Celsius. My tears will dry. Or be diluted by sweat. They'll powder my face before we do my close-up.

The rest of the day is a daze. Heat shimmers. Dampened conversations. Then explosive action in front of the camera.

I see Freddy with my little super-eight camera. I tried to explain the focus to him. Figured he didn't get it. With child-like enthusiasm he shoots everything. Rocks. Blades of grass. Ants.

Eventually he comes close enough to me to see the look in my eyes. He doesn't speak. Puts down my camera. Embraces me. I need this. Like water. Don't know if I can live without it. After a long time, Freddy speaks. Sometimes, when Freddy speaks, it's as if it's someone else's voice.

You're right, Coorda. We show the wrong way, to teach. We gotta do it.

I know Freddy's right. But at this moment I don't want it to be me. Don't know why it is me.

And then we're wrapped. Freddy and I are out of costume in a flick. Freddy flashes me his irresistible smile.

Can I drive, Bro?

Don't try your Jedi mind tricks on me.

I get behind the wheel. Gun it. Flog the hire car along the dirt track. Don't give a fuck. We grab some VB at the drive-through. Forget about our self-imposed quota. Go home. Nyandi. Big nyandi. TV blaring like some angry god no-one will listen to any more. Eat toast. VB. More nyandi.

Let's go for a drive, Coord?

It's dark now. We gotta get outa town. Away from the lights.

I'll drive. Freddy smiling at me.

Nah, I wave him off.

Climb behind the wheel. Dark as. Don't know the time. Don't care. Only call times for work are relevant. Even those are made up. Someone made up a clock. We all play along as if it's a real thing. But we all know it's nothing. All of us. At least it's a circle. We don't need Einstein and $E=mc^2$ to know that time isn't a straight line. Not out here.

Carn, Bro, let me drive.

Freddy is insistent. Consistent. You've got to admire him for that. I've had one VB. Freddy five. I'm driving. This is the job I signed on for. Even though I know jobs don't exist. So I drive. We leave Broken Hill far behind. Freddy never stops egging me on. I hammer the hire car. And then we are nowhere. But really somewhere. Slacker's grandmother's Country. We pull off the highway. I switch off the lights. Kill the engine. Freddy goes for a piss. Me too. We amble back to the car. The metal of the engine and bonnet ping and pop. Cooling down in the desert night air.

You can see our constellations from here, Freddy says.

Henry has taught Freddy this. Freddy is a good student when he wants to be. I look up. The Milky Way is so clear we could touch it. Caress it with our fingertips, or lips. It blankets us. I feel safe. Freddy tells me how to see Their constellations. I look. I search. I follow his instructions. But all I see are the stars. Their clusters. Their shapes. I look down. Embarrassed at my failure. We smoke nyandi. Freddy is patient. He gives me another set of instructions for my eyes.

Cast your net out from the other side of the boat.

I look up. I look through the stars, not focusing on the light, but on the dark. Something like looking at those 3D images in the Sunday papers, but on a vast scale. And stretched out across half the sky is the great Emu Spirit. I'm struck dumb. I'm on the road to Damascus, on my knees, rubbing the lightning from my eyes, wondering how long you can look and not see.

Look with heart, not eyes, Freddy whispers.

This is from Henry, too.

We are so insignificant under her sky. So tiny. Grains of sand in the desert. Freddy is still talking whisper-quiet. As the sky turns, the year passes, She lays her eggs. We know it's time to hunt for eggs.

I nod. So much knowledge can be destroyed. Swept away by gunfire. My body jerks at the memory of the rifle in my hands as this thought comes over me. My fiction. My reality. The present is the past is the future. I sit in the dirt. I've gone quiet. Freddy moves away to leave me with this. In this moment we are men. Brothers. Our love is a tangible thing. Thick enough to hack with a knife or a sabre.

Can I drive, Bro?

His voice comes from far away. From the silence of the desert. His teeth flash in the dark. I jingle the keys in my pocket. Me, the killer. I stand slowly. Hand the keys to the dead man.

We amble back to the car. Some roos are moving in the dark over the other side of the highway. And the sound of the tyres spinning on the gravel is like a swarm of European bees. They all sting. Hurt like fuck.

I remember the Woorabinda Dancers doing their Honey Hunt Dance. I saw them at the Maleny Folk Festival. The tallest fulla in the troupe playing the tree. These other Wadjigu fullas track the bees to the tree — then chop the tall fulla down. Then suddenly they're all getting stung. The surprise on their faces as they try to swat away the European bees. We all laugh. Before the Invasion the bees didn't sting.

What kind of invaders bring their own bees? Bees that sting? The kind who bring rabbits. Cane toads. Foxes. Horses. Camels. Pigs. Goats. Water buffalo. Influenza. Smallpox. Poisons. Guns. They finish off the dance with big shake-a-leg. Butterfly Dreaming. Them Queensland fullas.

The hire car roars up the highway. The desert air rushing past.

Lights, Bro.

I hear my voice from far away, sounding tinny as if speaking from the bottom of a huge empty Milo tin. Freddy finally switches on the lights. I glance over at the speedo. My anxious eyes. 140. 140 and rising.

Fuck!

I look to Freddy. He isn't even looking at the road. Jiggling with the Hank Snow cassette in the car stereo.

Fuck!

I look ahead. The corner is rushing up at us like Royal Marines screaming up the beachhead. A fist cocked for the king-hit.

Freddy!

I'm screaming now.

I'll do the fucken music!

But it's too late now.

Freddy!

Freddy looks up and jerks on the steering wheel. The tyres squeal in protest as they lose their grip. And we're off the road. Spinning end around end through the red dirt. I look out. There is only one tree for thousands of metres in any direction. The car is heading straight for it. Drawn like metal to a magnet.

Time slows down. I bring Liz into my mind. Pregnant with our daughter. Bring them into my heart. The car must hit the tree. My side. My door. I'm dead. Now I can't yell or scream. What's the point. I'm dead. No time, anyway. I think of my unborn daughter. I don't want to die hating myself for being stupid. But I'm gunna. Gunna die. Die a stupid gubbah death.

And then the car comes around. The tree ballooning up towards me. At the last moment the car spins twice as fast. As if a giant hand came down and flipped us around. Like my little brother and me playing in the sandpit when we were boys, laughing at the crashes we'd cause. We back into the tree at speed. The back window implodes, showering us with tiny squares of glass. The car travels forward. Back the way we came. Slides sideways to a halt.

And now I'm screaming. Time is running again. I'm yelling abuse. Punching Freddy.

Get out! Get out! I'll fucken drive it out!

I bundle Freddy out of the car. He lands in a heap. Amazingly the car starts. I drive back through the huge dust cloud we created and zip back across the tarmac and park. I don't know what I'm doing. The adrenalin has made me crazy. I drove straight back across the highway without even looking. The tyres have all been rubbing on metal. I don't know how it drove. I get out. I'm probably shaking. I don't know. Freddy comes over. The car is a write-off. A glance tells me that.

A few minutes later a car drives up, sees the huge dust cloud and our wrecked car, and stops.

You okay?

Yeah.

We haven't got a clue if we're okay or not.

They've got no room in their car. They promise to tell someone in town. Drive off.

I look up to the sky. Nothing has changed. The stars smile knowingly at me. If I was dead it would be the same.

Freddy smokes a cigarette. He sits in the passenger seat. He falls asleep. Leaving me alone in the desert. Alone with my stupidity.

I see some VB on the floor at Freddy's feet. I need one. I open the beer and drink. I turn it over in my mind. It was as if a hand, a huge spirit hand, encircled the car and spun it extra fast that last spin. Of course, there would be a logical explanation, a mud flat, or something, but out here I don't trust that kind of logic.

I look at the sleeping Freddy. I killed him today. He killed me tonight. Payback. Here we sit in Slacker's grandmother's Country. Two dead men. I'm alive. I'm alive. I'll get to see my daughter born. If I was paperbark, I'd tear myself. But now my insignificance hangs all around me like gunsmoke after a battle, beating like a heart.

My great-great-grandfather looked at these stars as he marched up the dusty, glary streets of Fremantle, in Wajuk Country. Chains clinking all around. The weight of those ankle shackles slowing each step. The first sweet smell of the bush beyond the glare of the limestone buildings invading his senses. The Roundhouse behind him, the gaol ahead. The same stars.

My beer is empty. I open another. I drink. Another. I drink. Lights. The headlights approach. Slow down. A 4WD. It pulls off the road. Parks behind us. Cops. I get out. I walk back to the cop vehicle.

G'day.

G'day.

Get in.

I climb into the cop 4WD.

What happened?

I came up the hill, swerved to miss a roo. Lost control.

The cop is trying to read me. I am blank. Not shielded. He'd pick a shield, a mask to hide behind.

I'm blank.

Where you from?

WA. Live in Melbourne. Doing a film here.

Your car?

Hire car.

Who's asleep in the car?

Freddy. An actor. The star of the film.

Been drinking?

Only since the crash. Nerves.

Ever been in trouble with the police before?

Am I in trouble now?

I'll have to breathalyse you.

I've drunk four stubbies since the crash. So it won't be an accurate reading of my levels when it happened.

I have to breathalyse you or arrest you.

He is steady. Not a threat. He can't think any way but rules and regs.

I hadn't drunk before the prang.

I have to breathalyse you or arrest you.

If I blow and I'm over, I'll fight it in court.

That's your affair.

If you arrest me, will you take me back to town?

Have to.

Can you arrest Freddy as well?

He's asleep. I can't arrest him. He hasn't committed a crime.

Nor have I.

But if you don't blow in the bag …

You've got to arrest me. Give's the fucken bag then!

No need to swear.

Give's the fucken bag.

The cop hands me the bag, pointy end first.

One long continuous blow, he says.

I smile to myself. Freddy is a didj player. He can do one long continuous blow that goes for twenty minutes.

I blow. The cop watches me. When it's full he takes it from me. I still have heaps of breath left. Drama school voice lessons. Don't empty yourself out. Ever. Or do it all. Suddenly. I silently exhale my bottom bit. The cop looks at the crystal. It hasn't changed. The cop is definitely disappointed.

Can you ring someone for me?

Who?

I take out the line producer's card.

Let her know. She'll get me another car.

The cop is starting to hate me now. He wouldn't know a shield if a thousand of them trampled his village, put his family to the sword and took his Country.

I'm going back to look at the skid marks.

Whatever.

I get out of the cop 4WD. He makes a call on his satellite phone. He drives off to check the skid marks. The main skid marks are in my jocks. I walk back to the hire car. Freddy is stirring.

What's happening, Coord?

Munarch.

Freddy's face goes ashen. I smile.

Told him I swerved to miss a roo. He's goin to look at the tracks.

Freddy looks to me, a question.

He couldn't track his own mum home from the pub.

We laugh.

He breathalysed me.

Question look.

Nothin.

Freddy is killing himself. The cop drives up. Pulls up right next to us. We stop laffin. I don't have to wind down the window. It's busted.

Swerved to miss a roo?

Yep.

The cop gives us what he imagines is a withering look. We're blank. Empty pages. The cop looks ahead. Puts his 4WD into gear and drives off without another word. We piss ourselves. Open the last two VBs.

Are those stars laughing at us now? Finally the beer is gone and we still sit by the side of the road.

Let's get a lift, I say.

Freddy nods. The next car that comes I stand and try to wave them down. They drive straight past. The next car stops but they have no room. The next two drive straight past. I sit on the crumpled car bonnet.

My turn, Bro.

A set of lights appear on the highway.

Freddy stands in the middle of the road, his feet straddling the centre line, arms above his head. As the edge of the light touches Freddy he starts to wave. It's a big V8. We hear it clearly start to speed up. The note of the engine winding up. Freddy doesn't flinch. The car comes straight for him. Flat out. Freddy isn't getting off the road. Freddy was born in the briar patch. At the last moment the vehicle moves just off the road and narrowly misses him as it flies past.

Freddy looks at me. Smiles.

The big F100 V8 hits the skids and backs up. A redneck and his Mrs.

Where yas goin?

Broken Hill.

Had a prang?

Yep.

Jump in the back.

The redneck gets out and lifts up the tarp. We climb in. He takes off at breakneck speed and doesn't vary this engine-roaring, tyre-squealing pace for the hour it takes to get back to Broken Hill.

We're freezing in the back. Crouched under the tarp on the cold hard corrugated metal tray. Looking out at the stars through a tiny crack in the tarpaulin.

He drops us home. At the unit. We have a smoke. I ring the line producer. She tells me to ring her in the morning to organise a new car. We watch telly. Go to bed. I lie awake for the rest of the night. Jumping at shadows.

Around five in the morning I get up and go for a long walk around the quiet streets of Broken Hill.

Blood alcohol .1788

Deep in the winter. I'm twenty years old. Wajuk Country, Perth. Haven't been to bed sober since I can't remember. Frightened of this dream where I'm in the coffin with my dead mate. Listening to the dirt being piled on. The sobs of our friends and family above the ground. Rain falling.

I go to this party. Even I know I'm a shithouse drunk — so I've packed a sleeping bag in my car, figuring I'll sleep where I drop. The party is a rager. I don't really fit in with these middle-class city kids, but I do a good imitation.

As my blood-alcohol level rises I fall in love with this red-haired girl. She is beautiful but wants nothing to do with a redneck fucker like me. She tells me I scare her. I don't believe her. I haven't fucken done anything yet.

I take the rejection hard. Turn nasty. I'm abusing everyone and everything. Destroy glasses, plates, chairs, tables, doors, a window and a mirror in the bathroom, eat several polystyrene cups and then regurgitate them — and then suddenly I'm driving. Driving fast.

I don't remember getting into this car. Only one way to go now. Flat out. I'm gunning it as I come up to these traffic lights. Don't want them to change before I get there. And then there is the tight right-hander to take me on to the freeway.

Even before I get to the lights, what's left of my brain tells me there's no way I can take this corner at this speed. Now is the moment to brake hard. I change down a gear and throw all my weight onto the accelerator pedal, as if I want to push it right through the floor and onto the bitumen flashing beneath the car.

As I hurtle through the lights, I drift too wide and the back of the car clips the outside traffic light poles. The collision catapults me sideways across the intersection. I bounce off a power pole which spins the car around and I travel backwards through a front garden on the other side of the road. The car crashes through a sandstone wall and smashes into a car parked in someone's driveway.

I'm still sitting behind the wheel. Strapped in. Facing back the way I've come. My foot is still pressed hard on the accelerator. There is no sound from the engine. Everything is deathly quiet. The streetlights are out. Traffic lights too. Everything has an eerie glow. Full moon. The power pole is leaning at an angle that'd make the Leaning Tower of Pisa jealous as a bastard.

Faark.

I open my door. Open my seatbelt clasp and pull myself out of the car. Something is hissing and popping near the front of the car. I finally stand on my feet. My knees are made of jelly. I hold myself up with both hands on the car. I can't afford to be arrested for drink-driving. Won't be my first time. Macca lives close by.

Fuck it. I'll do a runner and hide at Macca's.

I push myself off the car and start to move off. It's hard going. I can't get my feet to stay under me or to go in a straight line. My head is a giant football full of mud. I've gone about twenty metres and I have to stop for a breather.

Fucken long way to Macca's. Four or five blocks. Fuck it! Might drive.

I turn and weave back to my car, oblivious of the residents who've spewed out of their houses to see the wreckage. No lights. Power pole leaning at a dangerous angle. Two frontyards destroyed. Sandstone wall destroyed. Picket fence destroyed. Shit, don't remember hitting that. The parked car is a write-off. My car doesn't exist behind the driver's seat. Just twisted metal pinging in the cool night air. The diff is lying in the middle of the road — torn out by the concrete median strip and the now flattened Keep Left sign, this side of the lights. I don't notice any of this.

I yank open my car door and fall in. The key is in it. I turn it. The car starts. I put it in gear. Let out the clutch. Engine is revving nicely but the car doesn't move. All the tyres are blown, the back two unrecognisably folded into the twisted metal.

Why aren't I fucken moving?

There is a knock at my window. Knock. Knock. There it is again.

Woody Woodpecker, maybe?

My head comes around slowly and I see two cops standing there. I laboriously wind down my window. The window in my door is the only one not shattered or broken.

Ahh, Mr Plod.

Get out of the car.

You got a warrant?

Get outa the fucken car.

So I open the door and get out. I have to hold myself up by leaning against the car wreck. Blue and red. Blue and red. Everything is blue or red just for a moment. There are residents standing all around. Yelling out to me. Nothing pretty, I can assure you. I give them the finger.

Get fucked yourself.

The closest cop grabs me.

We're taking you back to the station for a breath test.

Why not?

Get the little cunt into the car.

The other cop comes over and cuffs me and puts me in the car.

The cops have a world-weariness about them. These same blokes have to knock on doors and tell mothers that stupid bastards like me aren't coming home ever again, or worse still, have killed a young family on their way home from holidays, or whatever. They're sick of it.

I watch them wander around the road. Looking at my tyre-marks. They get the tow-truck driver to drag the diff off the road. They shake their heads as they talk to each other. They talk to the residents. Eventually they come back and get in the car. I'm feeling small and weak now. I start coughing.

Cough. Cough. Hack. Hack.

All the way to the station in the city, I'm coughing. Finally, one of them cops turns around.

Shut up.

I got asthma.

(I heard you can get out of being tested if you're an asthmatic!)

Bull-fucken-shit!

We're in the city now. Must be getting close. That dirty little redneck in me wakes up, now. I could've killed myself and anyone coming the other way, and even people watching telly in their own lounge rooms — and I don't give a fuck.

Oh, you're a fucken doctor now, are ya? Who says cops are all big and stupid? This one here ain't that big — and this one here's a doctor. A respiratory system expert. His brother's a ear, nose and throat man.

Shut up.

Well, why don't you try and make me? You must know some good tortures if you're a doctor? None of that old-fashioned phone book shit on the side of the head for me! Let your fingers do the walking! Oh, no! I've got the doctor. Actually, I've got this acne problem. Two huge pimples. On my arse! And they're blue! Two huge blue pimples on the arse of humanity!

The car stops.

Should we squeeze them? The debate rages. Is that blue pus better out than in?

The back door is opened and one of them grabs me out.

The fucken Rum Corps never went away! Just keep changing their name. The fucken Rum Corps. Take everything off us, leave us with shit, control everything, lock us up if we ever get unhappy with the situation.

They haul me into the station. Just inside the door is a desk which is on some kind of riser so that the charge sergeant sitting behind it is above my eye-line. I have to look up to him.

I stagger sideways and nearly fall.

Breath test, Sarge. Drink-driver.

Okay. Process him.

I'm pushed into a seat. A plastic nozzle is presented to me.

One long continuous blow.

I dunno if I can, what with my asthma and all. Where's the doctor? I need a chit.

One long continuous blow.

One long prodigious throw and this game will be over!

Are you refusing this breathalyser test?

I blow. Long. Continuous. I haven't had asthma since I was four. I'm just a coward.

Stephen Motor, you are charged with driving with a blood alcohol reading of 0.1788. Process him.

Oh, yeah! Gotta lock me up! Australia's most drunken! I'm a dangerous crinimal! Lock me up! Lock em all up! When in doubt — lock em up?

This cop drags me over to the fingerprint desk.

Does he ever shut up?

The other one is at the typewriter with his two fingers going.

Don't fucken think so.

The cop holds my finger then rolls it on to the ink plate. I go all floppy. Then the moment he rolls it on to the paper I throw my weight behind my finger and drag it across.

It takes the cop by surprise and in the confusion he tries to twist my hand down and I manage to wipe his uniform with my finger. Now it's him swearing. Fell for the old floppy drunk trick. Maybe he's never seen James Brown — that floppy guy is gunna keep coming back fighting over and over again.

The process is repeated. This time my whole arm is in a lock so I'm powerless to stop myself from being printed. But I do let a few of my other fingers stray over the plate. The moment he finishes with me and lets go, I stagger sideways and steady myself against Constable Two-Finger-Typist — fingers first.

I'm dragged over to the photo spot. I'm holding a board. Or is it around me?

I'm trying to think! I need a drink! Ya got any beer in the fridge? Come on! We're all in this together! Wankers! Fucken wankers! Spankers! Where are my phone books? Yellow pages! Rock of ages! I paid my money! I booked this months ago. I don't wanna miss out on a bashing. A smashing. A midnight crashing.

And I'm standing in front of the big fat charge sergeant with his desk in the clouds.

Put him in three.

Three?

The cops look confused. The charge sergeant is deadpan.

Put him in three.

Yeah, put me in three. Three! Three! Then I'll be free. If youse can't count to three, I'll help you! It goes — One! Two! Three! Let's try that all together. There were three blue pimples, squirting pus upon the wall.

They drag me down the corridor. Doors creak open and thud shut. Big key rings jangle. Locks grate and click.

We stop in front of a cell.

Number three, I presume.

The door is opened and I'm shoved in and the door slammed.

Nice work boys! Tomorrow we'll count to four! Nighty night! Don't let the bedbugs bite! Don't forget to write!

I hear the cops move off down the corridor. They're laughing. What the fuck? The anarchist is funny? I stand there.

My face close to the cold steel of the locked door.

Then I get that funny feeling in the pit of my stomach. Cold. Tight. Feeling like I'm being watched. I slowly turn.

There isn't much light. Some of the globes have blown and no-one could be fucked replacing them. The concrete walls are covered in graffiti. Texta. Biros. Scratchings done with sharp objects or even fingernails. There are crude drawings of cocks, balls, tits and cunts everywhere. There is a detailed dot-painting of a lizard or a goanna on one wall. Done with something dark. Blood or shit. There is a metal toilet bowl overflowing with piss and shit and paper. It fucken stinks. There is a low wooden bench, or bed, I can't tell.

On the bench are two large silent forms in the semi-darkness.

Fuck. I'm not alone.

I freeze like a roo in the spotlight.

I'm definitely not alone. They stare at me.

Two big Nyungar lads. With the same attitude as the concrete wall behind them. I stare at them. One fulla has bare feet. His sleeveless shirt hangs open. The scarring on his chest and upper arms seems to catch what little light there is in the cell. The other fulla is wearing cowdy boots and a press-stud shirt. I don't know what to do. They stare. I stare.

Two hundred years goes by.

Then Bare-feet smiles at me and Cowdy-boots finally speaks.

Eh, Bro? Gotta smoke?

A cold freeze flashes through my body. I thought I was done with adrenalin for the night. I'm pulsing with it now. Is this a game? I'll wait. Silence.

Eh, Bro? Gotta smoke?

Finally I find my voice.

Sorry, Mate. Don't smoke.

Bare-feet's smile is gone now.

Silence.

Eh, Bro? Gotta smoke?

Sorry, Mate. Don't smoke.

Silence.

Oh, shit. Bare-feet speaks. His voice is like a deep church bell or a heavy old didj.

You don't wanna give's a smoke cause we're Nyungar.

Bare-feet sounds very sad about it all.

Sorry, Mate.

Is it cause we're Nyungar?

They get to their feet slowly, weary with life but absolutely determined.

Wouldn't matter to me who you are. I don't smoke.

They move closer to me.

If I had smokes, I'd give em to ya.

They are getting closer.

Give's a smoke! Fucken wadjula cunt!

And bang! They're on me. Crack. Crack. Crack. I'm goin down and that concrete floor is hard and those fucken cowdy boots are fucken harder as they smash into my ribs again and again. I curl up tight. Maybe I'm cryin like a girl. I don't know. It stops. Cowdy-boots stands over me and quickly rummages through my available pockets. He straightens back up.

Eh, Cuz. No smokes.

They laugh. It is pretty funny. I look up at them, standing over me. They look like they're waiting for a bus. They look around, bored with me now, as though they might suddenly see someone they know. They go and sit back down. I look at them. They're looking at me. Two little kids who've caught an interesting insect in a jar.

I slowly uncurl. Ow. I push myself against the wall and use it to get to my feet. Drag myself up. Takes me a while, but I get there. Bit of a sway up, though. I look at them. They look at me. Both smiling now. My face feels wet. Tears. Blood. Piss? Who knows?

Eh, Mate? Gotta smoke?

Their smiles disappear. I've got their fucken attention. I'm fighting to stay on my feet.

Eh, Mate? Gotta smoke?

Cowdy-boots stands up. Oh, fuck. Those kicks really hurt.

You don't wanna give's a smoke cause I'm wadjula.

Bare-feet stands too. Cowdy-boots takes a step. I lurch a step forward. I overact Bare-feet's sad voice.

Is it cause I'm wadjula?

They both take a step forward.

Give's a smoke! Fucken Nyungar cunts!

As Cowdy-boots comes in, I aim for right between his eyes with my right fist and give it everything I've got. I know I'll only get one in. I throw everything into this big punch. But there is no collision of fist and face. I miss his face completely and swing myself right off my feet. I corkscrew into the concrete floor and collapse.

Takes me a moment to shake this fall off. I'm bracing for a rain of hot blows when their laughter breaks over me like cool surf. I look up. They are laughing so hard. I sit up. I get to giggling. They are laughing and slapping each other. Bare-feet falls onto the bench and Cowdy-boots just collapses on the ground, both laughing and holding their sides as if they've been stabbed.

They are looking at me now, too. I spit out some blood. This really sets them off. And in their jiggling rictus of mirth, they act out my swing and fall down again. Eventually they calm down a bit.

Cowdy-boots is still giggling when he comes over to me. He picks me up under the arms and drags me to the bench. He puts me on it next to Bare-feet. After a few minutes the laughter dies away.

Give's a smoke! Fucken Nyungar cunt!

Bare-feet seems to laugh inside the words. He sets us off again.

Fuck, it went on for hours.

Finally, when our sides were aching so much from the big laugh and we couldn't possibly find any other ways to say our dialogue again, and we've talked our way around the last two hundred years, and the forty thousand before that, the cops come and let us out.

Outside the station we stagger off in our opposite directions without a word.

It feels about five o'clock in the morning. I thought I'd been in there for five minutes.

Nunga John Wayne and
something not right

Wiljali Country, Broken Hill. The day after Freddy wrote off the hire car we get a big new Falcon. Gutsy. We cut laps around town. Get noticed.

A big Nunga fulla with a cowboy hat and a red-checked cowboy shirt drives past in a red Ford ute. Nice ute. Looks like Nunga John Wayne. He stops across the road from us just outside the Bronx. He looks at us. Just looks.

Do I get a shield? Yep.

Freddy is wearing his mask. Fits well. Had it a long time.

What's behind the Nunga John Wayne mask? Who the fuck are you? What the fuck do you want?

I am blank. One tree in a desert with a highway running by. To this desert we are all insects. He looks at us. We look at him. He doesn't move. Very slowly and deliberately I turn to the front and drive off. Freddy is still looking. I can't read his emotion.

We pull up at Slacker's house. Slacker comes running out. We're never invited in here. I don't like it. Freddy pretends not to notice. Slacker worships Freddy. We go for a drive. Stop near the airport. Race the planes as they rip down the runway to take off. Make a huge red dust cloud. We have a smoke. Drop Slacker off. I'm over him. Something isn't right.

We get invited to another house. Have a cone. A cup of tea. Half the people in the street drop in.

Fly like a fucken eagle, they say by way of greeting.

It's a ghetto. People are surviving it. Behind us the huge slag dump has completely erased their hill. The boys laugh through the sad. At this time we hardly see any women.

I remember the first time I arrived in Katherine, Northern Territory. Jarwoyn Country. I see all the women sitting in one spot. The men completely separate under another tree.

Men's shade. Women's shade.

Our Jarwoyn guide says it matter-of-factly. Points with his chin. I nod like I understand. I don't. Not really. Not yet.

Later this Jarwoyn fulla tells me that the bus stop is in women's shade — so only women or girls catch the bus. Men gotta walk. Or taxi. I never knew if he was gammin or not. I only ever saw women waiting at that bus stop, though.

Nunga John Wayne drives past to see us on the verandah. Drives very slowly and deliberately. Everyone on the verandah watches him but he doesn't look at us. Makes a show of looking straight ahead.

Cups of tea or flagons

Next day we pick up Lloyd from the airport. He's excited to have travelled in a plane. But playing it cool. He loves the new hire car. We take him to the film production office. Everyone falls in love with Lloyd.

We've met a fulla who has invited us to come around so Lloyd can play with some other kids his own age. I never said nothin to the bloke about Lloyd having never spent much time with kids his own age. Why would I?

We drive to this footy oval on the outskirts of Broken Hill. The fulla we know is the under-14s footy coach. His team wins. We kick the footy on the oval surrounded by gum trees and slag heaps. We get invited back to this fulla's house. It's a hot day.

Back at the house there is a big mob. The adults are in the house. I find myself with a big mob in the kitchen. I can't see Freddy. I think Lloyd is still in the car. Everyone is drinking. They are talking about the police.

Fucken gubbah cunts!

Uncle Jimmo squeezes my leg.

Not you, Bruz.

Everyone in the room laughs. I laugh too. It's funny. First time anyone's acknowledged my presence at all. Skinny Celtic fulla surrounded by Desert Mob.

The kids are in the backyard. Lloyd is nervous of the Nunga kids. He sits in the hire car for a long time.

There is this old auntie there. We finally get Lloyd out of the car and Auntie pounces on him. Auntie wants to know his Mob. After a long discussion, most of which I can't follow, it is worked out that Lloyd is a distant cousin. Related up through the Wemba Wemba Mob in Swan Hill where Lloyd's mum is from. Once this is established, Lloyd joins in play in the backyard.

Uncle Jimmo wants us to meet some other uncles. No-one here is sober. Just me. I'm happy to move on when Uncle Jimmo suggests it. Even if that Old Man just wants to ride in the new Falcon. Freddy and Lloyd are in the back and Uncle Jimmo in the front.

We go to Uncle Jimmo's house. It's a very different atmosphere. Cups of tea instead of flagons. Country and western for hard rock and rap. As with the last place there is a photo of every family member on the lounge room wall. This is the same with Lloyd's Mob's places in Melbourne. Always a photo wall. Always family.

A group of Old Men sit in a shady verandah area at the side of the house. Freddy and I are invited to sit. I sip my tea. Keep my eyes down. Lloyd is in the lounge. He watches TV and is happy. Auntie keeps cake and tea coming. Out where we are the talk slips between English and Language. I listen.

There is talk about some site being desecrated by the town council.

Fucken gubbah cunts.

Uncle Jimmo squeezes my leg.

Not you, Bruz.

Everyone laughs. I laugh. It's still funny. Freddy suddenly jumps in to speak, to tell a story, but is told to shut up by Uncle Jimmo. Senior Uncle hasn't spoken yet.

Fucken shut up! Not your place! Shuddup!

Freddy sits, chastised, uncomfortable. The Uncles can smell the booze on him and don't like it. Sad more than angry. Smells like death.

It's suggested Lloyd should stay overnight so Auntie can spoil him. Her own son was stolen. Taken by the gubbahment. Never came back. I ask Lloyd if he wants to stay. He nods. Lloyd is happy. Perhaps he needs Auntie's cuddles. He's ten years old.

Crow feathers

We have to give Uncle Jimmo a ride back to the other place. We drive around, Uncle in the front seat, Freddy in the back. By now the partying is much progressed. Uncle Jimmo grabs a bladder of wine and two more fullas get in the car and we drive out of town.

I stop near where Freddy and I found the eagles. I find a dead crow. Even Pringhael Warkee (crow) is good luck. It reminds us to look for the creative spirit in our lives. I pick up some feathers. Take them back to show Uncle Jimmo. Warkee hasn't left any feathers for me for a while.

Uncle Jimmo is staggering now. He seems angry with me. I show him the crow feathers. He looks down at them. Screws them up with one angry twist of his hand. The same hand he squeezed my knee with in reassurance earlier on. In the circle of men.

Narcoo (no).

(Right hand flicks up and away.)

My feelings are hurt. I get into the car and wait. Uncle sits in the back. We sit in silence waiting for Freddy and the others to return.

They come back eventually. It's dark now. I drive back to town. Drop off the Mob. Freddy and I go back home to blaring TV, pacing, VB, nyandi.

Wurrung (Warkee) (Waa) — the Crow

Wudjari Country, Lort River Station. I'm about four or five years old. I sometimes drive around with Chaz Campbell. No kindergarten out here.

Chaz has one of those short-wheel-base Land Rovers, a .22 repeating rifle behind the seat, and a billy in a leather case in the glove box. The leather case has a little pouch on the side for tea and sugar.

I always have an exciting day with Chaz. We shoot the rifle and make billy-tea and drive flat out down bush tracks. Once we caught some mullet in a net in the estuary. Another time Chaz let me shoot a cow that had fallen out the back of a truck and broken its legs. One day we found a dead fox that Chaz had poisoned. You know, exciting.

This particular day I find the Land Rover parked behind Chaz's house near the duck pen, where Chaz is working. Not far away is this big shed. All them Wongi stockmen are there. Maybe they live in that shed. Reckon they did.

I'm drawn over to the shed, like an insect to a campfire. Them fullas see me. Skinny lil wadjula boorai comin over for a look.

Bart Billon, to me he seemed to float across the ground. He sees me and calls out.

Aaah! Wurrung! Wurrung! You my Wurrung-boy!

And Bart shuffles in the dust — a little dance — his arms behind his back, hands together down low, elbows out, flapping like wings.

The way Bart moved his body gives me a shock of recognition — I know exactly what he means. It is like a flash.

Crow!

Like that Dream moment with Mum and Uncle Kumanjai Presto in a film we're making years in the future, of leaving my body and seeing the blue stones. Like Uncle James singing me back to Country in that plane.

All them other fullas around Bart break into laughter, pointing to me. But I don't feel embarrassed.

Then Chaz steps out of his duck run and all those fullas go quiet and fall back into the shadow of the shed. I turn and wander over to the Land Rover. Chaz climbs into the driver's seat and I haul myself up into the cab.

I don't think Chaz even knew it'd happened. I had a secret. I knew something that Chaz didn't know. And I knew something about myself I didn't know before.

Hiding from the killers

Next day I go to pick up Lloyd. It's hot in Wiljali Country. He doesn't want to come with us. Auntie doesn't want him to go. There is a little girl there he is talking to. I drink a cup of tea.

Uncle Jimmo is there. Uncle wants us to take him for a drive. We go. In the new Falcon. He wants to go out Silverton way.

We cut some laps up the main street first. So everyone can see who is riding in a new Falcon.

Just before Silverton, Uncle tells me to turn off. I drive slowly down a hidden dirt track. Uncle tells me to stop just before a dry creek bed. We climb out of the car and stand silently for a long time.

Freddy smokes cigarettes. Uncle stares off into the distance.

Then Uncle starts to walk away. Down to the creek. Uncle looks back to me.

Come.

(Just with his eyes.)

I walk down.

It's taken me up till now to get used to Uncle's accent. I often miss things. Now it's suddenly clearer.

Uncle tells me where he was sitting with his family when the men with guns came over the rise. Uncle points with his chin to indicate the slight hill.

Who?

Police. Others. Gubbahs. Rifles firing. Old rifles. You know? Three-oh-three.

Uncle Jimmo is a small boy. His auntie gathers him up and runs. Bare feet pounding in the red dust, down through the creek. Up the other side. A tree has fallen over in the wind and ripped a hole open in the earth. Uncle Jimmo is thrown in. Gunshots cracking all around. A branch thrown over the little Wiljali boy. Auntie turns and runs back towards the creek.

Uncle never sees her again.

Uncle waits until dark before creeping out. The gunfire and shouting and screaming have died away. Fires burning all along the creek now. Cold soulless shapes of the killers gliding through the smoke and haze. The stench of burning flesh all around.

Uncle Jimmo walks to the outskirts of town. Long walk for a little Wiljali boy all alone. To his cousin's place.

I stand in the creek bed. The gunshots echoing all around me. The deep throaty shouts from the killers. I look at Uncle Jimmo walking back to the car. He picks his way carefully up the slope. Walks like Lloyd.

My eyes are watery, my throat is tight as a noose. Me, the gubbah film man with the new Falcon.

Freddy waits by the car. He gives Uncle a cigarette. Even from here I can see Uncle's hand shaking as he lights it up.

All around the bodies lie on the ground. Naked, their gaping wounds giving them no dignity. I wish the ground would open up and swallow them down. Swallow me down. Swallow down the shame stuck in my throat like the last survivor. I stand staring into the tree-hole. Uncle's hiding spot.

I walk back up to the car. I drive. Uncle seems lighter of spirit now. He points out features and tells me their Language names. What they mean. I listen. I nod.

Yeah.

Yeah.

Mmm.

We drive around the edge of the high country. It drops away quite sharply to the plain below us.

This high ground. When the sun was going down. Bathed in that magic changeover light so coveted by film makers. I'd been here a week earlier working on the movie with Freddy.

Freddy walking up the hill with Lloyd's limp body in his arms. The blood not yet dry on the dead boy. The tears stream from Freddy's eyes. A cold wind howls over the hill. Freddy shivering to his bones as soon as someone yells, Cut!

Take after take. Carrying the dead boy up the hill. The grief ripped out of him again. The child he couldn't save. The child he put in the firing line.

Is it himself he carries up the hill?

I'm standing off to one side in the fading light. Holding Freddy's jacket. He is shirtless in the shot. I'm weeping freely. It's my son he's holding. I can't allow this story to get a purchase in my world.

Now it's hot. Uncle directs us to the waterhole. We stop before we get there. We see the film set. We slow down and wave to everyone at the unit base. Soon they'll be doing the end stunt. Jump a truck off a cliff and then blow it up.

Freddy makes me stop. He picks a flower and gets it sent up to where they're shooting and delivered to the director.

We drive off. To the waterhole. We smoke nyandi. Look at the water. The birds. Crows. Parrots. Galahs. We look out at the flat country. Uncle Jimmo points out the station buildings thirty or forty kilometres away.

Down below we hear the explosion of the stunt going off. We see smoke from a fire. We find out later the fire got out of control. It doesn't matter. The film set is so small in the landscape.

We can see for sixty kilometres at least. Out near the horizon are the main buildings on the station where Nunga John Wayne is from. Uncle Firebrand's great-grandmother's Country.

After a while we drive back down past the set and into town. Uncle Jimmo takes us around to Uncle Firebrand's house.

Grog is the enemy

Uncle Firebrand is one of those remarkable fullas. A Wiljali man. A man among men. Most of us can only dream about being such a man.

A long time ago, when Uncle Firebrand was still young and angry, he was pulled over by a cop. Maybe he wasn't angry before then. Every man has a turning point. The cop felt it necessary to abuse Firebrand's ancestors. To impugn his manhood. To prod Firebrand with his finger. The cop woke up in hospital. Firebrand in prison. This is the way it is out here.

When he got out it was easy to get back in again. This is the way it is for Firebrand's Mob. And Firebrand couldn't help but notice all the other fullas like him. In and out. Out and in. No reason. So Uncle Firebrand came up with a plan.

He got with the Old Men. Bush Men. He began to connect up the young fullas inside with the Old Men out. When they come out, Firebrand organises for the young fullas to go bush with the Old Fullas.

When they're still inside he channels all their energy into health and art, Language and Culture. And then they never end up back inside. No government program. No funding. You'll never see Uncle Firebrand on television. You won't read about him in the newspaper, the weekend colour lift-out. Fighting back in his own way.

In five years he's had nearly a dozen successes. Young fullas who never reoffend. Broken the cycle. Changed their lives. The lives of their children and grandchildren. Uncle Firebrand.

When I first meet him he's standing on his front verandah in his rugby shirt, laughing eyes and tough as nails. We meet his son, Firebrand Jnr. Firebrand Jnr has a dog called Nyandi. Uncle has a strong woman. Three daughters.

On Firebrand's lounge room wall is a group of photos of family. Going back to an Old Fulla wearing the 'chief's' brass plate given to him by the gubbahs. Firebrand thinks this is funny.

A chief?

He shakes his head and laughs. This joke never wears out.

A chief?

Laughter.

Above the Old Fulla is an impressive Old Woman. Firebrand tells me she laid the groundwork for them to get the Land back. Their community pooled all their resources and bought the station on their own Country when it was up for sale. Paid money to own land that has owned them for sixty or a hundred generations. Now run by the Mob again.

We didn't know it but we'd already met the head stockman. The big cowboy who checked us out in the Bronx. Nunga John Wayne. Old Man Roo keeps a close eye out for danger around his Mob. That's how he got to be Old Man Roo. We'll meet him again, too.

So we are invited into Uncle Firebrand's home for a cuppa tea. No grog here.

Grog is the enemy, Uncle Firebrand says quietly, out of the blue.

Uncle's been there and done that and he'd fucken know.

Firebrand Jnr is the same age as Lloyd. I tell Uncle Firebrand about Lloyd. Uncle insists that Lloyd stays over. Firebrand Jnr and Lloyd run off with Nyandi the dog to do some little-boy stuff. The children are strong, attractive, independent. Lloyd is really in his element here. Except that Lloyd is used to being the toughest kid in all the circles he moves in. But not here. Here Lloyd is a city boy trying to keep up.

Freddy and I sit around a small table in the kitchen. We drink tea.

There is a commotion at the front door. One of Uncle Firebrand's cousins has come over. Charged up.

Firebrand's woman stands back. Gathers her daughters close to her. She knows what is coming.

Uncle Firebrand goes out. He picks up his cousin quite matter-of-factly by the scruff of the neck and the seat of his pants and tosses him off the verandah into the front yard. A six-foot drop. Auntie and the girls go back to watching TV and talking. Firebrand is cool as a cucumber.

Come back when you're sober, Cuz. You know the rules.

His voice is calm and full of love and understanding. Tough love. Uncle closes the door and comes back in.

We stay for hours. When we go home Freddy is quiet. Calm. Sitting on the couch instead of pacing. Cuppa tea instead of VB. Milky and sweet.

Desert herbs and Dream Language

We're back in the desert shooting. On set early. Cooked brekkie from the food bus. I go for a long walk. I find an old miner's or surveyor's peg; some kind of wooden marker with the broad arrow on it.

I'm thinking of my great-great-grandfather. The chains at his wrists and ankles. Constantly wearing away the flesh. The broad arrows on his uniform.

I finger the shilling I found on the first day. Step out of the car in the desert. Look down to see an 1880 silver coin. Refuse from the invaders.

A hundred years ago this whole place was crawling with diggers. Chasing the silver in the earth. Walking past Uncle Jimmo's Mob with their shovels and wheelbarrows and rolled-up swags. Sixty or seventy years before the massacre Uncle showed me. The soil is red. Bloodstains blend in easy out here. Soon be lost.

Freddy is in his lap-lap again. He is wandering around, talking to the crew. I'm not shooting. No cops today. I stay back. Just watching. Freddy is talking to the old boy on sound. Showing him something on the ground. A plant. He comes over to me. Smiling his impossibly huge smile.

Look at this, Bruz.

Freddy picks some leaves from the desert plant and holds it out to me. I take it. Sniff it.

Them Old People used to chew this. More better for long walk. Makes you feel different.

Freddy takes a few leaves and puts them in his mouth.

Chew for long time. Long time till pulp.

I put what he's given me into my mouth and start to chew. Freddy is wandering up to the high ground. I follow. We get to the top of this rocky outcrop. Step step. Chew chew.

Freddy sits. I sit next to him. We smoke a cigarette in silence. When did I start smoking? Can't remember now.

We're looking down at the film set. We chew the desert herb. I look down at my feet. See some ants working away. They've found a dead beetle and a bunch of them are carrying it home for tucker. I admire their teamwork. These fullas know each other well.

Look.

I look up from the ants to see what Freddy means. He points with his chin at the film crew below. Nothing much is happening. Actually, nothing at all is happening. There are people looking at flowers. Feeling the texture of dirt. Looking up at the sky. Wandering. I've never seen a film crew not working ever before. I look to Freddy. He is chewing. He exclamation marks it with his lips. The film crew are all chewing.

Them old people used it to make them feel close to the land.

After a long time someone is calling for Freddy. He's laughing. None of the chewers in the crew realise what has happened. Freddy goes down to do his shot.

I see an eagle a long way off. Up high and circling. I watch him riding the air currents. I wonder if he is the same fulla from the day of the killing. The tight circler. Maybe he's related to the huge bird with his strong spirit out the back of our accommodation.

Freddy is in his element.

The dazed crew are still being distracted by the wind and insects, the sun and the stunted trees and the land itself as they try to get the shot. They eventually get it.

We get an early mark and go to Uncle Firebrand's to pick up Lloyd.

Uncle Firebrand is organising some young men to go hunting.

Shoot a roo, bring tucker home for the family, feel like men again. Get respect.

I'm driving with the desert herb all through my brain and the car seems to have a life of its own. Which is probably lucky. My eyes wander to a solitary cloud drifting across the vast blue.

We drive up to the town lookout and look down at the big slag heap which many tourists think is the Hill of Broken Hill. Stolen Hill would be a better name for this town. Stole the real hill and replaced it with slag. The excrement of mining. Nothing will grow for a thousand years or so.

We take Lloyd to the go-carts. We're the only ones there and I pay for Lloyd to have as many laps as he wants. Lloyd tears around the track completely fearless. Laughs when he crashes.

The track attendant is impatient. He scowls as he runs out again and again and again to straighten Lloyd's car. And again.

And again. His crap attitude doesn't dampen Lloyd's enthusiasm for the race at all. Maybe Lloyd doesn't even notice. He definitely doesn't give a shit.

Afterwards we get some videos and go home. Kung fu videos. Skateboard videos. Basketball videos. Lloyd rides on the bonnet of the hire car as we go up the drive. He yells at me to go faster.

Faster! Faster! Faaaaaaaster!

Lloyd makes me laugh with his crazy bravery.

We eat chips and watch the videos with the volume up to a thousand and fifty.

I'm woken up at 3.30 am. Freddy and Lloyd are both yelling out in their sleep. My room is sandwiched between them. Both yelling in Language. No English. Some bizarre shouted dream conversation. Two different Languages. Yamatji and Wemba Wemba.

They settle down after a while. I decide not to get up. I lie there between them. Freddy speaks only a little of his Language while Lloyd speaks none of his. But in their dreams …

Your jeans and the sunset

Been on set all day. We're in the unit base, now. Both toey. We get a call from Uncle Backy.

Eeeeh! Yutupella, come over for smoke.

We go over. Motel room. Shooting the mission scenes tomorrow. Won't be a real mish, but everyone still has mixed feelings.

We smoke in the spare room. Backy rolls numbers that could kill a large horse. Backy is excited. He hops around and breaks into a step or two of dancing. An old owl. Toothless with huge beard, gammy hips, Backy dances with the spirit of a young man — before drugs stole him away.

Last time he was in Broken Hill was to make a movie many years ago. In that other life. In the Silverton Hotel there is a picture of Uncle Backy flanked by American movie stars. He'd got into trouble for galloping a horse and cart down the main street. Been drinkin long time. Barely remembers it. No alcohol now.

His Mob Wiradjuri. His tribal name Gumaa. Doer in the Dawn. Up before the sun every day, Uncle Backy is one of the most well-named men I ever met.

Uncle and Freddy talk about Language to use on set tomorrow. Rehearse little bit. It's like I'm not here. I know this is Trust. Later it would be edited out of the movie.

The photographer comes over. In her twenties. Overtly sexual. Locked into Setting Sun Land. On the set she fights with the director. Which makes it harder for all of us.

The Italian film star playing the lead role specifies no photos without permission — none during the shot or the shot set-up. Even though the director tells the photographer not to, she does it anyway. The Italian film star becomes angry and unworkable — all so some little publicity photographer can get a shot.

The photographer flirts with Freddy. With Uncle Backy. With me. Uncle says he's going to bed. We say we're leaving.

The photographer invites us to her room for a smoke and a vodka. We go. She gets us all strong vodkas. It's just a motel room with a big bed. Bare brown brick walls. Cosy as a cell. No other place to sit but on the big bed. She rests her hand on Freddy's leg as we share a joint.

Freddy goes to djillawah. She suddenly tries to grab me like she might kiss me. I explode off that bed like Kyle van der Kuyp out of the blocks. Spill my vodka on myself. I'm married-up.

What the fuck?

The door opens. Freddy steps back into the room smiling at some secret joke.

I decide to go myself. I go in without a look back. I put my vodka down. I have a piss and take a breath. I don't pick my vodka back up. I rattle the door a little, then open it to see them spring apart. Freddy looks at me standing in the bathroom doorway. Notices I've left my voddie. Her hand drops to his thigh.

I recoil like a shot got fired off.

I gotta go, Coord.

Will you model for me tomorrow? the photographer says to Freddy.

Freddy lights up, grabs her hand.

Yeah, what?

Just in your jeans. Your jeans and the sunset.

She looks at me.

What are you doing tomorrow?

Day off. Nothin. Chillin.

Can my brother and I and Freddy go for a drive?

Where to?

Wilcannia.

I suddenly feel real tired. Oh, you wanna have a little play, a little dabble in my world, do ya, darlin? I'm thinkin. Well, be my fucken guest!

When I speak my voice doesn't betray my sudden inexplicable rage. I don't look at her as I speak.

Come and get the car whenever you want. I'll be home.

I look to Freddy.

What're you doin, Coorda?

I'll come.

I get up and walk straight out the door. Not wanting to witness their goodbye.

Next morning the photographer turns up with her brother. He looks young, a sheltered childhood. Wet-behind-the-ears. He's come up from Sydney to visit the film set.

The photographer hugs me and Freddy.

175

He looks at me. He knows I hate being hugged by people I hardly fucken know. People with their eyes shut.

Him still lookin. You coming?

I look away. Take in the photographer and her little brother.

Nah. You go.

I look back at Freddy. He shakes my hand and jumps into the passenger seat. Wet-behind-the-ears is driving. They take off. I go inside. Roll a joint.

I've discovered a desert herb plant out the back. Near Old Man Eagle with his strong spirit. I put a clothes peg on my nose that I find under the sink in the unit before going out to pick some leaves.

The Rat would be laughing at me. That desert fulla. Why not just breathe through your mouth, Coorda? His little head-shake means, 'fucken gubbahs'. His smile tells me he means it with love. But that's a long way off yet.

In the car Freddy is already telling a story. Opening a VB.

Muriel-or-something

It's after dark when they get back. I hear the car and go out to see them.

Wet-behind-the-ears gets out. Looks paler than before. A bit shaky. Trying hard to smile. Failing. The photographer gets out of the car. She isn't flirting any more.

They have another passenger. She's been in the back with Freddy. A Nunga woman. Big and drunk. Hard as. Stinks as bad as Old Man Eagle.

Strong spirit, I think and smile to myself.

Freddy smiles vacantly at me. The photographer and her brother have gone straight for their car. They've let Freddy drive — I can still see the fear in their eyes.

Wanna come in for a drink?

I'm enjoying their discomfort. Ya mixin with people in The War Zone now, baby. How're the noble savages now?

The Danggali woman, Muriel or something, gets out. Brother and sister scurry. They're terrified of her. I look into the hire car. There is blood all in the back seat. Splattered all over the roof and the seats. Like someone been shot in there.

They'd been driving along. Freddy had hassled Wet-behind-the-ears for a drive. So Freddy was driving. He spots Muriel-or-something and her husband hitching. So he pulls over. Brother and sister are just so relieved to slow down even for a few minutes to pick them up that they don't complain.

Muriel-or-something and her husband get into the car stinking of alcohol, tobacco and stale sweat and urine. But, after only a few minutes of driving, husband and wife get into a serious argument. It quickly escalates and Muriel-or-something starts smashing into her man. She hits him a few big shots in the face and blood starts to fly.

Wet-behind-the-ears is cringing and sobbing by now. The photographer is screaming. Muriel-or-something yells at Freddy to stop the car. Freddy pulls over and Muriel-or-something opens the door and tosses her man out. She screams at Freddy.

Go! Go! Go! Drive the fucken car!

They drive away and leave him in a heap on the side of the road. They drive like maniacs. After a while Freddy pulls over and gives the wheel back to Wet-behind-the-ears.

They're pretty happy to get the driver's seat back from Freddy. Or so the photographer tells me later. Presumably in her own defence. She could've saved her breath. I couldn't give a fuck one way or the other.

They stop for a cask of Coolabah. Freddy and Muriel-or-something drink it. They're getting hotted up in the back seat by the time they get back to where I am.

Freddy and Muriel-or-something go into the unit. Freddy introduces us. Muriel-or-something is too far gone. I don't hear her name properly when she or Freddy says it. She doesn't give a fuck.

Freddy puts on my leather jacket. Liz's sister gave it to me. Freddy smiles at me, shows me the jacket like a model would, spins on his heel. Smiles at me as he comes around.

Deadly jacket, Bro.

Deadly, Bro.

Muriel-or-something turns on the telly. Turns it up full blast. I'd had it off all day. She gets a china cup to drink wine from.

Smoke, Bro?

He nods. I roll. We all smoke. Muriel-or-something hogs it, then sucks too hard and makes it burn one-sided. Does it every time. If it only lasts one or two rounds, I roll another. What's the diff?

I'm going to bed, Coorda. We got early start.

Ooo.

He nods. I go to bed. Freddy and Muriel-or-something argue for hours. Then they go to bed and fuck loudly. I can't sleep. With Old Man Eagle, Muriel-or-something and Freddy in the next room panting away, how can I sleep? I'm lonely.

Someone comes for Freddy at five. It was three when I last heard them. The car horn beeps. There is no movement from Freddy's room. I get up. Go out to the runner. Put on my work face.

He's just coming.

I clap my hands. Rub them together. It's fucken freezin. Sun not up yet.

Lovely morning.

She smiles, unconvinced. I go in. I knock on Freddy's door. No way am I going in.

Freddy! Freddy! Freddy! Motorcar!

Yo-Yo!

Something falls over and breaks. I hear him stand. Fall against something. Something else smashes. Muriel-or-something swears. Freddy comes out shirtless. Bare feet. His breath is unbelievable. And the stink from behind the door …

Get a shirt, Bruz. They're waiting.

Freddy just keeps walking past me and straight out the front door. Straight out into the headlights as if walking on stage in front of a thousand people. He dances a few steps.

Yaaaaaa!

Get a shirt, Bruz.

Fuck it!

Freddy jumps into the car with the runner. The runner isn't sure what she should do. Freddy's mask goes hard in the cool morning air.

Come on! Let's go! Let's fucken go! I got a fucken movie ta make!

She looks to me for guidance. Little bit nervous now.

The volume on Freddy's mask is turned up to eleven.

I nod to her. She drives off. I go inside.

I have to go at seven!

I yell out to Muriel-or-something. It takes forever.

… Yeah! I'm going to work! You have to go!

… No! Ya can't stay here! I'll give you a lift as far as I can!

… Come on! I'll give you a lift!

Muriel-or-something sits in the back and says nothing. I have to pick up Uncle Backy on the way. Uncle gets in the front. Muriel-or-something has a bag with her. We get to the turn-off where we have to go. I pull over to the side of the road.

I'm turning here.

No! I wanna go Creedon Street!

I'm turning here.

I wanna go fucken Creedon Street!

Here.

Take me to Creedon Street!

I'm turning here.

Take me to Creedon Street!

Uncle Backy: Get out the fucken car!

Muriel-or-something and me both jump! She turns and gets immediately out of the car. Slams the door shut like it's the door to hell. I drive off. A little shaken.

Jesus, Uncle got a voice like stockwhip cracking when he needs it.

Uncle is instantly back to his usual affable self, humming little riffs under his breath and dancing with his shoulders. After a while, driving in the dawn, he speaks.

Where she from? Freddy?

I nod.

He wanna be careful, that lad. They got Law out here.

I nod. I drive.

The leather jacket Freddy was wearing the night before was in Muriel-or-something's bag. It takes an hour of questioning Freddy before I piece it together. Even then I feel like he hasn't been straight with me. Did Freddy sell the jacket? Muriel-or-something had no money. Give it away? Trade it? For what? Was it stolen? How did Muriel-or-something know to hide it from me?

Ya gotta learn not to get attached.

Between the men

King is flying up to Stolen Hill for his last scene. The crew are all nervous. Producers, director, everyone. Sheltered childhoods.

King is calm. He's moved on. What happened between him and Freddy was a personal honour thing. I know it. Freddy knows it. And it came from love. Tough love. Maybe King knew what a prisoner Freddy could end up because he'd ended up like that. Traded in third-world Perth for first-world Melbourne. The compromises are far too many.

When King eventually tells me his side I just listen. I've never known King to lie.

I take Freddy around to Firebrand's place. I get a hundred dollars from the producers to pay Firebrand for having Freddy for the day. Firebrand doesn't want the money but I insist. This is a job that I'm getting paid for. The film has a budget of six million dollars. I reckon they can handle it. Firebrand gives half the money to his woman and then we drive to another house. A banana's worth of nyandi.

There is an angry young Danggali man here. Dressed like a skateboarder. He takes us through the turn-of-the-century miner's cottage. Many floorboards have been pulled up for firewood. Plaster is peeling. In the hall there's a group of photos on the wall next to the flag. Old People. Young People. Family. We go out to the backyard. Littered with rubbish. Two car wrecks. The angry young fulla goes to the shed. Outside the shed are two new spears he is working on. Firebrand picks up a spear and looks along the shaft for straightness.

This one strong, says Firebrand.

We go into the shed. Angry young fulla pulls out his bong. We all have one. We buy. Have another cone. I drive Firebrand and Freddy back to Firebrand's place. Firebrand takes us via Uncle Wombat's house.

Uncle is a snowy-haired Old Fulla. He is talking about hunting for roos. He shows us his old single shot .22 rifle. Exactly the same as my dad's. Uncle is going out tonight. Freddy says he'd like to get one to cook up at the wrap party. Uncle says he'll see.

Don't want to take too many.

I'm thinking about the petrol station in the middle of the night last week. I fill up. Walk in to pay. Standing by the counter is a bloke drenched in blood. Conversation stops when I walk in. I pay. Leave. Conversation starts up again. Outside is the bloodied man's ute. About thirty or forty roo carcasses hang off it. All beheaded. Executed. Why didn't I notice the roo-shooter's ute on the way in? Desert herb makes my vision selective. I chew some more.

I drop off Firebrand and Freddy and drive home. Well, to the fucken accommodation, anyway.

I drive out to the set. King is there. Defiance in his eyes. I greet him warm.

No prob with me, Coorda.

(Just with eyes.)

We shake hands.

Can I borrow your car, Bro?

The crew are watching. No trust there. Just fear.

Look closer, I'm thinking — and you will see. Things are not always as they appear to be.

I chuck King the keys.

I'll be a few hours, I say.

King looks down at my police uniform.

Jeez, you're an ugly munarch, Coord.

King flashes me his big smile. We both laugh.

Drive safe, I say. Stay under 180.

King laughs. Playfully punches me on the upper arm.

Yaaaaah!

King gets in the hire car and takes off. Tyres spinning on the gravel. I wander down to the old police station to put my head in the sand. This is my only speaking scene in the film.

The crew call me Clint Eastwood because all I do is grimly look into the middle distance. Usually holding a gun. There is a tracking shot. Complex. My boots are too squeaky. They put felt on the soles. Still too loud. Down to socks. I nail it every time. But it's complex. Sixteen takes. Patience.

The day before, one of Lloyd's shots was twelve takes. He did it better in the hotel room with Freddy and me. Out here the crew make him nervous. So many gubbah faces. Lloyd is only used to being around family.

I finish up. King is back with the car.

The film people were concerned that I'd been careless in letting King have my hire car. Everyone was worried that King would track Freddy down and bash him again. Not out of concern for Freddy's safety. Concern for the film. Just business. I explained what I knew of the history between Freddy and King.

King doesn't know Firebrand — so wouldn't have looked there. I doubt King would confront a man like Firebrand if it came down to it. Not out of fear. Just commonsense. In fact, Firebrand and King are similar, despite walking separate paths.

Before I left his place Firebrand told me: If I see him, I'll fucken flog him.

Firebrand's natural instinct is to protect those he knows and loves. He reads Freddy as a lost man searching for a way out. Freddy isn't very different to the fullas Firebrand works with in the prison system.

It's not like that, Uncle. It's between the two men.

Uncle Firebrand nods. He doesn't look overly convinced.

After I pick up Freddy he's gotta go back to the set or production office or something. He arranges a lift home.

So I go home. I sit in front of the TV. I watch it as if it's on. It isn't. I need stillness. Quiet. I sit. I smoke a cigarette. Make a cup of tea. After a long time I turn on the TV. I have it very quiet. As if it's on in another room. I suddenly look up and see Freddy standing there. Right in front of me. Between me and the TV. He gestures a greeting with his hand, open and low, fingers spread.

Fuck.

I didn't hear the door. See him come in. What's wrong with me?

My eyes flick to the door. It hasn't been opened.

Flick back. Freddy is not there!

Fuck.

What is going on with me? I don't move. My eyes and mind get into a heated argument. I'm wondering if I'm just too tired.

A few minutes later the door opens and Freddy comes in. Goes to the exact spot between me and the TV. Where he was before. Exactly. Or where I saw him before, anyway. Everything shifts into slow motion. I do the hand gesture with him. I look down at my hand just as it completes the gesture. As if my hand was working independently of the rest of me. With my other hand I go to sip my tea. Suddenly everything is in fast motion and I nearly choke to death. Freddy whacks me on the back a couple of times with his open hand to help with my coughing fit.

You alright, Bro?

What were you thinkin about a few minutes ago?

What, Bro?

What were you thinkin about in the car on the way here?

Just standin in the lounge room.

I get up and make Freddy a cup of tea.

That exact spot?

Yeah. Just here.

Last night in Stolen Hill

I tell King I'll see him back in Melbourne. And he is gone. Lloyd too. Back to his family. And it is the last night in Stolen Hill. There is a crew party — at the next location it'll be a cut-down crew. Drinks and food at the big hotel in town.

Freddy and I have one last appointment with Uncle Jimmo. Uncle Wombat has organised for Freddy to speak to the petrol-sniffers' support group. Freddy used to live in a park. To the kids he is a Yamatji Elvis Presley. They respect him.

Uncle Wombat will give us a roo to cook up bush way for our trouble. The crew are looking forward to Freddy bringing in a roo to cook.

I've been on set for an hour or so longer than Freddy. He promised me he'd stay home. Which he does. But when I arrive back it's clear that Freddy has demolished the best part of half a carton. Slurry and staggery.

I pick him up and we drive over to Uncle Jimmo's place. Drive in silence.

Uncle Jimmo comes out. When he sees Freddy's state he is really pissed off.

Let's go, then, says Freddy.

Uncle looks at Freddy with disgust. Freddy persists.

Where these petrol sniffers at?

Uncle Jimmo gives me a withering look. I look down. Shame job.

How can we fucken go?

What?

Freddy is genuinely surprised.

You're fucken charged up!

Freddy tries to meet Uncle's gaze but can't. Uncle goes inside to ring Uncle Wombat. We aren't invited in. We wait outside. Standing on the gravel driveway.

We can still go, Freddy says lamely to me.

How can we fucken go?

I repeat Uncle's question.

I look away, up the wide deserted street. We stand in silence. Freddy restless. Me still.

After a long time Uncle Jimmo comes out.

Take him home, he says to me.

I walk back to the hire car. Freddy doesn't move.

You're fucken useless to me charged up!

Uncle turns and goes back inside.

Freddy watches him go. He comes over and falls into the passenger seat.

Let's go home. We got a party to get to!

I drive off. Back to the motel unit. Freddy and I smoke joints and make a plan. In and out early, we say. I plan not to drink — so I don't hold back on nyandi.

We spruce up all deadly and go. Stop at a front bar across the road because Freddy sees a mob of young fullas from the Bronx. I fall off my wagon and have a couple of beers.

We go to the party. Big room. Even with us all there it still seems half empty.

This hotel stood for a long time. Since the silver rush. I look through the windows to the street. Maybe someone else sat in this bar with this silver shilling in his pocket. Maybe those police and others came here for a drink after their work at the creek. Or before. You can do anything on a gutful of grog.

Uncle Jimmo's dry laughter comes to me on a gust of wind.

Dempulla couldn't find me. Dempulla couldn't track their lil sis to the fucken dunny and back.

It's too far away anyway. They would've been drinking before they went.

A few of the crew are disappointed there is no roo to cook. I get the feeling they never really expected it. My mind is wandering. I find myself alone at the bar. This woman from the crew comes up and stands close to me. Too close. She asks me if I dance. I look away and down as I wrestle my loneliness. Smash it down.

Not tonight.

You sure?

Yeah.

Wanna drink?

Nah.

Freddy has moved off to get some food. There is silence. She looks for my eyes. I'm looking away.

Did you go to rushes?

Nah.

Wanna get some food?

Nah.

You wanna go into the other bar? It's quieter.

What?

You wanna go into the little bar?

What?

I might go in there.

What?

Now she's getting bored with me. One of the young grips comes over. I go over to Freddy. Nod goodbye with little vague smile, eyes averted. Freddy watches me come. Smiles at me wicked way.

Whachu doin?

Points with his chin.

Nothin. Married-up.

Thank fuck, I'm thinking. Don't shit in your own nest.

Freddy is laughing at me.

That wasn't easy, Bro.

I laugh.

Easy now.

We look over to see her touch the young grip's wrist. She leans in to talk to him and her breasts brush his bare arm. We see the crackle of energy from across the big empty room. Ya can't stop a steam train. Just stay off the tracks if ya don't wanna get squished.

Freddy is bored. The Italian director hasn't arrived.

We're both ready to go when she finally gets here. On the arm of the Italian film star. She stays close to him. Freddy only had a moment. Italian film star goes home. Director goes home. She's doing what the producer told her to do, pay attention to the film star. Freddy doesn't take it too badly, considering. The director and film star aren't on together. Least we don't reckon so. He just wants to command her time. Leos.

European movie stars. What can you do?

We eat. We drink. Dance a little. We go. No goodbyes. Be discreet is my message to Freddy. Do what you want. What you need. Don't let them see you do it. A six-foot-two Yamatji stands out.

We end up at a disco. So much for going home. A big empty shed with young kids dancing in a seething bunch at one end. Drunken wadjula kids with no rhythm.

We've heard of a late-night bar so we go to find it.

We only walk a little way and we see it. On the edge of the town block. Just across the road is a huge wire fence around the big slag dump which used to be the Hill. We go in and get a drink. Do a couple of shots. Beer chasers.

It's wall-to-wall local Mob in here. I stand out at the bar. Apart from the barman, I'm the only gub in the joint. I'm swaying a bit. My head is buzzing. Fullas are playing pool and yarning up. Cigarette smoke hangs like a dozen twilight fires by the creek. I order another shot to try to cleanse the taste of burnt flesh from my throat. Uncle Jimmo's massacre story has been swirling around me like a willy-willy all night. I light a cigarette myself. Suck hard. I'm lost in my thoughts. I lose time.

When I look up Freddy is toe-to-toe with this big fulla. From halfway across the bar I can hear Freddy's belligerent tone. He's telling the big fulla how hard he works. How hard actors work. How station work is all piss-easy. Not a real job.

I look around the bar. Fullas who hadn't noticed me before are now checking me out. I look down. I see boots. Lots of fucken boots. The whole bar is full of cowboy boots and jeans. I look back to Freddy.

Fuck.

That's Nunga John Wayne Freddy is talking to. Old Man Kangaroo watching out for his Mob. These men have big hard hands from the work. Steady eyes. Strong backs.

Shut up, Freddy. Just leave it. Shut up.

But Freddy's got his finger out and is prodding Nunga John Wayne in the chest.

You don't know shit about working hard!

In the corner a group of young fullas stand up to get a better view.

Time we were gone, I slur to myself. A parody of Clint Eastwood.

I finish my beer. A fulla near me with a long thin scar on one side of his face steps closer to me. His eyes are direct. Telling me not to move.

I push myself off the bar, brush Scarface off, and am at full-pelt in four steps. I hit Freddy running. Grab him by the back of the shirt, both hands — and propel him with everything I've got towards the door.

Nunga John Wayne lunges for me and misses. Freddy keeps his feet and I shove him again. Right out the door this time. He staggers sideways and almost goes down in the street. I grab him by the shoulder. I'm running and dragging him with me. Now I'm screaming.

Go! Go! C'mon Bruz! We're goin!

I drag him and run as his legs wake up and start to run with me. Behind us the bar is emptying out onto the street.

We're running like mad bastards now. The cowboy boots behind us an urgent clatter. We run. We turn a corner and go. We run. Legs pumping over bitumen and concrete. We cut through the night air like escaped convicts, desperate, afraid, but kind of enjoying ourselves. We see a big brick wall. We hear our pursuers coming around the corner. Without thinking or talking or breaking stride we throw ourselves up and over the wall. We land and instantly go still. Working to control our breath like Uncle Jimmo hiding in his tree-hole.

Our pursuers approach and slow down. Stop.

Talk among themselves. They move off. Good strong men. Just showing us the door. Outsiders are trouble.

We wait. They go. We look at each other. Laugh silently like steam trains. Chug along the cold steel desert track.

Ha! Hahahahahahahahahahahahahahahahahahahahahaha!

We're lying on the ground. We turn to see where we are. In the inner yard of some motel. There is a pool. Everything painted powder blue. There are some lights on. Then we hear it. Someone is getting a pounding nearby. She is moaning like a police commissioner, him as eager as a footballer making his league debut. We smile at each other. Take a step. Same thought. We come up slowly and quietly under a window.

Oh, Lord.

We know the voices. The two crew members from the bar earlier. Freddy sneaks a look. I can't. I just listen. The fucking inside has a frenetic desperation. Freddy eggs me on to look.

Have a look. You know you want to.

I can't. I'm on a different path. Even if I want to. I'm not gunna.

Not today, Zurg.

Let's go.

Freddy laughs and follows me. We have the long walk home. Even if there were any cabs, they wouldn't pick us up.

I'm drunk and thoroughly disappointed in humanity. I've always been a lousy drunk. Still am. Something Freddy and I have in common. I'm disappointed. Angry. You can waste a lot of energy fighting the wrong fight. The wrong people.

We get home eventually. Into the flat. We drink another VB and smoke a joint and go to bed.

The next day there is a complaint from the accommodation management to the film producers about some drunk gubbah shouting and being an arsehole at three in the morning — waking up the motel guests by kicking doors, throwing things in the pool and screaming obscenities. I don't remember any of this. I just laugh. I've crossed another line. I don't give a fuck what these gubbahs think of me.

Our sad, lonely laughs

Freddy and I get up early. Shit, there is a whole bunch of stuff in the pool.

We gotta head up to Andyamathanha Country for the last bit of the shoot. Near Wilpena Pound. We drive out of Wiljali Country and just cross the southern tip of Malyangaba Country on the way.

We put the dead eagle in the boot. An hour or so out of town we find a good spot near a big tree and a creek to lay him down. His strong spirit wouldn't want to leave his own Country.

We drive on. Come across a crew truck broken down. We take some essential gear into our car. Drive on. Freddy smokes nyandi. I refrain. Need my head now.

Into Andyamathanha Country. Something strong for all of us there. Freddy is excited. He has some kindred for this Country through his great-grandmother.

He wants a drink. Maybe he's scared like me. I can't stop him. He's a man. I can't have one. I'm driving. I'm driving my own ship. Sailing it up a foreign coast. I'm telling my Royal Marines to stand to. It's what I'm trained to do. Gunna build a prison. Take someone's Country to build it on. I'm waiting in the hold. The chains are still heavy on my ankles. I didn't have them on before the ship. I feel sick. I'm longing for sunlight. I don't care what happens. I've gotta get off this fucken ship.

We stop the car just short of Wilpena Pound. A huge Old Man Roo stands at the fork of the road. Not afraid of us. He stares us down. We just ran from him. Last night. He knows we're scared. Freddy looks sad. Sometimes when ya drinkin, ya can't remember things blow by blow. Just come back to you in snapshots. Like ghosts. Flitting here and there. Dancing in the firelight. Like Ned that night in the Toorak Road apartment. (But that hasn't happened yet.) Old Man Roo's gaze is unbroken. Freddy turns his head very slowly and deliberately and looks ahead. I take off. When I can't see Old Man Roo any more I look ahead.

We find our accommodation. Unload. Have a VB. Have a smoke. Dark now. We walk to find dinner.

We hear a rustling in the bush. Freddy is walking just in front of me. I see Freddy's hand stiffen in a discreet gesture. I stop dead. My eyes scan the darkness ahead and around. I'm tensed for the crack of a rifle shot. I'm feeling for a weapon I don't have. I blink my eyes. Squeeze them gentle as a trigger squeeze.

Freddy smiles back at me. His eyes flick to some bushes just off the track. We don't move. It's the lovers from the powder-blue motel room. Fucking on the ground. We listen for a moment then move on silently. When we're on the other side we laugh our sad, lonely laughs.

Sacred Site

Drive out to the set early. Cereal in our room. Pack up. Sleep somewhere else tonight. It's not far to the set. This is the heart of Andyamathanha Country. Down near the dry creek bed there is a carpark and a sign in English and Language. Andyamathanha Sacred Site. I'm surprised there is no-one here. No People of this Country.

There is the thumping of a generator. Water is being pumped from a truck. A thick rubber pipe carrying the water snakes away up the creek-bed. The script called for water. Freddy and I get out and pick our way along the creek bed. It cuts into the hill sharply — so that very quickly we are dwarfed by high rock walls on either side of us.

Cut into this rock at seemingly irregular intervals is a series of incredibly precise rock carvings. Freddy and I become unsure. We halt our progress by the apparently chiselled designs.

Men's place, Freddy says quietly.

It's quite cool in the cleft of rock. We hear voices up ahead. We continue to walk, following the rubber pipe through which water is flowing. The walls of the tight canyon begin to open out. Freddy goes on. I hang back. I'm still not sure. Up on one side the sheer rock has given way to a steep slope littered with boulders and tough little trees. Someone is up there, scouting for a camera position. The first assistant director walks past me.

How long we here for?

Three, maybe four hours.

I nod. I grab some biscuits from the tea trolley and up the slope I go. Slowly and deliberately. When I feel tired I stop to look down into the natural cathedral below. I can see Freddy down there.

Freddy is making the whole place vibrate by humming his deep baritone hum, his hands and back flattened against the ancient rock.

I get to the top and just keep going. Go in a big circle with that place at my centre. I'm looking. Don't know what for yet. I find some desert herb. Start chewing. Keep walking. It's hot now. I'm sweating. I circle around the Site. Respect with distance. Clockwise, because this is my Celtic heritage. I look at the plants and sand and sky. I look at prints and signs left by any animals that moved through. Live around. I smile at the birds. Nod at them like passing friends in the street.

After a long walk I sit on the top of a ridge. Well, just below the top. A soldier would never expose himself on the top of a ridge. Old habits die hard.

I sit and look out across the lower ground. I feel a slight breeze blow across my face. I turn and a young roo bounds over the ridge. She sees me and stops. I nod my g'day to her. She watches me for a bit. Then takes two long slow steps. Her pouch opens and out tumbles a little fulla. She nibbles at some fresh shoots. Rained a few days ago. I sit. The little fulla looks at me. They both come a few steps closer. Still eating. She looks up. Looks me right in the eye. Holds it, then looks away. The young fulla piles back in and she goes away in an orderly fashion. Not hurried. Just steady. Bound. Bound. Bound. Gone. Back over the ridge.

I sit for a long time. Lost in the serene beauty of those big brown eyes, this day, this place. Then I walk back down to the hire car to wait for Freddy to finish.

In the carpark are some Dutch backpackers getting ready to hike up to the Sacred Site.

Ya weren't doin it for me

Shooting finishes and Freddy travels with someone else and I drive the producer through Wilpena Pound to the Parachilna Hotel. The same producer who hauled me in for a dressing-down all those weeks ago in Melbourne. Now her opinion of me is changed. She talks about how sexy the men in the film are. Something for everyone. The Yamatji. The Nyungar. The Italian. I'm thinkin, what about the redneck? Ha!

Her husband drives a car in front of us. He drives very fast. He gets a puncture. We stop and I help him change the tyre. I notice a big scar tree near where we stop.

In the bar at Parachilna there are two geologists and a few stockmen. A couple of spunky young barmaids.

I have a drink with Stephen. I haven't seen him for a couple of years. Since he played the Spirit Dancer in the boxing-tent play in Melbourne. Stephen is Nyawaygi man. Coastal man. Shake-a-leg man. Stephen's big Land Claim is about to go through in Queensland. He is very excited.

Stephen and Mum's brother, Henry's uncle, are sleeping in demountable out-rooms. I have a big double suite in the main hotel. The rooms are dug into the ground to make them cooler.

Stephen ends up sleeping in my bed. We share a nyandi.

Freddy is off with the director. Talking. Sharing wine.

The hotel cooks bush tucker. Everyone is happy.

The next day is our last day of shooting. We drive out to the location. A red sand dune in open country.

I'm dressed as a cop. Freddy is shirtless, just jeans. Stephen is wearing feather booties. Carrying a spear.

I stand with Henry's uncle and smoke cigarettes. I can't look at Stephen dressed this way. Libby has explained to me how not to look. How to control curiosity. Even picturing the feather-foot in your mind can get you into water way beyond your depth. Or sand. Deep deep sand.

Freddy is hung-over and short-tempered. Freddy is also distracted. He can hear children laughing and playing just beyond the dune. He asks me if I hear it. I'm not sure. I go for a walk to listen. To look. I find some emu feathers. Several times I think I hear giggling on the wind. The wind is cold. Cutting straight through us as if we are wraiths, not really connected to this earth.

In the car on the way out Freddy talked about visiting the Community. Just talk. We both know we're not gunna go.

We finally finish shooting. Freddy finishes before me. By the time I've walked across the dune a couple of times with my hunting rifle on my shoulder, Freddy is a tiny speck in the distance. Just walked off. Hard to spot in the fading light, as if he is part of the country. The unit base where the cars are is kilometres away. He's headed there cross-country.

I wait for the 4WD to take me to my car.

There are signs of emus all around. I wanted to hunt for a new egg but now I've run out of time.

Freddy and I get into the hire car and drive back to the hotel. It's our last night. We eat dinner. Get drunk in the bar. Take over the stereo. Take over the whole place.

Stephen is trying to chat up the barmaid. I ask her star sign. Virgo. I tell Stephen not to waste his time. He decides to anyway.

Freddy and I, the director and the Italian film star eat dinner together. We drink wine.

Later in the bar, Freddy does a striptease. On the bar. He's hard to miss. He's good too. Bump and grind. Grind and bump. He gets down to nothing but with his hands he does a fan dance — so that the crew never get to see the business. They just think they do.

The director and producer are turned on by the display. The crew shout and stamp and clap their approval.

Finally Freddy gets down off the bar and gets dressed again.

Deadly, eh, Bro?

Ya weren't doin it for me, Coord, I offer.

We both laugh till we're sore. I go off and have a smoke with Stephen. Then we're out of nyandi. Gotta drink. Stephen goes back into the bar.

The Virgo barmaid is stacking stools on the bar so she can mop up. It's 3.00 am.

I'm going to my room for a drink. In the foyer are the powder-blue-lovers. He is sobbing. Leaning against the glass doors weeping. She stands nearby looking uncomfortable. What did she think was gunna happen?

Stephen comes back to my room eventually. Virgo girl went to bed. We smoke cigarettes now.

I go to knock on Freddy's door. He and the Italian director

are in bed together. I'm drunk. I stagger straight in and sit on the bed. They tell me it's a secret. That they haven't done anything. We'll all laugh about this much later, when Freddy and the director get married.

We've gotta leave in a couple of hours. When the sun comes up. Stephen and I sleep in my double bed.

The laughter from the children of the dunes echoes in our room until way after sunrise.

The only gub in the photo

Wurundjeri Country, Melbourne. A year has passed. All things are circles — no beginnings, no ending, round and round.

I remember Henry, my djaambi, at the first reading of his war script. Not The War. Another war, Kokoda war. Australia's first major independent battlefield success story — achieved by such unorthodox means that the soldiers on the ground even left high command way behind and were later accused of being cowards.

This is Henry's uncle's story. Djaambi. And his mate, Gubbah Djaambi. A story passed to him. Story of two mates from different cultures fighting a war together. A war with many fronts.

You can see why this war would interest a Gunditjmara warrior. A man who's been fighting for Country since drawing his first breath, when he wasn't even a citizen in his own Country.

George had told me about this script reading. We were smoking cigarettes in the kitchen in St Kilda. Late at night.

I reckon you'll like it. I reckon you'll get on with Henry. Real well.

When?

Tomorrow arvo.

We smoke.

And now here we all are, cramped into this tiny little shirt factory turned into a theatre. A sweatbox by any other name would smell as sweet …

I meet Henry. Have I already met him? It's hard to know. His eyes sparkle with friendship but they watch me like a hawk. All over me. I've seen this before. The look in those brown eyes. When I was in uniform myself. All my instructors were Vietnam veterans with those penetrating eyes.

I settle down. I'm to read the part of this old gubbah with old gubbah attitudes who has to swallow his pride.

We're all sitting on chairs against one wall. Facing the audience. There's about thirty people there. Invited people. From the film funding bodies etc. Me, George, Mark, that Murri fulla who used to live with Lucy, sister Joline, Henry, all these other Kooris, all waiting. Waiting for Freddy. I haven't seen him for a while. Freddy is playing the main role. We're pretty sure he got on a plane an hour or so ago in Sydney. Heading here. Pretty sure.

Henry is unfazed. Actually he appears to be in his element. Cracking jokes. Not worried. The punters love him.

Eventually Freddy strolls in. All smiles. Picks up the script. Never read it before.

You right? Henry says.

Yeah. Freddy smiles.

And we begin the reading. Mark is taking my role.

Is Henry watching me when he tells me who'll read what?

Freddy and George are electric and the story sings around

the room. Some of the audience cry when Freddy dies. They burst into spontaneous applause at the end.

The film industry people are beaming. So is Henry.

Afterwards we're having coffee and smokes outside. Someone takes a photo of us all.

Henry is loving this. You get this particular energy when you consciously walk your path. Embrace it.

In the picture I look pale, of course, but determined. I desperately want to play Freddy's mate. I feel I'm born for this role. I never noticed the determination until years later. I was masking it from those around me until I knew the lie of the land.

Same as not noticing that I was the only gub in the photo. I was so used to seeing it that I didn't see it any more.

Two teams

Wudjari Country, WA. I'm sixteen and playing in my first and only premiership-winning side in the local Esperance association. And my dreams come true. I play on my mate. Give him a bath. I get the girl at the end of the day — Joanna Steel. She runs up and kisses me even before my tears of joy have dried on my face.

I swap jumpers with my mate and my team do a lap of honour before the huge crowd of maybe a hundred and twenty. Our coach is Tony, a softly spoken Nyungar fulla.

Tony's appointment at the start of the season is a stroke of genius. We always had a talented side. Our problem is that the team is made up of fifty per cent wadjulas and fifty per cent Nyungars and Wongis. So if us wadjulas get the ball we only ever kick it to other wadjulas. The Nyungar and Wongi players would only ever pass to their own mob. So we'd have two teams out there.

It was always a joke among us that our nation had economic sanctions in place against South Africa because our gubment objected to apartheid. South Africa could just as easily have economic sanctions in place against us. Apartheid is in full swing in Wudjari Country.

Nyungars and Wongis confined to The War Zone. Us to the peace. All we lack are the signs in English and Afrikaans. And when we play Newtown, who also have a mob of Nyungars playing for them, there'd be four teams out there.

Tony has the idea that we have to link the groups together. He chose me to be the on-baller/link-man from the wadjulas and Jackson Murray to be the link-man for the Nyungars and Wongis. Jackson is a Fairhaven lad.

Tony never speaks openly to us that this is actually our role, but he has a way of making us understand it very well. Tony knew what made us tick. Wadjula and Nyungar alike.

Tony never really gives a half-time or three-quarter-time address. Sometimes he says a few words, but if he has something to tell a player he goes up to the player and says it quietly in his ear, while gripping or touching his upper arm.

I played like a man possessed. Jackson too. All season long. We won the grand final against our archrivals. Beat the sons of rich farmers and the local gubbah establishment. Except that we're only boys. Just sixteen years old. We become tight. Me and Jackson. All of them. We're never able to socialise outside of school or footy, but on the field we're tight nonetheless.

I was very curious about Jackson's last name. The Murrays were the original land owners in the area, who still maintain a tight grip on the money and power structures within this remote community. But I never felt right about asking. To me it would be the ultimate crime for the invaders to take even the people's true names, but history tells me that this is a practice as old as our European warrior culture itself.

Years later Mum, Henry's mum, would explain to me how

they had naming days at the mission in Gunditjmara Country. In order to stop the People speaking their own tongue, they had to be stripped of any tribal names or titles. The People would line up and a gubbah with a big book would tell each individual what his or her new name would be. And their children must also take this strange name.

Many of my own mob, Irish convict mob, changed their names to make them sound less Irish. Distance ourselves from the convict stain. (Didn't work!)

Later on, people at the mission would be tested and punished if they didn't know their names. Their gubment name. Gubbah name.

This champagne bottle is a rifle

I don't fucken know.

George and I are drinking somewhere. Daytime. So probably the kitchen in St Kilda. Boonwurrung Country.

Up behind the Junction Oval is a Scar-Tree that has been there long before this kitchen and this St Kilda. A meeting place.

George decides he wants to visit Henry. Henry is in a recording studio around the corner. Well, ten minutes away. So we jump in Liz's '71 Falcon and drive around to see him.

Henry and a couple of others are just sitting around. Not working on any music. Henry is pleased to see us.

Henry gets a phone call. Talks for a bit then hangs up. He beams at us.

We're going to the shop!

George inclines his head upwards, short and sharp, and his lips purse ever so slightly.

Champagne!

Henry sweeps out of the studio with us in his wake. We walk to the shop. The sun is still warm. We feel good. Marching up that street together. We go into the shop.

The shop assistant gets a real tight moom when he sees me walk in with that large Gunditjmara man and that huge Ngarrindjeri man.

Henry is cracking jokes so fast that the lad forgets to be scared and gives us the champagne. We march back to the studio.

We're in the streets of Port Melbourne. Marching down to the dock. Getting on the boat bound for New Guinea. This champagne bottle is a rifle in my hands. Why did Henry give it to me to carry? There is a ship waiting for us. Take us away to the fight.

We get to the studio. Henry gets another call. He talks. Hangs up. Breaks into a huge smile.

Got it! Got the fucken first bit!

We pour the grog into plastic cups and drink it down and laugh. All laughing for different reasons. Henry cause it's on now. George and I because we're happy for him — also, we wanna be in the fucken film!

And I ain't playin no old bastard, I catch myself thinking.

Henry looks at us and smiles, as if he heard my private thought.

Have to start auditions, he observes drily.

George and I look at each other. Smile. Look back at Henry. Smile bigger. Our faces must surely bust. They do. Go up like grenades. We all laugh. For different reasons.

Henry is one of them fullas. His Dreaming path is all around him. Alive and pulsing. Sometimes moorroopy and frightening to this skinny gubbah.

Moorroops are ghosts or spirits. Henry is one of those men who has them dancing all around him. I didn't know it then, but it is a world I would have to embrace. To openly love through my fear.

We fear what we don't understand. We destroy what we fear. This fight with my fear is *the* fight.

I felt it when I stepped into the ring with King and the old trainer encouraged us to fight. Really fight. I was afraid of being hit. I was more afraid to hit back. To hit. To hate.

Sometimes in my work, when I open the doors in my psyche, or whatever, to hate — like when I leaned against that rock in Wiljali Country, took aim at Freddy with a high-powered rifle and pulled the trigger and watched him crumple into the dust — it can really affect me for a while afterwards. And that's work. I didn't want to do it in my life. I'm still learning how to hit with love.

Like that night I had to face it with King, my Coorda, in front of the audience in Eora Country. Had to be there for him.

Had it all the time

So Henry starts auditions. The shirt factory theatre in Carlton. Run by people long friends of the People. The first gubbahs in Melbourne to acknowledge the traditional owners and the sacrifices they had to make so that we can stand here.

I turn up. I'm feeling confident. I know this character. Know this world. This is where I'm from. Where I'm going. I know my acting skills are honed to it. And maybe — little bit — Mr Reckons-he-knows-a-lot-about-Kooris.

Only one direction for this bullshit to travel in. After the first half-hour, I'm humbled. My knowledge is a tiny thimble of water evaporating in the desert, awaiting the arrival of Burke and Wills.

I become convinced that everyone else is communicating in a secret way that I don't understand. I feel a step behind. I don't get all the jokes. Don't understand all the shifts in the talk. I'm reaching out now.

George is reaching too, for something different from me. We share our reaching like a meal.

I'm standing outside smoking. Sucking like I'm at my mother's nipple. George is there. Freddy too. Henry. We smoke in silence. We look over our shoulders. We catch each other's eye and laugh.

And it goes on. And on. Audition after audition. My woman, Liz, is fucken sick of hearing about it, I'm sure.

I dunno when I started thinking of Liz as 'my woman'. I mean it the same way the People say 'my Country', as in the Country I belong to. Fullas say 'my woman' same way. Liz is the woman I belong to. My woman.

Sometimes we sit at Henry's house. Dark and cold with no fire.

Henry sings a song about the mission. I go to the kitchen so no-one sees my tears.

Sometimes Henry, Freddy and I go for long walks with Henry's dingo. The dingo is crazy. But who are we to throw stones? He affects all of us with his crazy up-play. We're looking for the spoor. The path. The track to walk along. We've gotta walk after them Old Fullas. Honour their story.

Henry takes photos of Freddy and me in the park. In the picture, Freddy and I are up against the solid green background, we look out, we look like someone else. We are in the heart of Men's Business. Story Business. My spirit is singing. Waking up all over again.

In this time we love each other as men. Brothers. Would give our lives for this Mob. This story.

But Henry is giving nothing away.

Freddy is confident. He laughs and says things to reassure me. They don't.

And we're back in the shirt factory and suddenly there is a bubble around us as we work. It stops being an audition. Rehearsal. Work. Gone somewhere else now.

Henry creeps around us. Like Old Man watching his young dancers. I can see him with a big stick in his hand for some serious teaching, too.

And then Henry calls a halt. Says he has to go. We depart.

George and I go and have a drink. We're sweating on it. If we don't get these roles now, we aren't going to. We sit out the back of George's place in Collingwood. The sun is hot on our Irish and Ngarrindjeri skins. Henry calls us up. We laugh.

Ya wanna have a drink down the pub?

Fucken oath.

We go to Henry's local. Everyone knows Henry. A fucken celebrity. A mob of young fullas play pool. They worship Henry. He buys us shots of sambucca. Sambucca you can't see through.

What else?

We get really blind. Henry tells us we've got the roles in his film. He's grinning like a Cheshire cat. I could take a fucken swing at him. I look to George. He could, too. Except that we're both so fucken happy! And besides, to take a swing at Henry would be the actions of a very stupid man.

We laugh and embrace each other. I've never auditioned for anything so much before in my life. Nor will I ever again. Maybe never wanted anything so much before.

This would hit me at two in the morning two nights later when I realise what Henry had done to me. He wanted me to be hungry for the cross-cultural friendship — not content in it.

I rang him straight up and abused the fuck out of him. Called him everything under the sun. Only interrupted my abuse to ask: Did I have it all the time?

You had it all the time.

And I'm back into abuse. I can still hear Henry laughing down the phone. His voice all gentle when he says goodnight.

Goodnight, Djaambi.

For now, in this pub, Henry's local, the last thing I remember is saying goodbye to Henry. Then watching him leave and having the floor suddenly rushing up at my face. I grab hold of this golden rail on the bar to stop my pointy Celtic nose from smashing into the tiled floor. And hanging there, like a monkey, unable to move, I look up and grin at Henry who is standing in the doorway like a Gunditjmara Gary Cooper. And laughing. Swaying a little. But maybe that's down to my eyes, too. Laughing. Laughing.

Soon it seems we must be ready

We rehearse in a community hall. Freddy and I drive in together every day. Freddy loves it when I turn up in Liz's old Falcon.

Boss car, Coorda.

Boss car.

We stand outside the hall and share cigarettes like old soldiers. We stamp the gravel with our boots. Our spines are ramrod straight. Shoulders squared. Our thoughts are on the green machine.

Henry is an old soldier. He knows how to train men. We get rifles to practise combat drills with. The old .303s. The weapons Uncle Jimmo once described to me.

We are just getting the hang of the guns and getting a sweat up in the hall when we're interrupted by the entrance of Myrtle and her make-up buddy, Dianne.

Henry introduces this striking Boonwurrung woman to us as the make-up and special effects artist for the film. Myrtle flashes a smile at us boys and they go off to set up the hair-cut station in the change rooms.

Henry cracks a joke. He looks after the women, then turns back to see us men all standing open-mouthed, still staring after them. We all laugh at Henry's comment.

This is the way with soldiers. Something about the rifles in our hands which speak to us of the prospect of not returning from the war, of lonely jungle gut-shot deaths, which makes us really appreciate beautiful women.

One by one we file in to get our 1940s war haircuts. Now we're feeling it.

I get that tingle around Myrtle. Not that sexual tingle. Something else. Us blokes are all married-up anyway. Like our paths are connected. Or have been. Or will be. Past. Present. Doesn't matter.

Tingle. Tingle.

Uncle Kumanjai Presto comes in to rehearse. His health has deteriorated further since I last saw him but his spirit is stronger and stronger. I struggle to look Uncle in the eye. Because of what I have to do in the film. My fear. Uncle feels it. Gives me his warm smile.

The film editor comes in to the hall to meet us all. Observe the rehearsal. She's listening for rhythms. Looking out for body language, eye contacts. She knows that to work across cultures she's got to soak these things up. At least have an overview about the different levels of communication going on all the time. I know it because it's all I can think about. We gubbahs have to work a bit harder at cultural disciplines, observing taboos or protocols.

And we try on costumes and soon it seems we must be ready.

After work Uncle's beautiful daughters come in to visit him. I'm hanging around with Freddy and George. Henry had to go to a production meeting.

I speak to Uncle later. Put my foot in my mouth. Say something very stupid. Presume knowledge that I don't really have, and assume an intimate relationship with Uncle (on a family matter). Uncle lets it pass. I drift away. My real embarrassment will come later when I realise what the fuck I said. Trapped by my own arrogance. I realise I've got a lot further to travel down this path than I've already come. Maybe it is the energy of the character bleeding through to me. Putting my foot in my mouth despite good intentions. It certainly brings me down a peg or two.

They know how to treat their war veterans

I'm sitting in the big empty community hall with Uncle Kumanjai Presto. We're rehearsing with Henry and Freddy and George. Uncle is telling us a story, laughing his way through it:

I go to walk into this bar in Wodonga. They won't let me in. In those days it was sometimes come in, sometimes piss off you Mob. I noticed that I was wearing an old army shirt. Dunno where I got it. I slept on someone's couch that night after hitching down from Sydney so I might've borrowed it from him. It wasn't mine. So I say to this barman, he's got ex-army written all over him: Mate, I didn't go to Korea so that I could come back here and have you tell me I can't drink in here! He gives me another look. He's not sure. Third Battalion, I say. He hesitates. Fuck you, Mate! I say and turn to go. Well, he's grabbin me and sayin he's sorry, it's just been a misunderstandin, he says, Third Battalion, eh? So I go inside and he buys me a drink and he starts tellin me all his World War Two stories. He tells the blokes in the bar that I'm ex-Third Battalion, been to Korea, and they all buy me a drink and tell me their old warries. I'd met this bloke once, he told me he'd been in the Third Battalion in Korea. That's all I knew. But luckily they were just so desperate to tell their own stories. I got charged up, got invited back to some bloke's place for dinner. Ya can't come in if you're …

Uncle laughs.

But they know how to treat their war veterans …

We all laugh.

… them country boys.

Uncle cackles at the memory.

Moorroop blessing

The first day of shooting comes along and I'm not scheduled to appear. I'm on the back-up day if the weather turns bad.

I have a good night. Get up. Start our day in St Kilda. Coffee. Stewie and Lloyd off to school. At about ten to ten I decide to take my daughter Charlotte for a walk to the shops. If anything was gunna happen, it would've happened by now. I get ready. Strap Charl into the papoose. The phone goes. Film producer.

Where are you?

At home.

How soon can you get here?

Where are you?

Narre Warren.

Forty-five. Hour tops. Hang on, I'll need directions.

And in a moment I'm on a four-lane highway in the car. Going flat out. Things got changed. I should've been rung earlier. Halfway there I pull over. The producer is waiting for me in his car. He takes off and I follow him.

We go quite briskly. When we finally get there we have to drive off the main road and through the bush to the location. Gunditjmara Country. The make-up bus is there.

I get made up by Myrtle. She has made her make-up bus a sanctuary. It is happy and full of joy. Mum is there. Uncle Kumanjai Presto too.

Myrtle and Freddy have just realised that they are related. Freddy's cousin is married to Myrtle's sister.

We get driven to another location when we're ready. An old scout hall. Inside, the crew have set up one corner as the barracks.

Us fullas joke around outside. We do a rehearsal. We're all holding back for the take. Like racehorses in the cage, ready to jump.

The take comes and we're all out with it.

We all feel this other presence in the room.

Once, when I was a kid, my mother got very emotional in church one Christmas Day. Sweating in the little outback community church, my mother suddenly burst out weeping. From down deep. The spirit of my grandfather appeared there in the church that day. The grandfather I never knew. Said prayers with his daughter in church on Christmas Day. It was very real. Well, the feeling now in the scout hall is something like that.

As they start resetting for the next shot, I go and sit next to Mum on a wooden bench at the back of the hall. Maybe it is a church pew. Can't tell in this dark corner.

Henry says I'm a big sook. He's probably right. But Mum gives me a look.

You feel him, Son?

Maybe there was a hint of surprise in Mum's voice. I could be wrong. I know she means moorroop. Sometimes it's best not to voice certain words at certain times.

I nod. Looking down.

Mum nods to herself.

It's alright, Son.

And it is. Alright. We nail that scene. Henry is rapt. It's working.

Heads up!

Favourite game

In a car. Driving around Port Phillip Bay. Boonwurrung Country. The runner is driving me in to the bar scene location. Roughly the path that William Buckley walked a hundred years before. Before the city. Before the Invasion.

The runner has his radio up full-blast. The song of the moment. Fills up the space in his little old car like firefighting foam. The guitar drones on with driven inevitability.

Wownw — Wow — wow
Wownw — Wow — wow
Wownw — Wow — wow — Wownw
And I'm loo — sing
My fav — rite game!

The runner has just finished working on this ad for Jaguar cars with a budget of six million dollars. We're making our short feature about the struggle for the soul of our nation for a hundred grand. Sooner or later all Australians will realise that the struggle for Land Rights and an equal place in our society facing the People is a struggle for all of us. We're all in this together. The struggle for Australia. The issue has been hijacked by the politicians. It is a moral issue, not a political one.

The guitar drones on, the notes bending all around us like sunbeams through glass prisms.

Wownw — Wow — wow
Wownw — Wow — wow
Wownw — Wow — wow — Wownw
And I'm loo — sing
My fav — rite game!

I get into uniform. Make-up. My shoulders go back. The country is young again. We have a chance to change things. If we have the guts to embrace it. I get a coffee. My back is straight. Legs are young and strong. My eye sparkles.

There's this old gubbah actor Henry has cast to play the barman. This fulla is an English migrant, been in the country twenty-five years or so. He looks a little uncomfortable with Henry's Mob buzzing all around, getting on with their film-set business.

The old gub sees me and his eyes light up. He comes over. Does the actors' dance with me. I'm not even in that world any more. He starts.

How ya goin?

Good.

Been busy?

Flat out.

We drink coffee from polystyrene cups. I give in. Why not?

You?

I've got my theatre restaurant now. Five nights a week. Doing well.

Oh. Good.

I'm staring across the road at the little old pub we'll be shooting in. He follows my line of vision.

This'll be interesting.

What?

I hear myself ask him, but my voice comes from far away. Like I know what's coming. I glance at him. It's coming all right. The Gub Club. I can tell by his sideways eye-flick at Willy, the young Murri assistant director who walks past.

Once we get inside the bar …

I let him trail away. I'm not helping.

If they start drinking …

I sip my coffee now. Look at the ground.

They can't help themselves …

I notice the lattice-work of angry-red exploded capillaries in his nose and left cheek. I take out my pre-rolled cigarette.

Just can't handle their piss …

I light up.

I'm going to have a look, I say, as though talking to myself.

I walk off without a look to him. If he wants a Gub Club meeting — he's talking to the wrong gubbah.

Inside, the bar is a hive of activity. Setting up lights, camera, video-split, arranging extras — it's all happening. Henry is in his element. Greets me warmly. Freddy and George come in.

Look at us here, would ya? Gang of fucken misfits. Alcohol abusers all working sober in a pub.

The irony of it cracks us up. We laugh and laugh.

So we all come in and start to shoot the scene.

The barman refuses to serve Freddy and George. He won't have Yamatji or Ngarrindjeri men in his bar. Fifty years ago I probably wouldn't have been allowed in either. Used to have signs on the windows: No Nyungars. No Irish. No Dogs.

Scene is going okay. The take finishes. The Old Gub says something under his breath. I feel George and Freddy stir beside me.

Youse couldn't fucken handle it anyway!

He is loud. I don't even know what he's talking about. Not specifically.

What?

It's Freddy. He'll kill this cunt. I grab him by the sleeve.

Later, Coord. Not now.

Did any of youse really fight overseas?

Oh, fuck. This gub is as stupid as he is fat and old.

Rather get pissed, wouldn't ya?

You'll be catching spears with ya fucken chest in a minute!

Henry from across the other side of the bar.

Funny thing is about this line of abuse, these other fullas could all drink this Old Gub under the table with one kidney behind their backs.

Couldn't throw if you were pissed!

I wouldn't fucken bet on it!

Not a bet I'd take.

We do another take. Djaambi comes up to me and speaks quietly in my ear after the take.

We'll do one more. No hate in your eyes, Brother. You don't hate this gub — you love your brothers.

We learnt this in the army, Henry and I. Something about the Australian psyche. Aussie soldiers don't fight against someone, they fight *for* their mates.

We do the take again. This time, Henry is happy.

The old gub goes home without realising how close he came to having a broken bar stool jammed up his arse until it knocked his teeth out. He probably thought he was being funny. Or probably he was just psyching himself into the character — I do it all the time — or experiencing character bleed without realising. Anyway, there are no hard feelings. Made the scene go real deadly.

I get taken home by the runner. Retracing Buckley's route. This was all swamp and wetlands then, where them Old People made tidal fish traps — then smoked big mob of fish to keep long time.

And the radio is playing our favourite song of the minute. We sing along. Even with the guitar

Wownw — Wow — wow
Wownw — Wow — wow
Wownw — Wow — wow — Wownw
And I'm loo — sing
My fav — rite game!

Don't blink or you'll miss it

The shooting seems to be going well. In the hills above Melbourne. Land of the Kulin Nations. The bush is dressed by the art department to look like jungle. Like Kokoda, New Guinea.

The sun moves across the sky. All the People know that fulla. I'm hearing the phrase from Djaambi's song, 'Condah Mission'.

We are the keepers of this land
We are the children of the sun

Shooting again and the light starts to go. The calculations for the schedule haven't taken into consideration the developing deep shadows among the big trees in the afternoon. Someone has fucked up. Suddenly we're all under terrible time pressure.

Henry quickly realises we need another shot to make the battle sequence work. We're going flat-out now. Flat out like a lizard drinkin. The gaffer is gunna try for a huge spottie — a midnight sun — but we don't know for sure if it'll work. Need a shot of me firing to kill a Jap and save Freddy. Henry comes over to me.

Run in there, kneel and shoot.

Okay.

Let's go … and, action!

I'm suddenly unsure. It's like I haven't fired a weapon for ten years. Looking through my telescopic sight at Freddy in that other film, squeezing the trigger, watching him crumple into the red Wiljali dust, seems strangely blotted from my memory, from my entire history, in this moment of love for my Yamatji Coorda, as though it never really happened.

Run where? Aim where? Shoot what? I run in. See the threat to Freddy. Prop. Take a kneeling fire position. Fire! See the Jap dead. Reload. Get up. Run on.

Okay. Let's move on.

I wanna do it again.

It was good. Move on.

Henry's older brother Mal speaks. Mal is a great man. Without him, none of this would be happening. He's the one who fought the behind-the-scenes battle to get the funding to make the movie in the first place. He's always been generous and open with me, despite him not being very close to many gubbahs. I'm embarrassed now. An ex-soldier who fucked up the weapon firing.

I think I blinked, Mal.

Blinked?

Both eyes. When I fired.

Might still work. You were shitting yourself. That's good.

Henry is moving the camera for the next shot now.

He won't use it. I wanna do it again.

But Henry has moved on. There is no time.

I'll look at it.

231

Mal goes to the video split. He watches it back. I smoke and watch him from the corner of my eye. His head drops sharply and suddenly.

Shit. Yeah. Ya blinked.

Fuck.

I kick the ground.

Fuck. Fuck!

Then the midnight sun comes on and we finish the last scene in crazy half-darkness. But the light has saved the film. Even the half-dark battle will work in its insanity. It is true. Can't argue with the truth. We're all gripped with the darkness now.

We go back near the unit base for the last set-up. One scene. Two shots.

Freddy and I hear Mal telling Henry there are five or six minutes left and no money for overtime for the crew or pick-ups.

Set up the shot. Here.

Henry indicates the camera direction with his hand aimed at Freddy and me, his forefinger and pinky extended as if giving us the cuckold sign.

The director of photography and grips literally run to do their jobs. Freddy and I rehearse. We know it's a one-take situation. Our hair is standing on end. It feels all moorroopy.

And Henry is talking to me. I'm weeping quietly in the darkness and hoping Henry isn't noticing and I'm not really sure what he's saying until I hear:

You ready?

Yeah.

I feel my lips move but I'm pretty sure it is someone else

speaking. I go and sit next to Freddy. George is gone. Shot down. Never see his wife and kids. Never see his Country again. We're in this crazy bubble now. In the Milky Way.

Action!

Cut! Print. It's a wrap!

Freddy and I amble away from the light. Henry is still working like a dog. We all look like shit. Luckily it's too dark for anyone to notice. And we don't give a fuck.

Freddy and I light up a joint and sit by the dirt track in our uniforms. We smoke in silence.

All this floods back to me. Years later. I'm in The Lighthouse in Gunditjmara Country. It's been converted into a restaurant/bar. Time folds into itself. Like brandy into cream in a Russian sweet. Sitting next to Mum, having dinner. The wind howls outside like an insistent child who wants to play. We wash down our hot curry with cold beer. Djaambi is singing. He suddenly looks up over the body of his guitar and smiles at me. Into my eyes. My spirit.

I had this dream last night
We were young and in uniform again

And we were young and in uniform again. Freddy and I and George. With a war to fight. War of attitude.

Gum leaves, trains and crying babies

The old railway station in Healesville, Victoria.

We are welcomed to Country by Auntie Mary, a Wurundjeri Elder. Auntie tells us about the gum leaves of the area and their significance to her People. How each leaf is the spirit of them Old People. How spirits cannot be destroyed — only transformed or transfigured — from the Land to the People and then back to the Land again. This Country is us. We are this Country.

I'm remembering the gum leaves in the ceremony for the wader-birds under the West Gate Bridge conducted by Wurundjeri Elders and Maori Elders. The wader-birds migrate from Melbourne and New Zealand to Japan and Russia each year and back again to breed under the West Gate. Because that area is now industrialised their habitat is under threat. The Elders held this ceremony to strengthen the birds and raise awareness.

A big mob of us were given small branches of gum leaves to carry and then sit on during the ceremony. First we had to sit on the ceremonial border of Wurundjeri Country and wait to be invited in. We see the smoke from the Elders' fire and down the hill we move. Then when the dancing, singing and other business with the Elders is happening we sit on our gum leaves, until we rise to do our bit. The ceremony finishes with this Old Wurundjeri Fulla making a joke. To his People, the wader-birds could be a sign of death, 'So I'm, you know, taking my life in my hands here!'

Liz and Charlotte have come up to be extras in the big going-off-to-war scene.

We cannot help but think about those real men who departed from this railway station some fifty years ago. Left their families and Country — many of them would never see home again. Men who went to lay their lives on the line for a nation that didn't even consider them to be citizens. Some of these men would return to find that their children had been stolen by the same government they'd been away fighting for. Most of the actors here are Stolen kids.

I look up from where I'm sitting, surrounded by a big mob of fullas, all of us in uniform, the smell of terrible optimism in the air. I see Liz on the platform with Charl in a pram from the period. Liz beautiful in a green dress, green like the rolling hills of Ireland, like the waving gum leaves of the Wurundjeri. My heart is sore with love — how can I leave them to go and fight this stupid gubbah war? But how can I stay and live as a slave, or hold my manhood cheap compared to those who are prepared to go and fight?

The heart of the civilian soldier in time of national crisis. Not a distant story. Close. We grew up with this story cracking and popping over our heads like machine-gun fire.

Henry's uncle is a decorated returned soldier, several bravery awards, the first Gunditjmara man to become a commissioned officer in the Australian Army, first of any of the Mob from this country. When he returns from the war he has to live with his family in a rat-infested hovel in Port Melbourne and can't get a job in this nation that he'd put his life on the line to defend. In desperation, Uncle rejoins the army to fight in Korea. The army doesn't care about his heritage — just his ability as a warrior. Not called 'The Fighting' Gunditjmara for nothing.

Later in the day and my own reality has really begun to slip. Slip-slidin away. Uncle Kumanjai Presto is in town. We'll shoot the coming-home scene in a couple of days.

I feel it coming from the future/past with a kind of dread in my bones. Though it is an easy dread. It all has an ease that flows through me like wind in the gum leaves. As though my course is being directed from way beyond.

Mum is there to reassure me, but I can hardly meet her eyes either. I stand alone on the platform, waiting for a train that will never come. The Capstan goes to my lips. Out comes a match and it strikes. Waru. The fire touches the end of the cigarette and my eyes go across the train tracks to the rustling gum leaves as the smoke fills my lungs. Behind me, way back, out of earshot, they are setting up the camera. I feel their eyes on me.

What's he doing?

I couldn't turn and look at them even if I wanted to. I know they aren't there.

Rehearsing.

Henry's voice chimes like a tiny bell in the wind.

The loneliest gubbah in the world.

I smoke. Steady myself on my cane. My wounds are old but

still ache through my blue suit like cooking fires on the beach in winter.

And then we're wrapped. Go back to the motel for a rest — then into town for dinner at the pub. Big old country pub. Locals aren't overly excited to have us there but they need our cash.

Charlotte is only six months old or so. She isn't overly impressed with the pub full of loud film people. In fact, she gets quite upset and has a big squawk. Liz can't settle her and is getting a little worried. Maybe we'll have to head off.

Suddenly Uncle Kumanjai Presto is right by our side. He grabs the crying Charlotte from her mother.

Now, you listen to me, young lady!

Uncle's voice is mock-stern. Charlotte instantly shuts up and listens. Staring up into Uncle's big warm brown eyes. Uncle nurses her like a pro. He *is* a grandfather. He carries her off to a quiet corner of the room. Talking to her all the time. After five minutes or so, Uncle brings her back and hands her to me.

She'll be fine now.

And she was. The pub got noisier and noisier but it didn't worry my little girl. She listened and watched and snuggled in to me and her mum.

Ya gotta read to her. Every night. I read to mine from the moment they were born. By the time they were one, I'd open the book and by the end of the first page they'd be gone. Off to the land of Dreams.

Thanks, Uncle.

Soon it really is time for us to go. We go back to the motel and get our little lady into bed.

The motel is better than the one in Morwell. But only

marginally. The decor certainly hasn't changed since 1973.

We smoke cigarettes in the cold night air. We brush our teeth vigorously. We curl up together with Charl. There's nothing like the warmth of a family sleeping together. I never want to leave this bed.

Later on we hear the others come back.

As the pub got close to closing, the gub producer decides to get everyone home and insists on giving them all a lift in his Merc. All the Mob, that is. Wasn't worried about any gubbahs drinkin late or muckin up.

By the sound of things, Freddy and George stay up drinking all night anyway. Probably in response to being rounded up and driven home. And they are a people pretty used to being rounded up and driven off.

No, I guess you never really get used to it.

Dad's story: Sunny in the dust

I'm telling my dad about writing this book. About how it is bringing up memories long forgotten. Dad laughs. Tells me this one:

Lort River Station, Wudjari Country, late sixties. I'm nearly four. My little brother is eighteen months old. Chaz Campbell the head stockman comes home with Dad for a cuppa tea. With Chaz is Sunny, one of the Wongi stockmen. As they enter our yard, Sunny stops and stands outside the gate. Dad tries to get him to come in as well. Explains that he is welcome to come in the house for a cuppa. Chaz tells Dad not to worry about it, Sunny would prefer to wait at the gate. Has probably never been inside a wadjula home. But Dad does worry about it. My dad has one of those true Christian hearts, and really does love all men equally.

The People had become citizens in their own Country less than two years before. Maybe nothing much has changed for the likes of Sunny and Bart.

Dad and Chaz take off their boots at the back door and go inside. But they had barely begun to drink the tea and eat the cake that Mum has served up when they hear this terrific commotion from outside. Screaming and squealing and growling, the dogs all barking and going mad. Dad goes to the back door and see me and my little brother locked in a fierce play-fight with Sunny. He's rolling in the dust with us, oblivious to getting filthy; we're all over him, he's getting punched, he's got one of us in a headlock, we're squealing and screaming with happiness and excitement and Sunny is laughing with pure joy. Dad watches for a moment before Sunny feels his eyes on us. Sunny sits upright like a schoolkid who's been caught doing something naughty. His face goes back to the blank expression he wears in the company of wadjulas, and his eyes go down. Us two little kids fall off him like leeches touched with a hot match. We all three of us sit there in the dust with the same blank looks on our faces. Dad smiles and goes back inside, and us kids start clamouring for Sunny to fight us again.

He's your mate

Deep in the bush in the hills above Melbourne. All Kulin Nations Country here.

Feels good to be in the scrub again. Not that this lush greenery is anything like Wudjari Country, where I grew up, or Balardung Country, where I did a lot of army training.

We shoot some patrol stuff. Feels good to move slowly and soak up the mood of the bush. To hold a rifle. My eyes move in a grid pattern. Scouring the foliage for any sign. Where my eyes look, my weapon points. These protocols were learned here on the Kokoda. Perfected in Malaya and Vietnam. Lucky for Henry and me, we were too young for Vietnam.

Always Henry's voice. Just outside the bubble. Talking us in like game. Maybe them Old Fulla Gunditjmara Men talked the whales in. Sung them in close to the shore. Then hundreds would feast.

Henry's the backbone of every scene.

We stop for lunch. The catering is fantastic, as usual. I have this lovely chicken curry with cold spiced beans. The real lads on the Kokoda Track didn't have this sort of tucker.

I go over to the green room bus to relax. I take my shooting schedule out of my bag to check out the order of this afternoon's events.

Shit. What scene is that? I didn't notice that this morning. Or last night.

I step outside and look around for Henry. He's gone back down to the location. I grab my smokes and walk back along the track to the location. I see Henry there, talking to Smokin Joe. He's a gubbah fulla who operates the smoke machine (and the least likely to ever get mistaken for Joe Frazier in the entire known universe).

I wander up to Henry. I have the schedule in my hand. Yellow paper.

We didn't rehearse this.

Henry looks at me as if he doesn't understand English. (It's been a hundred years, or so, since the missionaries forbade the Gunditjmara to speak Language. Which meant, of course, don't speak in front of the missionaries.)

We didn't rehearse this.

Nu.

Henry walks off. Leaving me standing.

Then we're on patrol. There are Japs. Blam! Freddy's head explodes. He falls in slow motion.

Cut!

Oh, fuck! Oh, fuck!

I go and light a cigarette. They're checking the gate.

Gate clear!

I see Djaambi standing just up the hill from me. I can't look at him.

I go up the hill. Freddy's new wife is there. The Italian movie director. We look down to Freddy lying motionless. Myrtle is attaching the beautiful wound that she's prepared. But Freddy doesn't move a muscle. I explain to Freddy's wife that when I had to shoot him (in that other film, her film), I imagined that I was killing the self-destructive part of Freddy, the drinkin and everythin that goes with it. But now? We stand there weeping. Soon the shot will be ready to go.

I go down to Henry.

We didn't rehearse this, Djaambi.

I know.

How do you want me to …?

He's your mate. You work it out.

I turn to look at Freddy lying still on the ground. I turn back to Henry. He is gone. The loneliest gubbah in the world turns, and walks back down the hill. The stunt guy wires up my hits. No remote controls here. I'll have wires trailing out of my boots back to the stunties' controls.

Action!

I see Freddy hit. I run. I scream his name. The explosions go off in my chest and hip and down I go. And I'm crawling to Freddy. Pull him onto me. Screaming for help. Calling on them Old Fullas. Openly calling on them spirits to help me. All I got. And soon there's a big mob of old soldiers all around. Standing in groups, throwing cheeky smiles at me. Nothing can upset them. But me, I'm screamin inside. The sarge takes off Freddy's dog tags. I have to cover the head-wound with my hand because the dog tag chain brushes against it and almost dislodges it. The Sarge gives me the dog-tags. And I'm howling now. Lost-everything-don't-give-a-fuck howl. The only hope left in my life — those dog tags in my tear-and-blood-soaked hand.

That night we go back to the hotel. The crew are quiet and gentle with me. Like I really have lost a mate.

We're staying at this grand Spanish-style motel-villa complex. My room has a spa. I swap rooms with Freddy and his wife. What am I gunna do in a spa by myself? Give it to the lovebirds. The newlyweds.

The sarge and I sit in Henry's room and smoke until the early hours of the morning. Henry wrestles with editors and producers and film labs and funding bodies and budgets and women trying to fuck him. All in a night's work. The sarge and I sit in the corner and watch it all like it's on TV. This is the behind-the-scenes nitty-gritty that the actors usually don't see. Shielded from it by the everyone-loves-you protocol of the set.

Planting seeds

Shooting is near the end of the Kokoda business. In the hills of the Kulin Nations.

Early in the day it becomes clear that the money is getting very tight. One of the producers decides that a good way to save money is to axe Willy, the young Murri fulla who has come down from up north to learn from Henry.

The news spreads quickly through the cast and crew. None of us would be here if someone hadn't given us a chance. A go. Good go. If they hadn't believed in us. Freddy is staunch.

We're standing near the make-up bus on the side of a dirt road. Down the hill are pines. All around us are spindly gums. We're also surrounded by dozens of extras in broken-down uniforms with bandages and blood all over them. The walking wounded for the next scene.

Let's go to the fucken pub.

Eh?

No money for our brother. Let's just fuck off until the money comes back.

George's character is dead but he's on set, of course.

We all agree. Even if it puts Henry in a hard predicament.

Freddy explains our position to Henry. This gig can't just be about us. We all want to plant seeds. Got to. So that when that seed grows things will be different. Better than what we were born into.

Henry nods sagely and communicates this to the producers. Henry doesn't comment on the language Freddy has used — planting seeds, that's Henry talking. Maybe he's smilin inside.

Mal and the gubbah producer are talking in hushed tones away from the buses. They both make several phone calls. How did film sets work before mobile phones?

Anyway, there is this strange fifteen-minute hiatus. We smoke cigarettes and talk to the women in the make-up bus.

Henry makes a command decision and cuts the next scene, the one all the extras have been waiting for. It's a schedule thing. Command and control. As essential in a battle as choosing the ground on which the battle will be fought. Henry must win. And we're shooting again.

The Murri lad, Willy, is still with us. Still being paid. Still learning.

The scenes go well. Edgy and nervous. Maybe it was just what we needed. We play with our smokes and our weapons. Death sits in our circle. Offers to light our smokes for us. We light our own. We're not afraid of the other side — me, Henry, Freddy, George — we got too many friends there.

We've also all had this overwhelming experience of discovering that certain events are being engineered, way beyond our understanding, by powerful spiritual forces way beyond our control. There is no such thing as coincidence. Coincidence is denial. Simplistic. Everything is linked. Them Old People knew that. Knew time wasn't a straight line forty thousand years before the European culture produced Einstein.

We've all got different understandings of it. And we've all challenged them spirits too. Maybe that's what brought us together. Well, we know who brought us together. Henry. Up to us what we do now.

Freddy does a fantastic pick-up for the low-light battle sequence.

Freddy's new wife drives us home. The hills slide past my window. Looking at these hills is like looking at a beautiful woman. I blow my smoke at the trees. We're driving down into the sunset.

Waking dream in Uncle's eye

This day starts early. Before the sun is up we are already driving. I'm smoking already and staring at the hills. Thinking about that line of hills in Andyamathanha Country. Freddy tells me to look with my heart. See the People lying down. Sleeping. And the picture shakes and I see them Old People sleeping. The curves of their faces and bodies. Big Mob. Old old Mob.

The runner is talking. I can't follow it. My eye roams the Country in the growing dawn. Looking for people sleeping. Looking for men pointing rifles at me. Or spears. Looking for where to site my machine guns, where I'd dig my rifle-pits, where the threat would come from.

We finally arrive at the location and I have breakfast. Bacon'n'eggs. Make a sandwich with my toast. Can't seem to taste anything. Sitting on my own. Not noticing much around me now. Getting dressed. In costume. Smoking a cigarette. Capstan.

I need this stick to walk. This stick was carved from the tree under which Henry's Uncle was born. His Uncle the warrior.

And Henry is talking to me. He's kind. Leads me like I'm his Nana. I can't look him in the eye. I force myself to when I need the message. And Henry's talking and Mum's there and Uncle Kumanjai Presto and sister Joline.

We go through the motions of rehearsal. Our strange little family: Gunditjmara, Indinji/Komet, Yorta Yorta, Yamatji, Wathaurong and me. No-one looks at anyone. Not really.

And finally we're into the takes.

I step up and hold out my dead mate's dog tags to his dad.

And now I look Uncle Kumanjai Presto fair in the eye. And something happens. Something really full-on. I'm gone from my body. Freed from it in one short sharp rip. I'm somewhere else. Country. Blue stones. The hills. The sparkling water below. Faces all around. All looking. And pain. And joy. And flying. And millions of images of the People, as many as stars in the Milky Way, each new image a whole movie-length, crowding into my head and heart.

And suddenly I'm back here again and looking into Mum's eyes and she takes me into a sacred mother–son place and I'm saved. I'm okay.

Henry seems happy. But sad too. You know.

Up the hill a bit from the railway line there are two men hugging. And there are two big burly railway blokes openly weeping. All the crew are quietly howling as they pack up their gear.

I'm howling again just writing this down. That's how much of a sook I am.

And then I'm driven home. I'm drained — like I've been at a funeral all day. Crossed some other line.

Years later, I'm sitting in a hire car at the Mission in Gunditjmara Country with Mum's brother, Uncle William, telling me about the blue stones that saved his People. The gubbahs couldn't get through that stone country on their horses to hunt the People down.

And when I look to where Uncle points with his chin, I am shocked to see them. Those rocks. The colour. The colour of the rocks shocks me. I go back to that crazy waking dream in Uncle Kumanjai Presto's eye. The colour takes me back like a trigger. I've been shown the door to a whole other universe. A universe as real as this physical one we can see all the time.

But even after seeing the rocks, which I had seen in that dream, it didn't hit my conscious mind until we were driving out the front entrance of the mish that I knew I'd been here before and would be again. And I don't mean in another life.

I said to Mum once, as we were driving past Convincing Ground — that terrible place where the Gunditj Mob were taken during the Eumeralla Wars to 'convince' them to give up the fight and consequently their land, and from whence no-one ever returned — that I'd started to wonder if reincarnation might be clan related. That souls may be continually reincarnated into the same family. Mum said she could see my point. And it's why I had been given the full spiritual journey out to the mish, sign-posted with eagles, crows and old man echidna. Maybe I fought in the war against the Gunditjmara. Maybe that's why I've returned.

We gubbahs aren't used to moving in such a spiritual landscape. We've depended too long on our intellects and worried too much about what can be scientifically proven, instead of the truth of feelings.

Hair and Land and fucken bruising

What you've gotta understand about my djaambi, Henry, is that he laughs more than any man I've ever met. A man who has experienced many hardships, many, many horrors, who has 'seen the world through a mother's tears — something no man should see' (from a song by Djaambi called 'Who Made Me?').

Henry is mischievous. At the wrap party for the film I learned the hard way one of his many tricks. If there is a stage and a microphone, Henry has an amazing knack of calling you up to the stage at the most inopportune moment possible.

The party is at this upstairs bar at a local pub. The first time I'd been in this bar was ten years ago, when it was a gangster hang-out. Large Mediterranean gents in ill-fitting suits with clunky metal bulges in their armpits and pants. Now it's a trendy function room.

And it's been a hard, stressful and joyous shoot. We need to let our hair down.

I'm at the bar with George and Freddy and other blokes. We're knocking back bourbon'n'cokes like water and bloke-talking it up. There are no women in our circle, so it's fuck this, and fuck that, and this fucken bastard, and that fucken cunt did this, or fucken did that. And right at that moment when I'm mid-redneck swear-rave, I hear:

And welcome to the stage, Mr Stephen Motor!

I hear my name and look up.

What?

Carn, Stevey! Get up there!

At first I think if I just remain where I am, everyone will be right and get sick of waiting for me and someone else will grab the mic. There's a room-full here who would all love to make a speech.

Stevey! Stevey Wonder! Come on!

Oh, fuck. He's fucken serious. So I walk unsteadily to the little stage. Step up.

Thanks.

I take a breath. Look at the room-full.

You know, Henry said to me once, when a gubbah comes into the Koori Community, he gets *fucken* bruised badly on the way in, *fucken* knocked around and bruised like *fuck* on the inside, then gets really *fucken* bruised on the *fucken* way out!

I pause. The room is quiet and still. Not quite the response I was expecting. Finally someone puts me out of my misery.

There are kids here, Steve! Language, eh?

I can see Henry at the bar. He is getting a scotch and coke, short glass, no ice. Has his back to me but his shoulders give away his giggle. The colour drains from my face. (Which is really saying something.) I've been inappropriate. I thought I was still at the bar talking with my mates and my brothers. Henry turns to face me again. He stops giggling to take a drink, pouring it into his huge smile.

Always be ready, his eyes seem to say.

Hurry up and wait.

Anyway, I'm sorry about my language. I just want to thank Mum, Uncle Presto, Djaambi, Brother Mal, Freddy, George, Joline. I was born to play this role. Thank you from the bottom of my bended heart.

I go back to the bar to the sound of sporadic applause. Sweating hard and feeling foolish.

But two can play at this game, and so Freddy, George and I have come prepared.

All through the shoot, Henry would always be saying funny shit to wind us up. His favourite was something like: Don't worry about me, I'm just a lonely old Koori with no hair and no land. Don't worry about me. I'll be right.

One day I decided to count how many times Henry could say this. I stopped counting after twenty. Of course, because of the absolute conviction with which he says it, it gets funnier and funnier each time. I love a running gag.

My dad used to have lots of running gags when I was a kid. My favourite saying of Dad's used to come out every time we had tomatoes. We grew our own on the station, so that was fairly often.

There's nothin tomata with that, Dad would say.

The funny thing is that I was about twenty-five and visiting Mum and Dad when Dad said it again.

There's nothin tomata with that.

And I suddenly roared with laughter. Even now I'm giggling. The running gag that it took me twenty-five years to get. Nothin the matter! Well, you probably got it first time. My brothers did. Mum too. Everyone except me.

Anyway, so when Henry looks nice and relaxed, we slip out

the back and put on these huge afro wigs. Then we come out dancing, me, George and Freddy. We do the Elvis thing, 'Heartbreak Hotel', but with different words.

Since my hair has left me
I've found a new place to fit
It's down the end of a lonely road
At the Koori Hair Fusion Clin-ic
Oh baby so baldy, I
Oh baby so baldy, I
Oh baby so baldy — I could die!

Guitar. Dance moves. The whole kit and caboodle.

Then we present Henry with one of the huge afro wigs and a little ceramic container full of dirt with a little Koori cocktail-flag standing proudly in the soil. Hair and Land. Henry is jarred right up, too. You shoulda seen his face. He wasn't expecting nothin. We all fell about laughing. Laughing. Laughing.

The ammo dump is on fire

Henry gets invited by the Melbourne International Festival to do a version of his two award-winning films on stage. One is the Kokoda story, the other is the first telling of his story of the Royal Commission into the deaths of his People in custody.

First day of rehearsal always feels like a family reunion: Mum, Henry, Freddy, Joline, Uncle Elmore and Robby. Feels like it because that's what it is. We smoke out the theatre. We sing and dance and ask the spirits to bless our project.

We're also doing some of Henry's poetry.

One poem would start with a performer in silhouette — looking like the archetypal noble savage, standing on one leg, holding a spear, pointing at the sunset; then the lights would come up to reveal a gubbah (me), holding a broom (I s'pose this makes me the noble gubbah). Then I break the image, start sweeping and speak the poem — a playful romp of racism through this story of a woman who gets pregnant to a Koori fulla, and how this old, old fulla loves the child and reckons he's the grandfather.

Working with Uncle Elmore is always a ride. He is so naughty on stage and often improvises whole scenes in front of the audience. And, of course, the audience love him for it.

The play dealing with Henry's time as a field officer with the Royal Commission into the deaths of People in custody brings me into another circle. A grieving circle.

By now I've identified that look in Henry's eye from our first meeting. I've seen it before. In the eyes of the Vietnam veterans who taught me to be a soldier. Something happens to eyes that have seen too much. Too much fighting, killing, brutality, death, grief.

As the rehearsals and the season of the plays wear on, it's like the heat is getting turned up on that fire burning through the ammo dump in some lonesome valley deep behind those dark-brown Gunditjmara eyes. And it's a cold heat.

The effort needed to hide the toxic smoke and fire and the occasional explosion from the fire gets bigger and bigger. We all deal with it differently. Freddy kind of shuts down. Cool, calm, eyes down.

Uncle Elmore is talking to his family on the phone a lot now. We hear him speaking Language into his mobile in the alleyway beside the theatre. On stage he starts to play songs that he hasn't sung for thirty years.

One night I'm sitting in the wings watching him out there. He is using my clap-sticks — a present from the Dreaming Festival. Freddy is into the final scene now. There is a storm raging all around. Sparks fly from Uncle Elmore's clap-sticks. We hear rain striking the ground. Smell the wet dust. Uncle sings. Lightning flashes down by the creek. The theatre is gone. I hear *dozens* of voices singing. Clap-sticks all around me. I look around. Can't see anyone in this rain haze. Anyone but Uncle Elmore. Just a Ngan'giwumirra man singing and dancing. Sweat flying off him, lightning sparking from his sticks, feet striking the ground rhythmically, shaking the earth as with the approach of some great beast or spirit. Bang! Crackle! Lights out.

Uncle comes off stage to where I'm sitting. Puts the sticks in my hands. The sticks are hot. I can hardly hold them. Uncle Elmore beams at me. The applause thunders through the tiny theatre which used to be a courthouse.

I bin play Lightning Dreaming.

I nod. Sure fucken did.

Half-time now. We get changed. Ready for the second play. Go outside for a smoke. Henry is there.

Hey, Djaambi.

Henry doesn't look up. Like he's really concentrating on the red-hot tip of his cigarette.

Hey, Djaambi.

Henry just looks at me. What in the police force they'd call a target glance. Fuck. I take a little step backwards, as if to say: No threat here, Djaambi ...

Goin djillawah.

When I get back Henry is gone. I see Robby.

Where's Henry?

Pub.

What?

He didn't seem too good, Bruz.

We'll see him after.

But we don't. I ring him later that night. No answer.

Don't see him at the show again until closing night.

I've been off the piss to support Freddy but tonight I want to have a drink. So Freddy goes home to his wife. I stay for one or two. We crave what destroys us.

After a few I catch up with Henry. We hug. Talk for a bit. But I don't know where Henry really is. Not here, that's for fucken sure.

I thought it'd be good for him to get his story up there, out there to an audience, share the suffering. And the audience sure as hell couldn't get this story from reading between the lines of newspaper stories about young lads dead in police custody. Now I'm not so sure. Not sure about too much, actually.

Sometimes I wonder how Henry can talk to any of us gubbahs. He must often be gripped with the desire to stick a bar stool into my head. I look like those who've done it to him and his People. But that's gubbah thinking.

Outside the wire

Boonwurrung Country, St Kilda. I get a call one morning, early. Few weeks later.

Eh, Coorda, it's me.

The deep timbre of Freddy's voice unmistakable.

Hey, Coorda.

Just got a call from Henry's house.

He alright?

Don't sound like it.

Give's ten minutes.

Ten minutes later I pull up outside Freddy's place in Port Melbourne. Freddy's wife hands me a coffee as I come in. Good coffee.

What's goin on?

Dunno, Bruz. Reckon we should check it out.

We get the address and drive over. Not his old place. New woman. New place.

Freddy and I arrive at this quiet suburban street. The house is a thirties Cal-bung — no renos.

We walk straight into the house, front door wide open. This

gub woman is standing in the kitchen in a daze. We wander through, gingerly calling out.

Hello. Hell-o!

We're walkin so careful. Like we might break something.

Another gub woman appears. We introduce ourselves.

This is a side of Henry's life we know nothin about.

Freddy and I listen to the story in silence. War story. Eyes on the floor. The woman eventually finishes talkin. The two women wait awkwardly for our response.

In the early seventies, world politics came to my sleepy hometown when this young local lad came home from Vietnam. He'd finished his national service.

He got an old rifle from somewhere, a Lee Enfield .303, and camped down at our local beach, Yonda Quagi (place of big emu). No-one ever saw him down there. But we knew he was there. When we'd drive down to the beach there'd be dead stuff all over the place. He shot anything that moved. Everything. Brumbies, roos, emus, seals, seagulls, dead shit everywhere.

No-one says anything against this lad. He comes from a good family. Used to be a horse breaker.

As a community we begin to deal with how wrong we've all been. About the United States, about domino theories, about Vietnam. Look what they're doing to our sons.

Freddy and I examine the floor, carpeted with broken glass and crockery. We don't want to see the fear in the eyes of the women.

Where is he?

They look at me.

He rang from a hotel. Can't be too far away.

Freddy and I nod. Shuffle our feet in the rubble.

What's your number here?

I write the number down. Freddy and I look at each other. Shake our heads. We're not thinkin anything. We've wrecked a few houses ourselves. Walk back out to the car. Liz's new work car. Get in and drive.

The first two early openers are no-goes. The pokies not even warmed up yet.

We decide to go to Collingwood. There's a couple of bars there we know. One where we had a rehearsal for Henry's political activist film script. No go. I ask at the bar.

We try every pub on the way. Six or seven. Some of them aren't open yet. I peer in the windows anyway. Henry is the sort of fulla to know owners and bar managers well enough for them to let him in. Draw a blank.

Freddy calls the house back. Henry has rung. Sounds like he's deteriorating fast. Hard to tell though, unless we see him or speak to him ourselves. We're starting to get worried now. Don't want to leave our brother lost outside the wire. At least he knows we're looking for him. He's not alone outside the wire. We're in the backblocks of Collingwood, and we've checked every bar here.

I've got an idea.

I'm flooring the little Honda down this backstreet. We come to this tight left-hander and turn. Even though it's a two-way street, there definitely isn't enough room for two cars to pass each other. Too many cars parked down one side of the street. These streets were never designed for cars. And hurtling towards us is a two-tone orange and cream '81 Falcon. The driver and passenger are both big heavy-set men. Ponytails. Tattoos. They stare straight ahead and their expressions don't change as we suddenly come around the corner. Maybe they even speed up. Really hard lookin fullas. We don't need this.

I brake hard and slam the Honda into reverse. We flick back around the corner and the Falcon flies past, missing us by a bee's dick.

Freddy and I note their heads as they zoom past. We did the rightie. They were hard cunts and … BANG!

We come to a sudden halt. I look in my mirror to see that I've slammed into a taxi. Damn. I hop out to survey the damage and the Pakistani taxidriver comes running up to me, screaming abuse.

I apologise.

He screams abuse.

I accept all responsibility.

He screams abuse.

I suggest we swap addresses.

He abuses me.

Look, I'll just move my car. I'm blocking the street, I say in between insults. I'm getting a little bored with the way the conversation is progessing.

I jump in and drive just around the corner. There is no damage to the taxi. My left-hand back panel is hanging off dangerously.

As I go round the corner the Pakistani taxidriver runs along next to my car, madly threatening me for driving off and trying to pull out a notebook to get my rego at the same time. We haven't got time for this shit. I get out, write down all my details and give them to him. He's still desperate to argue the point. But doesn't really know how to do it because I keep accepting full responsibility. I know what I did. It was either the taxi or the two heroin/speed dealer/armed-robber types in the '81 Falcon. I'm not stupid.

Freddy and I find some gaffer tape in the boot to secure the back panel so that it won't hang out to the side or scrape on the back tyre.

The taxidriver is still trying to argue with me as I get into the car and drive off. I'm the one who should be pissed off. That panel is gunna cost a few grand that we haven't got. Doesn't matter. We got a brother who might be in trouble. Outside the wire.

Anyway, we drive around for half the day before we finally accept that Henry doesn't really want us to find him at the moment. I gotta get home. Feel a bit stupid now that we didn't find him. I got my own family to worry about.

Freddy catches up with Henry later. Motel room. We drove past that motel a dozen times.

Thought he might really do it. Naah. Too much dancing left to do.

Holding on too tight

Weeks later. It's a cool day in St Kilda. Henry and I are drinkin in the POW (Prince of Wales Hotel). We sit on bar stools and stare out at the rain falling in the street.

Across the intersection, towards the beach, is the Koori Park. When I first arrived in Melbourne, ten or so years ago, I sat on that bench there. Then there was no landscaped, manicured garden with totem poles. Just the old toilet block. Some of the Mob had painted a huge flag on the wall and various other murals. The Parkies who lived there wanted us all to know that the place was cared for, owned.

This old Uncle came and sat next to me without a word. I bought a few stubs of VB and we drank and smoked together. Mostly in silence. Two friendless men from two different worlds. This Uncle welcomed me.

I was waiting for my old army mate to finish work. I'd be sleeping on his lounge room floor in Elwood for a couple of months.

As Henry and I looked out into the rain, the tears were forming in my eyes. We talked about the day Freddy and I came lookin for him in that motel room. Henry tells me about finally catching up with Freddy later that day. I haven't felt like throwing it all away for a long time. Not since …

You're holding on too tight, Henry says from nowhere.

You can fucken talk, I mumble into my beer.

And I tell him all about Pringhael Gil. How he was taken. How I blamed myself. How I mourned too long.

I can see grief in the way people walk. Hold their hands. Look away too quickly. (A line from Henry's play.)

We talk about our grief. Do these spirits freed from this world want us to hold on to them?

Henry explains how his Mob will not use the names of the dead. Unless the prefix Pringhael — Spirit — is applied. Others might say Kumanjai to denote the spirit of the person and not the person. Many people won't use the names of the dead. Let them go. They don't want us calling them back. Holding them here. They want to fly. Free.

We get the feeling that there's all these dead fullas sittin in the pub with us. Listening to our conversation. Nodding gently and smiling their knowing smiles.

In a second, hours and hours have gone past. Henry and I are drunk. Sober drunk. Some fullas by the pool table sneak looks at Henry. Talk under their breath.

We gotta go now, I comment vaguely.

Henry will kill these fullas and not even work up a sweat. Time to move on. Drink up and go. We both accept the inevitability of the cards dealt to us.

Didjeridu

One day, out of the blue, George turns up at my front door in St Kilda with this didj. Decides to give it to me. It is a beautiful didj. Big. Heavy. Deep. Turtle-design paint-up. Part of the design is actually carved into the wood as well.

Not our traditional instrument.

His voice is a deep Ngarrindjeri drawl as he hands it over to me. I'm gobsmacked. This is obviously a valuable and precious thing. George never says where he got the didj. He is beaming. His generosity seems to surprise and amuse him. I am honoured. I pour out some bourbon'n'cokes.

So I start learning to play. I have brilliant teachers. Uncle Elmore drops in every time he's walking past to give me pointers. Elmore is very excited when he first sees the didj. This is his cousin's paint-up. He knows this design. Elmore is happy to think of his countryman again. They were close when they were kids. He is a good teacher. I worry about not mastering the breathing.

Don't think about it at all.

Elmore always seems to be smiling.

Don't think about it at all. It'll come.

And he talks to me about tongue and lip positions for Language, to be used when playing.

King drops in and teaches me about rock'n'roll rhythms. Dylan talks about notes and particular kinds of drones and noises.

Anyway, I started playing the didj a bit. Freddy would often come and have a play. I'd watch, listen, learn.

One night Myrtle drops in to St Kilda. With her are her brother-in-law, Freddy's cousin Arthur, and Rocky, this Palawa fulla (from Tasmania). Arthur is Yamatji man, of course, but because he is married to a Boonwurrung woman, he has a strong association with the Tasmanian Mob.

Boonwurrung became related to the Palawa Mobs: Peerapper, Tommeginne and Pyemairrener, through the rape camps of the sealers and whalers, as well as the missions and prisons of the English invaders.

The women are in the lounge room and I'm in the kitchen with Rocky and Arthur. They've both just walked out of a big stint in the bush. Both got big healthy beards. Clear strong eyes. A very direct way about them. These men are staunch. Strong in the Law. Proper.

Liz and I joke later that to us gubbahs they're like Jedi knights.

We drink our tea. Have a laugh. A yarn. A smoke. Rocky tells me that if ever I'm in his Country he'll take me bush. I thank him for his generosity.

Thanks, Bruz.

For what?

The offer?

I'm havin a cuppa tea at your place, aren't I?

Yeah.

How many places do you reckon make us feel this welcome?

Rocky gives me a huge bud that he grew himself on his own Country. I twist one up with it.

Arthur starts telling me about a trip to Germany he once took:

I'm walkin down the street there and I can hear this didj. Not good didj (laughs), but didj. So I'm lookin around, finally I see this fulla up against a lamppost in the street. He's playin this didj. Got a little Turkish rug he's sittin on (laughs) and, you know, got a hat out. So I go up to this fulla, I explain to him that me, I'm Yamatji man. That in my culture the instrument has deep spiritual and religious beliefs attached to it and the playing of it. And I ask him straight out to stop playing.

Wha'd he say? He speak English?

(Laughs)

Probly better than me.

English isn't Arthur's first language. Probably his third or fourth. Arthur is from Meekatharra, so ahead of English is Watjarri, Badimaya, Tjupany, maybe even Yinggarda. His language skills as a child often saw him acting as an interpreter for Elders at multi-lingual meetings — years before he learned English.

No, this German fulla, he just nodded politely and waited for me to walk off. Then he just started playing again (laughs). I stood at the next lamppost down and wept. Dunno why. Couldn't control it. When it stopped, I just walked off.

And I do confess to getting a strange feeling — now that Arthur brings it up — at the wrap party for Henry's film when

I saw all these gubbahs crowding around the edge of the stage. I pushed in to see what they were all crowding around, it was a didj. They were all desperate to have a go. Have a blow. To prove they could play it, or something. It had a weird vibe, if you ask me.

Anyway, because of my respect for Arthur, I couldn't play that didj again. From that moment. Once I told this to Uncle Elmore. He could have said, Don't worry about what he said. Elmore had never had a problem with me playing it before. But he didn't. Elmore lives under the Law too. He didn't want to disrespect another fulla's Culture, I reckon.

Some time later I got to make it right. Freddy and I are doing this play with George. George has secured all the money for the project himself. George is good like that. He wrote and directed the play and got the money to do it himself for this festival in St Kilda. Not one to sit around sipping cafe lattes. He just did it.

Anyway, something went wrong with the money, can't remember what, I got paid some of mine but Freddy dipped out, or hardly got anything, or something.

So I gave Freddy the didj. And in that moment I understood why George had beamed at me that day. It felt great. Really good.

Freddy would play it, too. Not long after, I sat in Freddy's beautiful back garden with his beautiful wife, big steaks in our bellies, and Freddy blowing and talking up the wood for us.

Charlotte loves it, too. Ever since one time when Chris Walsh, this outrageous Pitjantjatjara fulla, dropped in to St Kilda. Just after I got back from Broken Hill. Liz had Charlotte in her belly, six or seven months and growing. Chris was on his way to a gig at the POW. Had his didj with him. Chris suddenly picks up his didj and plays over Liz's belly. Oh, he played a beautiful song, too. Liz and Charlotte were in bliss.

Late one night I'm watching a doco on SBS about the Celts. There are these Irish fullas playing traditional instruments. One of them has what appears to be a long copper or bronze looking didj. I get a rush. Realise why I was attracted to George's didj. This instrument reverberates in my Culture, too. Maybe I'll learn to play one of those Irish metal didjes.

Fucken hell! Did you see that?

I'm doing this play in Adelaide, Kaurna Country. Invasion play. It's a cracker. Robby and Dylan are also there working on a film. Robby comes to stay with me in my digs. Safety in numbers. By coincidence my landlady drops in. Very proper. Descended from the squatters. Very polite. Straight as the Gunbarrel Highway. She pokes her head round the corner of the door, catches sight of my Yorta Yorta brother. Her eyes go wide and she gasps with a short sharp in-breath.

My brother is staying with me for a while, I offer with a huge smile.

Robby steps forward. Huge smile.

Hello.

Hello.

She nods and smiles. She and I move back outside.

Your brother?

Her voice comes out very thin and very high.

I nod and smile.

… Your … brother?

She hops from one foot to the other and back again, as though she is busting for a piss.

I nod and smile.

… Your … brother?

She is still smiling and nodding strangely and nodding as she backs away from the house in the Kaurna night. I go back inside.

Robby is laughing at me.

You enjoying yourself?

We laugh.

We both have a night off so we go to the movies. *Swordfish*. We admit right from the start that we're only going for the glimpse of Halle Berry's chest. The movie is what you'd expect. Product. We both come out satisfied. Mmmm. Good movie.

We go for a beer and then wander down to the taxi rank. Line of about eight cabs. It's a cold wet night in Kaurna Country. Not much action.

We wander down the line to the first cab. Robby goes for the kerb-side back door and I go the street-side. Robby's hand is just reaching out to the door when the cabby clocks him in his rear-view mirror. The driver slams the cab into gear and takes off in a headlong rush of tyre-squealing engine howl.

Robby and I are left standing with our fingers reaching for the doors of an invisible car.

Fucken cunt.

I'm looking on the road for a loose rock. There's nothin. I'm aching to lob one through his back window. Tonguing for it.

My head is full of Eloise Gallop and the best throw I ever saw. Wudjari Country. I'm thirteen and standing on the top oval after school. Going to athletics training. Hookie Hore was there and for some unknown reason he was giving these Wongi girls the shits. Getting stuck into them about their skinny ankles.

Eloise breaks from her group to have a swing at Hookie.

I'll make you piss in your boot, wadjula cunt.

Hookie looks to me for support. Us rednecks gotta stick together. Me, I'm blank like a sand dune cleaned by the wind. I'm standing next to Sulli. Hookie looks at Sulli. Sulli just smiles at him; if you're stupid enough to give the Wongi girls shit, it's got nothin to do with me.

So Hookie turns and takes off at a dead run on his fat legs down the hill and across the bottom oval. Eloise could easily run him down and snot him.

But Eloise only takes two steps after him. Then she stops and looks down. Hookie is still flat out, running for the safety of the bush on the other side. Eloise picks up a coondi (throwing stone) and looks up at Hookie's fleeing back. He's probably thirty or forty metres away by now. She weighs the rock in her hand. It's a moment etched into my memory in slow motion, like Cathy coming round the final bend in the four hundred at the Olympics. A tiny nod and smile to herself. Then draws back and lets fly. The coondi arcs up high enough to be silhouetted by blue sky for a moment, tracking Hookie like a missile, then arcs earthward and smacks into the back of his head. The blow lifts him up and dumps him in a messy bellyflop onto the grass of the bottom oval.

Fucken hell. Did you see that?

Bloody hell.

Eloise glares at us. Sulli smiles back.

Good shot, Sis.

Deadly, I agree.

Eloise steps back over to the girls. Laughs. The other girls giggle and turn away.

Sulli and I are laughing. That was incredible. Fifty-five, sixty metres. Made him piss alright.

For myself, I've always found skinny ankles attractive.

It's a long time before Hookie moves. This sets us off again. He sits up. Rubs his head. Priceless.

Anyway, Robby and I are left standing in the street in the Kaurna rain looking at each other like we're in a silent movie. We shrug. Get into the next cab. Next bloke is fine.

Fucken hell. Did you see that?

Bloody stupid, Mate. Took me half an hour to get to the front of this rank. Look at that stupid idiot. That's him, right up there. Left-hand turn with no indicator. Bloody stupid, Mate. Where we goin?

We go home and tip this fulla ten bucks.

Exorcisms in English

That night Robby and I have a beer, watch telly, talk about Halle, about her lovely ... talents, then go to bed at a reasonable hour; we both have to work the next day.

We're in bed. An hour or so goes past and we're woken by the jingling of keys and chains and the clumping of big boots. Both of us are up in a moment to see who's come in. Lights on. Look around. No-one. We shrug — back to bed.

A little while goes by. Then same thing. Jingle jingle. Clump clump. I get up. Walk out to the kitchen.

Robby is over it. He calls down from the mezzanine bed.

Spirits, Bruz. Restless spirits.

I go back to bed. This time I close out the noise. I've been in this place for two weeks. This is the first time there's been any such night activity. It's Robby's first night. It's gotta be him.

Next morning I'm up and off to work. I usually walk in. Clears my head.

I go across the road and look back at the building we're staying in. For the first time I notice the militaristic look that the modern renovations can't hide. And there is a double of it up the street, with a clearly discernible entrance between the two buildings — like a stockade.

I talk to the landlady on the phone at lunchtime and find out that the building was originally police barracks, or used by police, or something. About a hundred and twenty years old.

So these old wadjula jungais don't like my Yorta Yorta brother in their place. Maybe they conducted campaigns against the Kaurna, or the Peramangk, or the Ngarrindjeri from here. Or maybe it's something that Robby has brought with him.

That night we go to see Dylan who is staying around the corner with our Wongi sister, Kelly Sunray. We have a cuppa tea, a smoke and a yarn.

Dylan gives us some sap from a certain plant that he brought over from Pinjarup Country. He tells us to crush it and burn it to get relief from those old gubbah spirits keeping us awake.

While we're there, this other fulla, Sean, arrives. Dylan knows him from the film he and Robby are working on.

Sean organised all the young fullas for the football sequences. He works at a live-in high school for desert kids.

Some of them Desert Mobs want their kids to have wadjula schooling as well as traditional learning. Need people in the community who can read and speak English. So they come south to Adelaide for a few years.

Sean looks after the boys' dormitory. He coaches them footy and generally acts as big brother or Uncle. He reminds me of Uncle Firebrand: same intention, different path.

While we're there, Sean reveals that his grandmother was a Wongi woman. It's a vulnerable moment for Sean. He's not sure how he'll be received. He's never spoken of this in public before.

Dylan and Robby and Kelly are overjoyed to hear this revelation. Suddenly everything makes sense.

After Sean's initial announcement there is a little silence. Then Dylan speaks up.

Them at school know you one of the Mob, Cuz?

Sean shakes his head. Dylan embraces him. Kelly embraces him.

You're my own Mob. You're my brother.

We're all embracing and handshaking and backslapping and laughing — even lil ol me.

Do you know your grandmother's name? We might be related, Cuz.

Kelly is excited.

Nelly. But don't know last name.

Nelly. I'll ask my family when I ring tonight.

Sean tells us this story about the dormitory where the desert lads camp. Same thing. Spirits keeping everyone awake and giving everyone the shits. It freaks some of the younger kids out. So they get this Old Fulla from the desert, strong fulla with spirits, to come down and smoke and exorcise the place. This Old Fulla gets there, everyone waits outside. He goes in alone. He sing little bit to himself as he goes in — but once inside, with the doors shut, everyone can hear him shouting at the spirits.

You go! Get out! You leave now!

He talks them round a bit but mainly shouts at them to go. And all in English. This Old Fulla doesn't have much English. A bit of a shock for the Mob outside the door to hear him shouting in English. Eventually he comes out, nods to everyone. Talking in Language again.

Them fullas will move on.

Why you English talk, Grandfather?

Them fullas all wadjula. Big sick in chest.

Old Fulla bangs his chest. Pretends to cough.

Them fullas not too happy. They go.

And sure enough, the boys return to their dorm and there are no more hauntings.

They do some research and find out that the building was once used to house returned soldiers who were sick — they all had TB.

Anyway, Sean has to go. Some business to take care of. Dylan hugs him. Robby and I shake with him. Kelly holds him in a big embrace. For a long time.

Thanks, Cuz, she says very quietly to Sean.

Sean drives a flash red Commodore. Dylan gets him fired up.

Carn, Bruz. Give's a demo.

Dunno.

Yeah, Bruz. Fire her up.

So Sean gets in and takes off with the big V8 roaring and the mags spinning on the bitumen. We all clap and cheer.

Robby and I go back to the former police barracks and crush and burn the sap that Dylan gave us. It flames suddenly in little orange and yellow sparks and gives off the thick sweet smell of the bush by the river in Pinjarup Country. As I throw the crushed sap into the flame I fill my mind with thoughts to drive out them copper spirits.

That night them old troopers sleep well. So do Robby and I.

Learning the six-times-table

Watching telly. Kaurna Country. Ads. Can't sleep. I get up to go to djillawah. Look at the clock on the stove as I go past: 2.38 am.

Two-thirty-eight — shut the gate!

I slam my hips with my hands, thumbs up, fingers straight, palms flat and facing out. Standing in the djillawah, I suddenly say to myself:

Once six is six — make me a mix!

And laugh. Laugh. Laugh till my guts hurt. It's hard for me to complete my toilet, I'm laughing so much. Can't walk properly. Lean against the wall as I make my way back to the couch, giggles bursting from me like an underground stream breaking the dusty surface of the earth.

One day at school, all of Lloyd's class got homework where they had to make up rhymes for the times tables as a memory aid — your own rhymes are more personal, I spose. Lloyd has lived in street and park and laneway and been around his uncles and aunties and cousins heaps when they've been having a cone or two. His very first rhyme is:

Once six is six — make me a mix!

Cracked us all up. Even now, five years later, alone in the djillawah at 2.38 am.

Two-thirty-eight — make your own fate!

Once six is six — make me a mix!

Laughing. Laughing like a mad bastard.

Members only

George and I go to see Robby in a play at Trades Hall in Carlton. Wurundjeri Country. Robby is great in the play. Afterwards we decide to go for a beer. We stand on the roadside to grab a cab. The drivers see a skinny Irish fulla with a big Yorta Yorta man and a huge Ngarrindjeri man trying to hail a cab and they just drive on by.

I see. One of those nights.

We give each other the smile.

Let's walk.

Fuck it. Let's walk.

We walk down town. First place we come to is The Lounge. There is a short-haired bull-necked gubbah moron with a bow tie at the front door. We see him open the door to let in this skinny gub in an open-neck flowery orange shirt. We approach the entrance. Bow-tie closes the door.

Members only.

We stop. We look.

Members only.

We just stand there. No-one moves a muscle. I spose you wonder how many times you can listen to it.

If we were in St Kilda things'd be different. That famous Yolngu fulla got kicked out of that bar on Fitzroy Street and the bar went broke. Everyone voted with their feet. If this is the kind of place where our Yolngu brothers aren't welcome, especially someone from the world-famous Yothu Yindi rock band, we don't wanna drink here either. In fact, the next three businesses in that location went broke as well. There were plenty of jokes on the streets of St Kilda that the bar had been sung. After the place went broke the first time they forgot to lift the curse, so the next couple of businesses got it too.

Members only.

George takes a step.

What?

His voice is quiet. Controlled.

Bow-tie steps forward.

Robby and I step forward.

Members' night.

You said that already.

Bow-tie is starting to sound pretty unsure about his place in the world. He's starting to look very alone. He's decided George is the trouble. Obviously never been hit by a Yorta Yorta man.

Let's go to St Kilda.

Yeah.

Let's go to St Kilda.

We're only inches from Mr Bow-tie but he is gone now. He's not sure what to do about us ignoring him from point-blank range. We're not really ignoring him. Just looking right through him. Like he's not there. Like this nightclub isn't there. This street isn't here. And at the same time picking over his soul like crows on a carcass at sunset. Finally, Bow-tie takes a step back.

We haven't moved. Our eyes still steady on him. Through him. Past him. He looks like a roo frozen in the spotlight.

After a while we simply turn and walk off.

George is quiet. A tree.

Mealy-mouth little cunt, bursts out of my mouth.

Don't worry bout it, Bruz, Robby consoles me.

Maybe I always get little bit shame when other gubbahs are like this. I shake it off.

Still, woouur, eh!

We all laugh. Get into a cab at the top of a rank. He can't drive off then (unless he's a real crazy racist like that taxi driver bastard in Kaurna Country that time).

We ride the cab to the front door of the POW. George knows the owners. We get VIP treatment. Ushered in to our own table. Drink-cards all around. Everyone is welcome in St Kilda. No-one cares where we're from.

Easy to kill a man

Wurundjeri Country, Carlton. We get a crew together to read Henry's latest script. The most personal thing he's ever written. A new play about his time with the Royal Commission. The Royal Omission. The Royal Sweep-under-the-fucken-carpet. He's written about it before. But not like this. There's never been anything like this. This one is about what it was like to be him, is like to be him, a Koori man going through all this. It would turn out to be a work that would get under all of our skins and will haunt us for the rest of our lives. Sometimes good haunt, sometimes, you know, haunt haunt.

Same old theatre. Used to be a courthouse a hundred years ago. Half a dozen or so blokes sent to their deaths in here by some old gubbah in a wig, swigging whisky from a silver flask, warming his old bones by a fire in his room. The judge's room is now a dressing room. The toilets are the old holding cells. We all hate taking a piss. Never alone in there.

We're reading this script with George playing the lead. Playing Henry. The audience are interested parties and money people — government bureaucrats and friends and family and theatre industry folk.

Half way through the read we have to stop. George is falling apart. To see this huge Ngarrindjeri man tear up and start to shake is hard for all of us. Especially Henry. We take a break. Go outside for a smoke.

George comes up to me. Hugs me.

I'm sorry. My brother.

What for?

All that. Before. What's between us.

Silence.

(Don't really wanna go into it.)

George draws on his cigarette.

I'm sorry, my brother.

Thank you, Bruz. There's nothing between us now.

Brothers.

We hug again. I'm lost in the arms of the big man. Fuck, George could snap me like a twig. Nunga Marlon Brando. That's what they call him.

We go back inside and finish reading the script. It's a journey through hell. By the end of it we've dragged ourselves and the audience through the story, leaving us all bloody and torn, but strong too.

We go next door for a drink. Henry is rapt. We'll get the money to get a production up. We can all feel it in our bones.

The Rat turns up, too. Fuck, I'm pleased to see him. He wanted to be here for the reading but couldn't get an early flight from Sydney. He was staying with Henry when Henry wrote down this play. The Rat does a fucken funny imitation of Henry working. At the computer for three seconds, then up and pacing. Pacing up and down and smoking furiously. Pacing, smoking, pacing, smoking. Then stopping suddenly to say in a tense rasping voice, something like:

It's easy to kill a man.

Meaningful pause.

What's hard … is talking to his mother.

We're laughing at the Rat's delivery. But the content is like two bulldozers pulling a massive steel chain across the Sacred Country in our hearts, clearing everyfuckenthing.

Can't get a house because of native title

And then the Invasion play comes to Melbourne. In Melbourne the audience are more sombre. In Adelaide we had occasional hostile receptions.

One audience member stormed out twenty minutes before the end of the show and then waited in the bar area to harangue us — defending the actions of his squatter ancestors. He had this fairy tale view of our history; as though the Traditional Owners were happy to be displaced from their Sacred Country; as though there was no violence involved in the coming of the Europeans.

Politics is so personal. In Melbourne a Bibbulman woman who'd seen the play drily observed: Of course, if a Nyungar wrote the play, it'd be much more hard hitting. Many of the theatre audience, who'd squirmed during the play dealing with the true nature of Traditional Owner vs Squatter interaction, squirmed even more at this comment.

One night I come home after performing and turn on the TV to veg-out. All over the TV screen were pictures of aeroplanes being flown into buildings on the other side of the world. The world suddenly seems to be changing very fast. Our immediate reaction is that we want to be close to family now. I want my kids to grow up knowing their grandparents.

So our exile in Melbourne is over. We're going home to WA. It'll be hard to leave Lloyd, but he is back with his own Mob now and already has one foot in the Men's Camp. I'll see him when I come back for work. I'll have to come back to finish the journey I've begun with Henry.

So the family gets off the Indian Pacific in Kalgoorlie. Nighttime in Wangkathaa Country. Bart Billon's Country. This is our first stop inside the WA border on our journey home.

We have a couple of hours to visit my brother. He blows big holes in the ground. Goldmining game.

We grab a cab from the station. The cabbie is a big fat redneck bastard, of the big-fat-redneck-bastard variety.

They need a security guard to stop the fucken Wongi kids chucking rocks at the train.

I give him a look.

They got nothin else to do, he continues.

Stewie sits up in the back now.

What?

I turn to the driver.

Yeah, what?

He looks me over. Maybe for the first time. Trying to assess me. Can't work out why his patter isn't working. It always works. He's heard my country accent. Doesn't make sense. He decides to make an effort. Clears his throat nervously.

Yeah, to stop the bloody Wongi kids throwing coondis.

This is obviously the best he can do. Such an effort. These

Gub-Club blokes seem big on assumption and low on observation. Body language, eye contact, clothes, hair style, skin texture, the way you use your hands; there's a lot to see if you really look. Henry taught me this.

We drive over the bridge across the railway line. The big fat silver body of the Indian Pacific shines invitingly in the moonlight. I wish I had a big rock.

Kal is dying. Ya can't get a house because of native title.

Doesn't look dead to me. On the train on the way in we've been passing mines being worked twenty-four hours a day for the last few hundred kilometres. Not dead yet. Not the mines. Not the profit lines.

Over two hundred people in the fringe-dweller camps don't know about this huge power they have that the taxidriver is talking about. How much of the profits from mining their own Country do you reckon they see?

The rest of the taxi ride to my brother's is in silence.

Yupella prom Tanning?

Wajuk Country, 1980. Me and my two best mates are walking down the main street of Perth. Heading for the mall. We're up in the big smoke for Country Week Footy. Got an hour of free time before we have to meet up with the team and go to dinner, so we're goin for a walk.

We've only been out of our hotel a few minutes when we see this mob of Nyungar girls on the other side of the road, coming towards us.

They see us three and a huge giggle erupts in the group like a volcano. They're real country girls in singlets and skirts and we're sixteen-year-old boys and super-aware of every bump and curve of flesh on display, or hidden.

The tallest of the girls suddenly dances forward out of the group and yells at us from across the road:

Eeeeey! Yupella prom Tanning?

I dunno. It wasn't one of those moments where you think. I danced away from Pringhael Gil and Michael, summoned up my best Nyungar accent, body language and all, and yelled back: Naaaar! We're prom K'rata!

The tall girl falls back into the group and a massive giggle wave sweeps back and forwards through them.

Pringhael Luke and Michael are pissing themselves and slapping me on the back. You can get your head smashed in for shit like that. We waltzed away laughing. We could hear the girls repeating the joke over and over and laughing.

Yupella prom Tanning?

Nar. We're prom K'rata!

Laughter.

Maybe I'd made some joke I didn't know about. Katanning is south, near the borders of Kaniyang, Wiilman and Goreng Country. Karratha is way north, in Jaburra Country, near where Martuthunira and Ngarluma Country meet. Maybe it was just an icebreaker.

There's Nyungars around

Wajuk (Nyungar) Country. We move into this brand new place in East Freo. Walyalup — place of eagles. Just over the rise I can see from my backyard is where my great-great-grandfather got off the boat. Walking a rickety plank on unsteady legs to get ashore, wasted leg muscles struggling against the weight of the leg-irons.

We meet our new neighbour. She takes us into her house. There is a security-screen door.

Gotta lock up. There's Nyungars around.

Really?

We step through the front door and right in front of us, on a stained occasional table, is a framed photo of an Old Nyungar Fulla. I suddenly feel like I'm in the middle of a Monty Python script.

Oh, who's this? An uncle of yours?

The woman looks mortified.

No. We bought it in a shop.

They're probly looking for their uncle's photo.

Who?

The Nyungars.

What Nyungars?

The Nyungars who are around.

The woman gives me a look. Doesn't know how to respond. So she pretends it didn't happen. This is what us wadjulas do. What we're really good at. Pretend I didn't speak. Pretend nothing happened. None of it.

We tour the rest of the house in silence. We go home.

She would've paid twenty to thirty bucks for that photo. At the Freo markets there is a whole stall dedicated to such photos. How much do you reckon went to the subject of the photo?

Why do you reckon she wanted that photo?

Hockshops and a banana's worth of speed

Wajuk Country, Perth. I'm feeling the need to reconnect to People. Drive over to see Dylan. Dylan is Pinjarup/Wiilman man. Plenty of Wardandi rellies as well. Nyungar man.

I first met Dylan at the Festival of Dreaming in Sydney in '96, hosted by Eora Mob. Dylan was doing a play which he wrote and directed. I was on the balcony at Baba Du with King. Dylan was there. We got introduced. Dylan looked cold, I was hot. King and I had been performing the boxing-tent show. We were fit as fuck and jumping out of our skins. I was wearing a big warm coat that Liz scored when it was left behind and unclaimed at the nightclub where she worked. Dylan was wearing a light trackie top in the colours of the flag.

Wanna trade, Bruz?

I instantly take off my coat and hold it out. No time for hesitation. Dylan takes off his. We swap. We have a smoke. Even though I'm Irish, my godmother is a Wiilman woman. Two WA boys in Eora Country. We admire our reflections in the windows, each in the other's coat.

Deadly, unna?

Too deadly, Bruz.

Later on I'll give the trackie top to Libby because she tells me she likes it. What goes around comes around.

So I drive to Maddington to meet Dylan. Ring him before I leave. But by the time I get there he isn't there. Out somewhere. Down the shops. So, Charl stays with Dylan's woman, Trace, and I go to look for him. I ring him up. He gives me directions to the shopping centre. I drive down. Can't see him. Get out of the car. I ring him.

I can see you, stay there.

Don't you just love mobile phones? I look up to see Dylan coming across the car park. He's dressed warm and carrying a big heavy bag. Car amps and speakers.

Hock em, eh Bruz? Get fifty.

We drive around to visit a couple of fullas. They're all hepped up about a rock being thrown through their cousin's window last night. The Old Fulla looks ruthless but frail. The young fulla is contained. Lightning in a cloud. They say they know who did it. Some of the new ones.

We'll have to go with a fucken carload, says Dylan.

They'll have a fucken carload, agrees Ruthless-but-frail.

Lightning-in-a-cloud looks away. He doesn't give a fuck how many carloads there are.

Ruthless-but-frail gives Dylan a banana. He gives me the look I've seen many times from Lloyd's Mob. Don't have much to do with wadjulas. Don't trust em. Don't trust anybody, for that matter.

We drive to the hockshop.

Gubment is moving a lot of Nyungars into Maddington, says Dylan.

Why?

Keep us all together, I spose. Left here, Bruz.

Maddington is another world.

Prices are goin down. No one wants to live next to us, he says matter-of-factly.

I give Dylan a look.

Eh?

Rocks through people's windows, running through houses, fighting in the street ...

Dylan trails away to nothing, as though he loses interest in the thought.

At the hockshop no-one wants to buy his amps and speakers. I stand smoking cigarettes watching a steady stream of Nyungars arriving with TVs, stereos, cameras, drum kits, computers, computer games.

Dylan argues his case with the hockshop bloke. He's a big amiable redneck with tattoos up both exposed arms. The colourful tattoos clash terribly with the powder-blue short-sleeve office shirt with the logo on the pocket.

Dylan finally gets acceptance and a deal but has forgotten his ID.

We pile back in the car and drive home. In between phone calls from Ruthless-but-frail, Dylan looks around for something else to hock. He shows me his carvings.

Have a look at this, Bruz. Found it near the river. Three Old Men. They seen me before I seen them. A dish. Mallee root. This'll be a clock. You need a chopping board? Sure, you don't need another chopping board.

You already made me one.

Boomerang. Got this wood near Kal. You wanna buy a car?

Needs some work. A bloody bewdy. You drink herbal tea? It's from Spain. You have it.

We're working through the backyard and into the shed. I suddenly notice how fast Dylan is going. I shut off my mind. Trouble. Instinct. Never wrong. That's why it's your instinct. I hold the kilo of herbal tea Dylan hands me in a plastic shopping bag. He's turning over another wood carving.

Found this on the beach. Been in the sea for years. See the seals? The mother? The baby? Face is here. Eyes. Mouth. Shit, I've got some cameras.

We go into the house. Trace's mum has arrived. Charl is happy and contained. Dylan grabs a beautiful dark didj leaning in the corner.

Don't be stupid, Coorda.

Dylan looks at me. Confused. Maybe surprised.

There's gotta be somethin else. Don't hock ya didj.

It's just a loan.

Something else, Bro.

Dylan puts the didj down.

There's the video in the shed, offers Trace.

Dylan marches off to the shed.

Trace gives me a look. (Thanks, Brother.)

We go back to the hockshop. Video under arm. The stream of Nyungars with stuff under their arms continues unabated.

Dylan argues the price. This takes a long time. I smoke another cigarette. Finally we leave.

Dylan takes me to another house on the way home. So I can get nyandi. Weatherboard house. Gum tree with a big split in it out the front. It'll go in the next big wind. Tear the tree in half.

Dylan takes me into the house. Three lads. One has huge

tufts of hair missing from his head, the bare scalp an angry pink. One lively. One with eyes as dead as prison walls. I get introduced. No-one wants to shake hands. There is no chat. Prison-wall-eyes pushes three deal bags across the table. Poor here. Third-world Land. I'm from the first world. They can smell it on me.

What about a bud for me? asks Dylan.

Prison-wall-eyes just looks away.

I'm always bringing you customers.

I wait a moment longer. Nothing. I throw seventy-five dollars on the table. I could buy seven of these bags for seventy-five in my world. But I'm not in my world, am I?

Biggest deals in Maddington, says Prison-wall-eyes to no-one in particular.

I grab the deals. We go to the car. Give one to Dylan.

He wants to take Lively-one's car to sell to someone else. We go back to the pawnshop one last time. Then back to grab Lively-one's Commodore. Dylan jumps into the Commodore. He doesn't have a licence. Follows me home.

Meet me at the shopping centre, Dylan yells, and turns off.

I collect my daughter. She's happy to leave. *Antz* has just finished. She likes Trace. We say our goodbyes. I drive to the shopping centre. Dylan meets me in the carpark.

Drive round the back.

I drive round the back. Everything has gone into slow motion. I watch a Falcon with a big mob in it drive past. A Tarantino movie. The two fullas coming out of the TAB are in slow motion too. Dylan comes over. He is on a bike. He holds out his fist through the open window.

Take this to that other fulla.

My hand is already accepting what he gives me. I drop my hand onto my lap then glance down. A deal bag full of speed.

Fuck.

My daughter is in the front passenger side on her big blue booster seat. Dylan gives me directions. The directions of a man who's lived here all his life.

Why didn't I expect this?

Dylan and me, we've gotta talk.

I drive with the speed down my trousers. I take a wrong turn but see Ruthless-but-frail and Lightning-in-a-cloud standing out the front. Op-shop trousers held up with baling twine. Blotchy skin.

Nearly got lost. Get confused in a city.

Where you from?

Grew up on a station.

Thanks, Brother.

The Old Man's smile is surprising. Warm. He grips my hand. His eyes flick to my daughter. As though he sees my dilemma as clear as day. He looks at me as though I'm the gum tree out the front, gunna split in half in the next big wind.

Thanks, Brother.

I drive home to the first world. Charlotte falls asleep in her little car seat.

We should never have given them citizenship

That night we go to a party in Mosman Park. The other side of Perth. The other side of the universe to Maddington. We're dressed up. Our first Perth party since coming home. My old school mate, Les. As we arrive we're instantly bailed up by Norma. Les's mum. She wears gold. Golden hair. Golden jewellery.

We should never have given them citizenship, she says.

What?

Norma has just returned from a stint nursing at Jigalong. Palyku Country, close to the borders with Mardu and Wawal Mob.

They call me Sister, you know.

She shakes her head. Shakes it off. It seems funny to her. She tells us she gives this certain woman a catheter and drugs and sends her back. The woman wouldn't stay overnight. Norma complains to the doctor on his monthly visit but the doctor tells her she is doing the right thing.

One young mother lost three infants to sudden death syndrome — SIDS is always suspicious.

Norma sips her red wine.

One maybe, but three? And that same woman is now fostering another child. And one mother was very unhappy about her pale-skinned baby so she put it in the sun all day, naked, to toast it up.

I'm really struggling now. Feeling assaulted. Les is my best mate. And before, in the dark winter, Norma would offer me shelter. Give me comfort. A good mum. A good woman. Worked hard for everything she's got. So I've gotta really look at this a different way. It's the attitude, not the person. And this other loop too — it's not the experience itself but what conclusions are drawn. Which is about how you read the situation. Whether you know the map, or not.

I pour myself a glass of fifty-dollar wine and go to greet the host. Les launches into this story. Set in Broome, Jukun Country, with Yawuru to the south and Ngumbarl to the north. Les is fired up about this story. He's up there with seven mates. Fishing trip. They're all big working blokes. They want a pizza. Phone the order through and then walk down to pick it up. Les and another bloke are really hungry. They charge on ahead of the pack. They're walking along the streets when up ahead, on the other side of the road, they see a mob of local fullas. The locals see Les and his mate and cross the street to confront the out-of-towners. There is no talking. Just straight into the fighting. Les and his mate start out doing okay but pretty soon they're taking a hammering. Outnumbered. They're really copping a flogging when around the corner come their other five mates. The latecomers see the blue and take off at full sprint to join in.

Les and his mate suddenly get a new lease on life. Punching. Kicking. Ripping. Tearing. Blood. Screaming. Les's mates join the fray and quite quickly they account for the locals. They run to the pizza shop. Grab the pizza. Run home to eat. Lights off. Blinds down. In a few minutes there are four or five carloads cruising around — looking for them.

How could it have gone any different?

Les is asking me. I'm looking at him blankly. Blinking my eyes.

What else could we do?

Les goes out a day later and sees them in the pub. He buys a fulla a beer to diffuse any recognition blues. It works.

What else could we do?

Les repeats the question. Maybe he is asking the sky, not me.

I'm thinking about Maddington.

This is the second time tonight. Les is a man of infinite love. And a warrior, too. Would put himself on the line for me. Has. Many times. We go way back. And Les is talking a war story. What else can soldiers do but fight?

They don't wanna be helped, some other guy says, pulling me back to the surface.

Our policies must have failed, I say.

I'm not really sure what to say. I'm scratching in the dark. Why can't everyone see?

They don't want to help themselves. It would need thousands of policy changes, Robbie the Saab driving accountant says.

A change in our thinking?

I let it sink in. It does. I go after Robbie. He doesn't really believe what he's saying. I can see it in his eyes. He is the one I can change. Everyone else reckons what they reckon.

You might change one, says Henry.

If you believe in democracy, it's gotta work, I say.

We should never have given them citizenship, Norma repeats.

Then they couldn't drink.

Noel Pearson says that the welfare handouts haven't worked and should be stopped, I counter.

What about if we lost our citizenship rights as a result of supplying the liquor? I ask Norma.

Her gold jewellery flashes in the light. She looks confused for the first time. Usually everyone just agrees with her. The Gub Club. I've got my back to the wall now. I smoke and drink in the courtyard of the million-dollar home.

They'd all die from diseases if it weren't for me, says Norma.

You mean the diseases we brought, I counter.

The Yorta Yorta Nation was cut in half during the first two years of contact with the invaders, just from influenza. And this gubbah I'm talking to has the same name as my Yorta Yorta brother.

I hammer Robbie about attitudes dictating government policy and the opportunities to make real changes for once. I go in hard. Henry has taught me well. Once I saw that look in his eyes, the roo frozen in the headlights of the oncoming road train, I just couldn't stop. In the end Robbie has me backed up and is shouting at me, his finger prodding the air in front of me.

We just have to change our attitudes, he yells.

Change everything we've ever thought!

I top up our wine. In Maddington there are drugs, malnutrition, third-world diseases, and a pale blue Commodore with mags and a hole in the tail-pipe for sale.

Eventually Liz and I find ourselves at home. In our nice new house. In our nice new suburb. How the fuck did we get here?

Nar! We're prom K'rata!

Nyungar Country. Mid-1980s. I'm at this party with Les, my good old redneck mate. Not really a redneck; I just mean he's from the country and is crazy and we both got drunk and dropped out of uni simultaneously.

Lots of private school boys at the party. All wadjulas. Farmers' sons who'd been to boarding school with Les. I don't know anyone. I grew up on the land too, but owned nothing. Farmed nothing. Poor wadjula trash.

There is some talk about the price of wheat and soil additives, about roo shooting, tractors and the stock market. About a B&S in Kojonup. Kaniyang Country. I get interested because I was born just north of there, in Wiilman Country at Narrogin. Anyway, without thinking, I say to this young bloke: You from Tanning?

And I swear, he turns and beams at me: Naaar! We're prom K'rata!

And the whole room roars with laughter. Repeat it. Bunging on the accent, big time! Yupella prom Tanning? Wadjulas love doing the Nyungar accent. Naar! We're prom K'rata!

Laughter.

The first family to arrive

Night. Standing in the alley outside the Nyungar Theatre in Wajuk Country having a cigarette. Prison play. Dylan kills the role.

There's fullas smoking Blue Ox in the alley. Nyungar fullas with big beards. Hard faces. Hard hands. Warm eyes. One fulla takes time out to explain its value to me, once he's established where I was born, where I grew up. Holds out the blue pouch for me to see. Raises his eyebrows as he speaks.

This's the bossest smoke, Bruz. It's boss smoke.

This European woman I know comes up to me. She does PR for theatre companies. Haven't seen each other for a while. She starts talking.

… We're doing this play. It's in a National Trust property. Beautiful old homestead. Built by the first family to arrive.

I almost start laffin out loud.

What, the house is sixty-seven thousand years old?

What?

She's looking bewildered now. Other voices from the circle speak up.

Everyone always says forty thousand but that's wrong.

Who died fightin for that land?
Who honour that Country now? Proper way?
The People didn't arrive. The People were here.
The People are here.
True, Brother. The People are here.
True.
Too true.
The European woman tries again.
No, I mean the first, oh, …
The People are here.
Anyone got the time?
Six years.
Laughter.
With good behaviour.
More laughter.

Double-edged swords

I fly back to Melbourne to work on Henry's play. The one I did the reading of with George playing Henry at the Royal Omission. Only George can't do this show now. Some kind of dispute with the theatre company that I don't understand. I don't like to be away from my family, but you've gotta fight the good fight. And I knew moving to WA would mean more travel for work.

So we start rehearsing with Freddy in the lead role. On the first day we do our Ceremony. To recognise the people whose Country we're in. To acknowledge that those People have lost everything so that we can stand here today. To ask for the blessing of them Old People. To clean out the space with smoke. Get rid of any moorroop cobwebs.

Then we read the play and go through some of the songs before lunch. At lunchtime Freddy drives me home to his place. Freddy's wife makes us tasty focaccias and coffee.

Freddy has just finished shooting a film. Played a Nunga fulla in gaol. Hopeless gaol.

From the first moment in rehearsal for Henry's play it is obvious that Freddy is wound too tight. His wife is worried for him doing this role. I can feel it too.

Rehearsals are slow to start with. But the songs are already sounding good. And this Mob never been that big on rehearsing, anyway. Henry has picked a good team as usual. Later on, a gub critic will describe this play as the only musical tragedy that he's ever seen. A harrowing musical tragedy. Henry is a Gunditjmara man to the core and a performance without singing and dancing doesn't compute in his world.

There's a group of plays all happening at the same theatre. So suddenly all around us are these WA fullas. They're a tonic to a homesick Freddy — who hasn't been in his own Country for years now.

Freddy has this barbie round his place. We have a hoot. Freddy is an expansive host. To these young Nyungar and Nyikina fullas Freddy is a real path-maker. They look up to him. Freddy is in his element. Cooking up huge steaks. Playing didj. Singing Language Songs. Me, I suddenly feel pretty homesick too. One of these young Nyikina fullas eats two meals. Freddy is impressed. He can't stop talking about it.

Two huge steaks! Two platefuls of salad!

It's like a physical memory for Freddy. He well remembers eating big when there was a feed — dunno where the next meal would be coming from.

A few nights later I begin to realise what a double-edged sword this is for Freddy, having these fullas around. We're in the Punters' Club in Fitzroy. One of the last gigs before they turn another great rock venue into a clothing shop for women with pre-pubescent figures. Ned is playing. Belting out his songs in Pitjantjatjara.

Freddy comes up to me at the bar, drink in hand.

Sorry, Bro.

Freddy knows he can't drink.

No sorry, Bro, I come back.

I hold up my own drink. Freddy knows I can't drink.

Yaaaaaah!

We hug. I'm not my brother's keeper.

Freddy is teamed up with Livvo, this Gooniyandi man. I'm at the bar with Robby, my Yorta Yorta brother. I'm drinkin little bit. Feelin good. Like I'm surrounded by family. Not too many gubbahs here. Good. They make me nervous. Deep in my heart, like in Freddy's, those fucken police are galloping over hill and dale, swinging cutlasses, swinging stirrups, firing guns, wielding whips and rope. Burning down my Sacred Country.

It's a huge night. Like a family reunion. After Ned plays, he yarns with me at the bar. Has a beer. None of us should be drinkin. We're bein naughty after school. We been talkin for a little bit when he says to me:

What's your name again, Coorda?

Stephen.

The bar is loud. Canned music turned up.

What?

Stephen. Stephen Motor!

Peter Docker?

No, no, Stephen Motor.

Ned nods.

Kaltukajara, he says.

I nod. Then I look back to see him having a little chuckle.

This is a 'nothin tomata with that' moment for me. Like when I'm later at the Rat's place and he refers to one of his work colleagues as 'Nbandwe'. Well, see, her name is Alice.

Desert humour. Nbandwe — desert. Language name for Alice Springs area.

It's a year later, I'm standing in an office in Wajuk Country, Perth. It's an advertising agency, I'm auditioning for a role in one of their ads. On their wall is a map. And clearly marked is the Language name for Motor River in Pitjantjatjara Country — Kaltukajara.

When we were kids, we always joked that the river was named after Granddad. He lived in the goldfields of WA for years, from 1919, but I don't really know if he got as far east as Pitjantjatjara Country.

Next day at rehearsal, Freddy is a no-show. I can feel it all unravelling, but I got my own problems.

Spirits can smell ya

Henry wants me to play a Pringhael Koori character. I'm not so sure. Henry tells me it's time for this to happen. To cross the political line. Uncle Paulie, Gunditjmara man, agrees. But this is not a fictional character. A real fulla. Strong fulla. Lived and died in custody.

I throw myself into it. I go for the accent and the body language. Gubbahs love to do the accent.

I've been up this path a little way before, when I played William Buckley. Buckley was a runaway convict who lived with the Boonwurrung and Wurundjeri People for thirty years. I got taught some Language by them Wurundjeri fullas. Buckley escaped from the first attempt at settlement. When the wadjulas left because they were all fucken starving, they left him behind. Found him when they came back for a second try thirty years later. Buckley could no longer speak English — he'd become one of the People. As colonisation proceeds, Buckley suffers the same fate as the Boonwurrung and the Wurundjeri.

So I launch myself into playing this Pringhael Koori fulla. But near the end of the first week, I'm sitting on the metal fire-

escape stairs at the back of the brewery converted into a theatre.
I'm pale. Shivering in the cold wind. Sucking on my cigarette
like it's an oxygen mask. Henry comes out. Lights up.

You alright, Brother?

I look away. I can see cars chasing each other on the freeway
— all the way to the West Gate Bridge. I haven't slept for a few
days. Haunted by faces unknown. Unknown and therefore
terrifying.

I'm struggling, Djaambi.

I slowly get to my feet. Suddenly feel so old. Like I was born
in 1788. Henry looks into my eyes. He puts his hand over my
heart. Like I'm a horse and he's a vet checking me out. When I
was growing up on the station, oftentimes the station vet
would administer to us kids, the town doctor being so far away.

Them spirits probly don't recognise you.

Henry takes my hand and rubs it in his armpits.

They can tell me from my scent. They smell ya.

I rub my hands over my face and hair. Leaving traces of
Henry's body smell on me. To protect me. The rest of the day
is a blur — but that night I sleep through. And despite the
grog and nyandi, I dream. I dream.

Smell them Nyungars

Lort River Station, Wudjari Country. I'm about eleven years old. Shooting with my dad and my brothers. We're in the top paddock past Chaz Campbell's place. Low scrub as far as the eye can see, the bush getting thicker, with a few trees in the creek beds.

Earlier on we saw a big mob of emus. Over a hundred and fifty. Took off when they saw us. Running full-pelt. We couldn't see their legs pumping for the scrub — they seemed to float just above it — their tail feathers flowing out behind them and their heads high and proud.

My favourite way to hunt is on foot with my rifle. Especially in this Country. Coomalbidgup.

A few years later I'd have my first political thoughts about this bit of Country. I come up here to find the landscape as barren as the moon; the bush and scrub cleared by bulldozers. I get so angry I shake and weep.

Our station is owned by Chase Manhattan Bank. Over a million acres. Bought it from the government for fifty cents an acre on the proviso that they clear it and fence it and put up sheds. To clear this Country is to kill it. In a few years the topsoil will be all blown away and the waterways will all be salt. Between now and then Chase Manhattan Bank will make a lot of money. I don't know this then. All I know is they have no right to bulldoze everything. To drag huge chains. To rip everything up. Burn the rows of bush debris. No-one has the right.

Up until this moment it never really occurred to me that someone else owned this Country. Faceless men in suits who sit in high-rise offices in New York City. I thought this Country owned me.

Anyway, when you're hunting, if you're quiet you can get really close to grazing or resting roos. You've gotta watch for sentries if there's a mob.

Like me, the roos bob down to hide in the scrub. Once you go down you're invisible. But like me they get real curious and can't resist bobbing up for a look. Unlike me they don't have a pointy stick which makes smoke and little thunder and can kill a man instantly. Rip a hole in the head of a roo and smack him to the ground.

This day we're using the ute. Getting meat for the dogs.

We've just shot this old man roo, had to chase him. Took four shots from the .22 to bring him down. The ute finally pulls up next to his bloody carcass and us boys jump down. The first thing that hits us is his strong old man scent.

No wonder them Nyungars could smell him long way off, I comment.

Them roos could probly smell them Nyungars first, replies one of my older brothers.

We all laugh. Laughter that would haunt me for the rest of my life. Laughter that would make me ask why. We were station kids. We loved to go days without bathing. The longer the better. We knew about hunting and animals' scent on the wind. Our scent too. With our toothpaste and soap and milky diet and petrol engine, that old man roo could smell us a mile off. And none of us held any hate in our hearts. Only joy. Innocence. So why did we laugh?

Fitzroy Street Wanjina

Wurundjeri Country, Melbourne. After the second day with Freddy not at rehearsals, Henry decides he'll read the part so that at least we can all rehearse our stuff. Henry is playing the part of the character he created to portray himself in the days of the Royal Omission. Not a simple task, a straight path, an easy road. We do it, and no-one who was in that room will ever forget it.

Night-time is when my struggle kicks in. I got no-one to talk to. This night, I don't know what happens. I thought I went to sleep. When I come to I'm in Fitzroy Street, St Kilda. Blind fucken drunk. No fucken idea how I fucken got here. I'm burning with anger. Steaming down the pavement like a fucken locomotive.

I've had dozens of conversations with Freddy and his wife, about what's goin on with them, his work, their life together. I'm turning this over and over. What to say. I think I'm trying to help Freddy and his wife. But I'm confused and lost and in no shape to be helping anyone.

And then there's the play, to do the show or not. To be or

not to be. The character's issues as against our own issues. Henry's plays are about the life we've all lived. He's a conduit in this way. Me on the outside looking in. Freddy on the inside looking out. Henry on the inside looking in.

So I'm steaming down Fitzroy Street, burning holes in the concrete with every step. My guts and face are sore. I've been punched a few times and then thrown out of somewhere.

There is this Koori fulla sitting in a shop doorway. He sees me. He sees right fucken through me. Starts on me.

Eeeeh! Have a look at this useless gubbah cunt! With his useless gubbah walk! His useless gubbah skin! His useless gubbah jeans with his useless gubbah wallet! Full of his fucken useless gubbah money! Can't buy your way out of this one, cunt! Eh! Fucken gubbah cunt! Yeah, you! Ya fucken gubbah cunt. Don't look around, ya gubbah cunt! I'm fucken talkin to you! Yeah, you! What you lookin at now, gubbah cunt? Ain't got no gun now! Eh? Where's ya fucken gun now? Fucken gubbah cunt!

And I'm almost on him now and he starts to push himself up off the footpath. One hand on the pavement, the other on his bottle.

You weak gubbah cunt!

He is still half-up half-down as I reach him. His eyes blaze at me. I step right up to him and smash my fist into his face. He falls back against the glass shop door but somehow stays on his feet. I'm screaming at him.

Who're you talkin to, cunt?

Fuck. My hand is stuck. My fist has smashed right through his face and wedged itself inside his skull. I can't pull it out. I'm like a kid with my hand stuck in the cookie jar. No fucken cookies here. I kick him until he comes off my fist. Haven't totally forgotten all that fucken karate. He doesn't fall. There is a hole in the side of his face like he's been shot with a cannonball. He leers at me. I smash him with my other fist. That one smashes through the other side of his face. I panic again and kick him again and again to get him off my fist. He just stands there, smiling at me, looking at me with those huge bloody cannonball-wound eyes, like a grinning bloody Wanjina. I look down at my hands, bloody to the wrists.

I turn and move like Tony Soprano walking away from a hit. Still angry. Gotta go fast now. Get away from my shame. But it's riding me down like the cavalry. Wave after wave of horsemen riding through my camp, steel blades slicing into my family flesh, killing everyfuckenthing. Don't know where I'm goin. I stop. I'm on the overpass below the Esplanade Hotel, St Kilda. Watching the traffic below, blurred through bitter tears. My head feels like it's gunna explode.

And I'm in my bed and it's early in the morning. And I know I drank far too much to be fucken dreaming. I take my hands out from under the doona and look at them. They are swollen but clean. I look around the room. No big blood wipes. I'm jolted by a knock at the door. Freddy's wife. Upset. Him gone. Not gunna do the show. Fuck.

Just another fucken wadjula sticking his beak in

We're all in at work early. Drinkin coffee. Smokin cigarettes. Talkin quietly. I'm standin with my Tharawal brother, Lance, when Henry walks in. He's caught out. Confused. Maybe angry. The whole project is teetering on the edge now. He says a few things. Maybe we're all angry. Lance reminds us that our primary concern has to be Freddy's welfare. Thank you, Brother.

I go outside and get on the phone. I have a good idea where Freddy might be. His nephews live out west. Their father was in my brother's class at school in Wudjari Country, Esperance, in the seventies. I do love those big Nephews, with their Tupac clothing, their soft voices, their massive appetites, their casual ability to get all the money out of any phone box they encounter. Survivors.

I dial the number. Get a message from Telstra telling me the number is no longer connected. I try Freddy's mobile. Get his wife. She's beside herself. I tell her I'm lookin. I find out that this young Nyungar fulla is also a no-show in one of the other plays. This fulla was at Freddy's barbie and the Punters' Club the other night. I get his number from his stage manager.

Hey, Bruz. Stephen Motor.

Pete Modem?

Steve. Steve Motor.

Hey.

I met you at the Punters', watchin Ned the other night. And at Freddy's.

Yeah.

Lookin for Freddy.

Dunno.

Just wanna talk to him.

I dunno.

Come off it, Brother. Nothin heavy, I just need to talk to him.

Dunno where he is.

He's with them Wongi nephews.

Is he?

Are you there, too?

Nah. No way.

Listen, Bruz. You don't know me. I don't know you. I'm just saying you need to get him to call me.

He doesn't wanna talk to you.

Let him tell me.

He doesn't wanna talk to anyone.

I'm not anyone.

I can't.

Fuck. Don't shit me. I need to know he's alright.

He's alright.

How the fuck would you know?

He's alright.

Just fucken put him on.

Can't. He's not here.

Give me his number.

Can't.

Fuck. Fuck, fuck, fuck!

Pause.

Alright. You tell him Stephen Motor rang. To speak to his Yamatji Coorda. You fucken tell him.

Yeah, yeah.

Fucken make sure you do.

And when I ring off I'm fuming. This young lad doesn't know me. Known Freddy since he was a baby. I'm just another wadjula to him. Stickin my beak in. So they've closed me out. I go over to the shade. Eat two cigarettes in quick succession. Lance comes up to me.

Just another useless wadjula, I mumble and hurl my cigarette into the fence. It makes a shower of sparks when it hits. Doesn't matter what I do. I'll always be the invader. Soldier. Trooper. Prison guard. Cop. Teacher. Welfare worker. Killer. Rapist. Gubbah motherfucker.

Brother, Lance says gently, and squeezes my arm.

I turn and look him in the eye. My Tharawal brother.

Thank you, Brother.

What I might do

I know I can't play this Pringhael Koori character. All day I
want to tell Henry. The day is heavy. Like a funeral. Been like
this for a week now, if truth be known. As we all go deeper.

Freddy is still missing. Henry says he'll play the lead role
himself. I know he can. But I'm thinking about my Vietnam
veteran army instructors. What they're like late at night. Tellin
war stories. Drinkin. Always drinkin. Hearing sounds. Seeing
things. Jumpy as bastards. They get more and more unsettled
the more they talk about the blood. Dangerous killers, afraid of
their own shadows. Not afraid of what might be done to them.
Daring someone to have a fucken go. Afraid of what they
might do. They know how easy it is to kill. I don't want Henry
to do it. Can't see it being good for him or us.

Maybe I'm afraid to tell him. Don't want him to cut me out.

There is darkness all around us. Dogs barking around fires
built right up. We got the feeling those long tall ships are still
coming for us. Coming to destroy everything we've got.
Unstoppable as the sunset.

I'm at home. I'm staying with Keith, my best mate from
band days. We'd followed each other through hundreds of

shitty Melbourne underground and pub gigs, pumping out our post-punk-garage-blues-surf-rock. Never got a record deal but had a major laugh. Lived the rock'n'roll dream. One of the few gubbahs not of my blood I'll call brother. A big heart.

I'm sitting in my room, drinking. I rehearse in my head what I'm gunna say. I dial the number. Hang up before it can start ringing. Smoke another cigarette. My hands are shaking. I walk through the house. One more time to count the hanging points. Thirteen. Shit. Only got twelve last time. Someone was holding out on me. I dial.

Djaambi.

Moats.

How are ya?

Alright.

My bottom lip begins to tremble. I slam my fist into the wall.

What was that?

Nothin. Dropped somethin.

You drinkin?

Yeah. You?

Yeah. Wanna come over?

Got no money for cab, I lie.

I don't want Henry to see me like this. Shame job.

You by yourself?

Yeah. I'm alright.

Sure.

I'm crying now. Big fat tears running down my cheeks and dripping off my chin.

I know this is bad timing …

Listen, Moats …

But I gotta tell ya before it's too late.

What's too late?

I can't play this Pringhael character.

What?

Can't do it, Djaambi. He's all over me. I'm out of my depth. I've given it a go. I can't. I can't. He's all over me. He's …

Hey! Hey! Moats. It's gone. Don't worry. We'll get someone else.

What about the money?

We'll find it. It's gone. Don't worry.

I just can't, Djaambi.

Wha'd I say? It's gone. It's done.

Thank you, Djaambi. I just can't.

Gone now. You got someone coming home?

Yeah.

Gubbahs?

Yeah.

Pause. I hear Djaambi drag on his durry. I hold the phone out. Smoke comes out my receiver. I put it back to my ear.

You sure you don't wanna come round?

I'm safe here. He's a real mate.

You sure?

I get a feeling. There's something else about Djaambi's voice.

What else is happening?

I spoke to the Rat …

The hair on my body stands on end. The Rat was there when Henry wrote this play. I know Henry always wanted the Rat to play the main character. But the Rat had been unavailable for the rehearsal period. But now the rehearsal time is all but finished. I smile through my tears as I remember the

Rat's impersonation of Henry's hyped up writer-state.

Is he …? I stammer out.

He's coming. Be here tomorrow.

Oh, fuck. Oh, fuck.

The relief floods through me.

I gotta go, Moats. You call me if you need to.

Yeah.

Click.

Go really good way

When the Rat arrives we've got two days before we meet our first audience. I'm feeling much lighter of spirit.

Henry has got this Wiradjuri fulla, Little Big Man, to come and play the Pringhael Koori role I was rehearsing. He's a dancer and artist with no acting experience. Henry wants me to help him. He doesn't really need my help but I let him know I'm there for him.

When we do our Smoking Ceremony to start proceedings with our new members, Little Big Man gets the fire going. It's Little Big Man who is helping me. As the smoke wafts over me from those leaves I feel clean and pure, like my slate's been wiped clean. Little Big Man knows his character well. All this mob here know what being in and out of prison, the system, is like. Know how it affects every family member, not just the ones inside, or Stolen, or destroyed by some other means.

My mind has to accept what my spirit already knows — if it was purely an acting assignment, there is no reason why I can't do it. It's not just an issue of needing a Koori to play a Koori. That's important. But the days of gubbahs wearing boot polish on their faces in such roles are long gone. After watching George and Freddy get removed from this project by powerful forces way beyond our control, I would be a fool to ignore what's been goin on for me. This is not just a play we're doing here.

I'm happy to see the Rat. He's like a brother that I sent off to war, thinking I'd never see him again.

There's never been another character like the fulla he's playing seen on Australian stages before. On stage for over two hours. Talking most of the time. A massive emotional range covering every possible extreme. An Arrernte Everyman. A Nunga Jesus Christ. A Palawa Superman. A Gunditjmara Macbeth. A Koori Hamlet.

None of which seems to faze the Rat. He is a man shrugging on an old overcoat. An old overcoat made before he was born. Passed down by an old uncle. He wrestles with it a bit. Struggles to get it over his shoulders. Adjusts his body to the weight of it. Feels how warm it is. How it smells like an old friend. How beautifully it fits. How it is made for him.

And time for rehearsal is finished. In two days we're on. The Rat shuffles around the stage, his nose in his exercise book where he's pasted the script. He listens. He watches. We usher him around. At this point we know the show better than him. This won't last long. We tell him where to stand. Where to move to. What scene is next.

Everyone is deferential with the Rat. Like talking to an Old Uncle. This won't last long, either.

Henry is not like this, of course. An old soldier can't help himself. He has to patrol and probe for any weakness. This is how he's survived this long.

We're on a break. The Rat and me. Sitting outside the old courthouse. Henry comes out. He's just been in a meeting with the theatre producers. I'm smoking.

Stupid fucken habit, says the Rat.

Henry lights up.

How are ya? he asks.

Good, says the Rat.

I'll do opening night, says Henry.

Why? asks the Rat.

To give you more time, says Henry.

The Rat shrugs. Henry and I smoke.

Then you can do the next night, adds Henry.

Silence.

Somewhere, a few blocks away, a lone crow calls out from his rooftop perch.

When you're ready, adds Henry.

I'm ready now.

I'm just worried you haven't had enough time.

Fuck.

Think about it. I'll do opening night …

I'm not watchin.

What?

You can do it. But I'm not watchin.

What's the point, then?

What's the point?

Henry and I finish our cigarettes. Chuck em in the bin.

I'm fucken doin it, Djaambi.

Henry nods. He gets to his feet. Goes back inside. Maybe the tiniest hint of a wry smile in the corners of his mouth. This is how it is with Henry. The characters he creates come from such a personal place that you have to wrestle them away from him to play them.

Opening night. The Rat and I are standing in the dark behind the stage. The audience have come in. The house music is on. The house lights are coming down. No place in our minds for anything but success.

Break a leg, I say.

Kele mwerre anthurre, says the Rat.

What's that one?

Mwerre is good. It's like, walk good, you know, go really good way.

Kele mwerre anthurre, I try.

The Rat smiles at my pronunciation. We hug. Lights up. We're on. The Rat is awesome. I've never seen anything like it in my life. Learnt it in two days. Asked for three prompts only. A brilliant performance.

Little Big Man is strong as a mallee bull.

We get a standing ovation. We make them laugh and weep. Laugh and weep. Laugh and weep. Mainly weep.

And every night — singalong party

Settle in to doing this show. Nine a week. One day off.

Over the first few days it is noticed that lots of shitty little things and feelings have been happening. We get to thinking. Turns out half a dozen or so gubbahs were condemned to death in this building a hundred years ago. Maybe these lads aren't happy. Don't understand. Maybe feel left out. So before the next show we all gather early and smoke the place again. Things improve.

The show rolls on. Again and again and again. To us it's like Groundhog Day — but where the day is filled with loss, heartache, betrayal, murder and absolute futility. And funerals. Always funerals. Being part of this play is like going to a funeral every day. On the days when we do matinees — two funerals. And, you know, someone close to you, brother, close to you, sister. And, oh, the joy! The joy of surviving. Of speaking out. Of paying respect. A Healing Ceremony. Sorry Business.

And after every show, later on, when most of the audience have dragged themselves hence — out come the guitars, the sticks and didjes — and everyone sings and dances. Every night a celebration. We're all exhausted. But somehow elated. Every night I yarn to Mum.

She is there, flanked by her beautiful Gunditjmara nieces. I roll cigarettes for Mum. Get a drink if Mum wants one. Sometimes I notice Henry notice. He knows I'm paying respect.

One night there is this big party. People offering up songs. Party up and trade Culture at the same time. One woman offers up an Islander song, Muralag way. Livvo sings a haunting Gooniyandi (Kimberley) song and dances along.

All of us there, our breaths taken away. Swaying in that alleyway outside the theatre, hands keeping the beat, heartbeat, we see him go to Country for the song, feel it live in him.

And Mum inclines her head to me to come over, as the warm family applause dies down. I start to move over to her.

And Stephen Motor is gunna sing for us now! Thanks, Stephen.

I freeze. Look around. Everyone is looking. I'm not prepared.

I …

And then I breathe in and out and mumble a few words of intro and launch into this prison song. This is my Culture. I belt the fucken thing out. I'm trembling from adrenalin and the feeling of my Ancestors standing there in that circle, the weight of the ankle chains just a dream memory now — and everyone loves me, and in that moment I feel the warmth as a solid force, a wash, and I am full of it. I look up and suddenly feel a bit stand-outy, little-bit shame job, so I go to leave.

The Rat calls me over: Don't go walkin off like ya haven't got any friends!

Everyone laughs. I plonk down at his table. I was about to be all gubbah about it, but then I just opened my mouth and sang. Only worked cause I went full-blast. Mum musta known what'd happen.

And here's me trading songs too. I'm deeper into this Country now. And lost too. Lost in this Country. Henry warned me about this. But I never quite got what he meant. Whenever I do talk to my gubbah friends, I feel like I've slipped away somewhere. I can see and hear them — but they can't reach me, or … I dunno.

And every night we sing together. Sometimes cry again for joy. Sometimes for sorrow. All sorts of friends and family drop in and trade songs. Well, all family really. And it flows out of us. Healing ourselves now, too.

Looked after by family

By now we've switched theatres to a converted brewery. Boonwurrung Country. We do this matinee show. As the show is going, I'm struggling to hold back these huge sobs that are threatening to engulf me. All I can think is that the Rat is going to die. That he's gunna go all out. All the way. All the fucken way! I don't want it to happen. I don't know if I can stand at that grave.

When I look at Lance playing that young lad on the morgue table, I think it's really him. That he's gone too.

Out of control. I scrabble through my lines. Screech through my songs. Stamp through the dance. In the curtain call I can't look at anyone. That'd make me come apart. Come apart at the seams. Explode. Disintegrate into atoms and electrons and be flung into every corner of the theatre, like a traitor whose body is hung, drawn and quartered and buried in far-flung corners of the kingdom. So I look down and bite into my lower lip until way after it starts bleeding.

After the show I find my way outside. There is a tableful of Gunditjmara. I walk up and stand next to them. Desperate to feel inside the family. Feel the strength from the Clan. People look up. Henry goes his big smile. Goes to introduce me to the People I don't know. Oh, shit! Gubbahs too. Didn't notice em before.

You alright, Brother?

Everyone suddenly looks to me. Drawn by the tone in Djaambi's voice. I take a breath. Feel like I'm as thin as paper.

I'm a fucken long way from alright, Brother.

I want to look around to see who spoke. But I know it was me. I collapse and hug Henry, like a lost child hugs a parent on being found. Djaambi motions to Mum. And I'm walking away, well I can feel my legs moving me down the alleyway, Mum next to me. Mum, a tree.

Jesus, Mum. How could they do it? Fucken cunts.

Don't dwell on it, Son.

How could they do it?

Again my voice seems to come from some far-off place. A dry creek bed where fires rage and everywhere there is the smell of burning flesh. I want to dive into a tree-hole. Cover myself with branches.

This is the path we choose, Son.

A wind suddenly springs up and howls down the alleyway. For a moment I think the wind will lift us off our feet.

This is the path we choose.

Leaves swirl all around us. That wind blows right through me. Like I'm not there. Like the alleyway is gone. There is bush and wetlands all around. Just down there is the Yarra.

Mum talks. I begin to take a step towards understanding and that old wind just drops away the instant Mum stops talking. Stops so suddenly that the leaves howling past my face hold up, and then flutter straight down to land at my feet. Mum hugs me.

You see that?

I indicate all around with my lips.

Mum smiles. (Yeah. I saw it.)

Smiles. We walk back.

And later that same night, I'm standing in the same alley. Finished the second show. Done my two funerals. Had a nyar-ha. Got a beer in my fist. I'm just trying to loosen off a bit. I see Little Big Man with his woman. They're just leaving. Going home to the kids. Good People.

I'm yarnin to him and he looks like he's shivering in front of me. Really cold. I look down to see that I'm wearing this beautiful lined denim jacket that Freddy lent me because I was cold when I first came back over from Wudjari Country. I look into my heart to see that I'm carrying hurt from Freddy, and with a smile I remember my leather jacket and Muriel-or-something in Wiljali Country that time.

I strip the jacket instantly and give it to Little Big Man. For trade he rolls me a nyar. We smoke it together. I feel warm. My heart is warm for Freddy again. Not stained by those other hurts. And Little Big Man rolls a good nyar-ha, too. We hug our goodbyes.

There's this young gubbah girl there, hair up, tits out. And, you know, I'm away from my woman and kids. I'm in someone else's Country. I'm telling some bullshit story. I look down and notice this girl is drinking in my every word, and she leans in to laugh at something I've said, and her bare arm brushes mine, and she flicks her hair away from me and throws her head back to expose her bosom and throat.

Stephen!

I snap around at the voice. Mum. I laugh.

Stephen! Come here! Come here. Right now!

I saunter over like a teenager caught snogging behind the sports shed. I cross into a zone where I can't be followed. And I *know* I can't be followed. I play the game, too. Give Mum my best I-wasn't-doing-anything-especially-not-noticing-that-other-woman smile:

Yes, Mum.

Just wanted to see you, Son.

Mum flashes her wicked smile. Her nieces all laugh.

Just wanted to talk.

We both laugh. I take out my makings and roll two cigarettes. Hand one to Mum. Light it up.

In a while they'll bring out the guitars. For now, we smoke and yarn up. Lance comes over too. We feel like we're winning now. Really fucken doing something. I feel looked after. And so does my woman back in Wudjari Country. Twelve Countries away. That's all there is. Family. Just family.

Touching sorry scars

I always admired the apostle, Thomas. He would go down in history as Doubting Thomas, but I always thought that those early Christian clerics misread his actions. When Jesus appeared to his followers they all fell to the ground, prostrating themselves before the risen-from-the-dead Christ. But Thomas had to step forward and put his fingers in the nail-holes in Jesus' hands and the gash torn in his side where the Roman soldier stabbed him with his spear. The others could all live with blind faith but Thomas was the only one who was prepared to test his faith, not to believe blindly, but to know for sure that this apparition really was his master risen from the dead.

I'm sitting backstage in the brewery-converted-to-a-theatre. For the last week in the old courthouse-converted-to-a-theatre we'd been doing the show twice a day. All of us are frayed and torn at the edges like an old threadbare blanket covering a sleeping Parkie. I'm not sure if I can keep going. I don't feel tough enough.

Henry comes round the corner. There is a deep dark ring of pain around his eyes, too. Henry takes my hand and runs my fingers across the broad scars on his upper arms. The scars are like big sad mouths or sad closed eyes, cut into his teardrop shoulder muscles. Smooth and knotty at the same time, like thick silky rope blu-tacked onto his flesh — their silkiness belying the pain endured to receive them. To receive them willingly.

In a moment I'm scrabbling on the floor in some dimly-lit room. My best mate's eyes are beacons. There are blood and tears strewn all around like dead bodies dumped on a distant shore. In his eyes I see him lose his children. Make a choice to let them go so that he can stay and fight this war. In his eyes I see those Gunditjmara children buried up to their necks in their own sacred sandy beach. In slow motion, I see the boots of those gubbahs as they stride up and swing back ready to kick their heads off. I get to know every patch of leather and the laces of those boots as though they are my own grandfathers' or great-grandfathers'. All around are the wailing of women. Mothers wailing. Sisters wailing. Aunties wailing. Grandmothers wailing. Beating my skull like huge teardrops frozen hard like hailstones.

I see the pain of a man who is crushed by the grief of his People and when he comes home from the day's battles can't even hold his own children for fear of sucking the life out of them. I look down to the blades in our hands. I watch the pain flowing out with the blood. I know the only way to get rid of this pain is to cut it out. Don't know how I know. Just know.

I look back to the beacons. Shining eyes. Djaambi's eyes. And we're back in a poky backstage corridor of a theatre. I get myself to my feet. Blink away tears. Tears that seem so small and useless in this ocean of grief. A swell hits me, knocking me

338

against the brick wall. I stagger like an old drunk, then catch myself. I look to Djaambi. His eyes laugh at my little clown stagger. I grin back at him.

Soon the play will start. We can hear the audience shuffling in and talking. The low muffled talk of funerals. We all know we haven't been doing a play for some time. Never really was a play. The Rat brushes past me. We clasp hands involuntarily. Don't look at each other. Henry moves off to talk to someone else. A priest moving through his congregation.

Kele mwerre anthurre, says the Rat.

Kele mwerre anthurre, I breathe.

Scars on the gravel footy oval

School footy carnival. Late 1970s. We travel north-east from Wudjari Country to Malpa Country. To Norseman. I'm fifteen. It's a three-hour road journey for us. Schools come from all over south-east WA. Goreng, Nyaki-Nyaki, Kalaamaya and Wangkathaa Country. We're the defending champions in this lightning carnival. We fancy ourselves a bit. First game up. I'm playing half-back flank.

I run out on to the gravel oval in the sun. It's already hot. Ten o'clock in the morning. We do our warm-ups. Captains toss. I run to my position. We're playing this team from the goldfields. Wangkathaa Country. I'm a skinny wadjula kid. No testosterone rush yet. No body hair. Balls haven't dropped. High voice.

This fulla I'm playing on runs up. Bare feet, full beard. Thick ridges of scars on his upper arm. I just know they go under his footy jumper too.

What the fuck? I know straightaway he's got a higher pain threshold than me. Not afraid. Wadjulas have been coping with this thought since the first Land War in Tasmania. They couldn't beat that Big River Mob or them Oyster Bay Mob.

The leader of their warriors, Tongalongata, gets his arm shot off and continues to fight and conduct his warriors.

This young Wongi man puts his face close to my boy face.

You touch that fucken ball — I fucken kill you.

I stare back, unblinking. Give nothing away. That's what I've learnt. I've had my share of hidings. I'm not afraid. Not yet, anyway.

The siren goes and the ball comes out of the centre fast — straight for our position. I sprint for it. One thing I've got is speed. But he's right on my tail now. Can't outrun him. I'm coming up fast on the ball. If I scoop it up, I'll be driven into the gravel. I fumble it on purpose. It goes past me. That Wongi fulla grabs the ball. But I've slowed my pace for three steps and he runs into me as I'm turning to grab him. I use our momentum to throw him to the ground, incorporating our twisting momentum so that he lands flat on his back with me on top of him. The ball spills free.

I get up laboriously, pushing myself off him as if he was a rock I was sunning myself on. He looks straight at me. His expression doesn't change as I push him into the gravel to get myself up.

Shi-i-i-t.

I look up the field to see the ball go over the top to Pringhael Gil, who sets up Fender for a goal with a little give handpass. It goes through and we all erupt. I run right down to the forward-line to slap hands with Fender and Pringhael Gil. They're revving me up.

Inspiring tackle, Moats!

Killin im, Mate!

I run back down as the ball is returning to the centre. The

Wongi fulla is waiting for me. A faint smile playing in the corners of his mouth.

Soon enough the ball is coming our way again. And I'm caught in my own trap. He gets there first and fumbles it. I really take off. This is my chance to punish him. He looks like he's gunna fall over. I gather in the ball — he's miles away — take two steps, see Macca breaking away into the centre of the ground. I'll pin this pass on him — when, crunch! That big Wongi is all over me. Chops down on my arms, I spill the ball, his entire weight comes on to me and down I go. Buries me.

I lose bark from knees and elbows and have a little cut on my ear that bleeds like a stuck pig.

He gets off me, pushing me into the gravel as he goes. I shake it off. Stand up. We're tryin to act tough, but we're smilin, too. I feel like a man today.

So it goes all day. The ebb and flow. Game of blood and imagined manhood. My wadjula team-mates are winding me up, too.

You're a pig, Moats!

Bloody bog-Irish pig!

We win the game. At the end of the game this Wongi fulla makes a point of running over to shake my hand. For some reason I had this impulse to reach out and run my fingers across his scars. I didn't dare.

Suck out the hate

Wurundjeri Country, Melbourne. Come off stage after the Party scene. Three quick scenes in a row at the top of the second act. I remember the order of the quick-change scenes, where I don't leave the stage, by chanting their names like a mantra just before we go on at the top of the second act. Mama, Cold Cunt, Party. I use the mantra to psyche myself into the scenes.

I breathe with the greatest of care. Each time my rib cage expands to lower my diaphragm and fill my lungs with air, the pain in my left front side goes from dull ache fire to razor-sharp red-hot pokers in my flesh. My chest and arm muscles are sore sore sore. Bruises on bruises. A tiny sound escapes from the side of my mouth. I look around quickly. Frightened I've been discovered.

Sitting here in the backstage dark. It's the eyes of the women that fall on me. Serena, flower of the Wiradjuri, and Mary our mother/sister from the Yorta Yorta. I blink my eyes to clear the tears and they are both there whisper-close.

Alright, Brother?

They can see I'm a fucken long way from alright. I can't lie to my sister/niece or my mother/sister.

My ribs are broken.

When?

Dress rehearsal.

Shit.

Almost a week ago now. Maybe a lifetime away. I take a deep breath. The hot pokers go in. I like it this time. I wipe my tears.

Don't tell the Rat, I say.

I look into their eyes.

This is my business.

Those two women nod. Serena strokes me. Mary hugs me.

My boy. My boy, whispering on the wind.

I sit and gingerly run my fingers around my rib cage. I can move pieces of broken rib with my fingers. How the fuck did I get here?

How things begin is hard to know.

There was no song or ceremony or dance to commission me … but we all of us knew what had to be done, says Henry's character, Jack, in the play. I knew I wanted the stunt to be hard-core. I knew the Rat needed it as well as Henry and me.

So we talked it through. I wanted head-butts and kicks. Punching is for Lionel Rose, not Jack in a bar. A bar full of weapons. So we rehearsed up a head-slam into the bar.

On the third night in front of the audience, I'm on stage at the beginning of the next scene after the stunt (Cold Cunt). The Party. I'm half facing away from the audience. Mary whispers out the corner of her mouth, you're bleeding, Brother. The head-slam had made contact with the bar and I hadn't realised.

At an opportune moment I scooped up the tea towel from

the bar and wiped above my eye. We finished the scene and Mary and I left the stage with the giggles.

And for the two kicks to the guts, I had shown the Rat how to flatten his foot as he makes contact, and how to do it against my chest muscles. But then along came the dress rehearsal and the Rat's costume shoes are big heavy boots that can't really be flattened. And they're heavy enough to create momentum in the kick, or to make it hard to pull up short, in any case.

I've got something terrible hidden in my heart. From times long gone. Before I was called to this journey. Kidded myself that my attitudes were in line with everyone else's, that it was the company I was keeping.

And I know them Old People notice things. They notice what you bring to the table. What sacrifices? How far you are prepared to go. And for me; I'd take a hiding for Henry. For Mum. For the Rat. Hell, I'd take one from the Rat. I do every night. Because he needed it. Because hate can take you over if you let it build up. I took his hate. And Henry's. Sucked the hate out of those big leather boots as they smacked into my body and the audience gasped in shock. Screwed up their faces. Shifted in their seats. Laughed way too loud in the next scene, the Party, and I could feel their eyes flicking to me as I'm standing on stage with my frozen smile. The Rat felt it too.

Are you alright? You alright, Bruz?

Me, I was born in the briar patch. Certainly, when I had to change my shirt in the toilet of our dressing room so that the others wouldn't see my swollen blue and purple and green and yellow flesh, I did flash back to my childhood.

It was just yesterday that I sat in Dr Randwick's surgery and had to take my shirt off so the doctor could listen to my chest. I tried to wriggle out of it but I was only ten. As soon as my top came off I knew I was fucked. And I was. Doctor Randwick sees the bruises covering my arms and upper body. Me, I'm looking down. Not talking now. Shame. No questions. No answers. The doctor gets stuck into Mum who is beside herself with shock and embarrassment.

What can I say, Mum?

We go home. It's a long drive that day. It's a long drive every day. Of course, the good doctor's gone off at Mum, saying he will speak to Dad himself if Mum wants. But Mum knows one thing for sure; it isn't Dad. So we drive and I ask Mum to keep it secret. I beg her. She knows it's my brother. I know he needs to do it.

And I've got to the stage that I don't care. I've come through my fear. Many times. You face the fear each time — but you know the path now. Sometimes I conserve my energy for one big hit back. It's all I need. Something for myself. For him to know I can hurt him too. I never cry in front of him. Never make any outward show of pain. What I try for, anyway. Sometimes this fuels him to further violence but I don't care. Gone past it.

Mum tells Dad. Dad whacks my brother. Mum gets upset. Mum and Dad have a huge screaming match. It was the only time I ever saw them fight. Dad doesn't know what to do. Mum is upset for my brother. For me.

My brother is unrepentant. I get a bashing the next day. I shut up about it.

So I'm back to hiding my bruises after all these years. It's different now.

My brother has since apologised to me. The man sorry for

the sins of the boy. He rang me up at night from Wangkathaa Country, Kalgoorlie. I think maybe he'd just remembered it. Been buried. I forgive him. I never stopped loving him. I looked up to him. Wanted to be him. Be tough like him. Made me who I am.

I won't back down from the stunt. Despite the damage. This is against all that I know about acting. About theatre. But I'm no longer interested in those things. It's a means to an end. I'm a message. Nothing can touch me. I want to serve up the truth. I have to serve up the truth. That's all. I'll take the spear in the leg when it's coming to me. My Sorry Scar for Henry's pain and misery and the Rat's brotherhood. Written on my bones now. And this time I'll be the one who has to apologise. Apologise to the Rat. For not being up-front and straight-up.

The winter
(things hidden in my heart)

The winter of my discontent comes early. Discontent. Malcontent. Breaking over me like angry swirling surf. Dragging me down.

I'm nineteen and my best friend Gil gets killed. Life sucked out by that gum tree by the highway in Malpa Country. Norseman. Leaned forward to change the cassette in his car at the wrong moment.

I fall into a depression. An angry grieving which goes on and on and on and consumes everything like a cyclone, picks it up, whirls it round, smashes it up, dumps it.

One day I start drinking. And I can't stop. During this alcohol-fuelled burn-out I meet up with a kindred spirit, Les. We run around Perth in the early eighties being angry young men together. Drunk angry young men.

I'm in Perth, Wajuk Country, now cause I can't stomach Esperance.

Les and I are drinking. Been drinking for days now in this Wajuk winter. Been kicked out of three pubs in a row. The last one because we were both collapsed in the corner refusing to stop screaming 'Yuk' at the top of our lungs.

We go back to the college where Les is living as he drinks his way through uni. We go to the common room. There is a Clint Eastwood movie on the TV. An avenging policeman — judge, jury and executioner, you know the fucken drill. I don't know why but it sets me off. I am screaming at the TV. Screaming racist remarks. I'm not gunna soil these pages with those words. As Clint the hero cop executes an African-American alleged criminal without trial, I'm screaming encouragement. I'm proclaiming the superiority of my race. Cause we've got guns. We've got fucken guns.

I could lie and say it was Les. But it wasn't. It was me.

The Asian and the African students quickly leave. They feel the real threat. They haven't seen the Leses and the Mes of this world up this close. Well-fed-red-raw-angry-racist-redneck fuckers.

The night deteriorates and we really smash up the common room. The racist diatribe falls from my lips like blood in an abattoir.

The police get called. But, somehow we give them the slip and cut through the bush to visit some girls we know in another college.

The next day Les is called up to front the headman of the college and banned from the common room for a month. They call it being 'sent down'. The college is shamed. The Asian and African students have complained.

Some guy called 'Moats' is constantly mentioned to the headman. He was the one ranting and raving and becoming threatening and abusive. He is banned for life in absentia.

What the People first saw

The Rat is talking about this Old Fulla. The Old Fulla reckons:

Everyone always talks about what Cook saw, what Banks, what Sturt, Hume, Mitchell, Burke and Wills — but what about what the People saw? When they stood on the shore to see the pale men arrive — a boat full of dead men. Spirits, maybe.

They have a second skin they can shed like a snake. Underneath their second skin they are pale and shiny like stars.

They wear strange ceremonial headgear all the time. They can make their hands disappear. (Makes a show of putting his hands in pockets.)

They keep other men tied up like dogs. They beat their men-dogs with thick rope. They're very possessive about their men-dogs. Don't ever let them run away. Reward you if you bring them back.

They can attach themselves to a large beast and move swiftly across Country and then detach themselves at the other end.

They have pointy sticks which make smoke and little thunder and can kill a man instantly.

They drink this drink that makes them really strong and

brave to do anything, but makes them really crazy too.

They put things on their feet and can walk through fire and over very sharp rocks.

They can communicate without talking. A fulla comes in to the mission store and the man there might know his name, where he's from. They pass around little pieces of thin bark when they do this magic. (Makes a show of writing something down, passing it to someone else who reads it.)

He knows my name? That I'm sick? I didn't tell him anything?

He looked at that thin bark and he knows my name. He's reading my mind or that other fulla that I told my name to, but that was last week.

These must surely be powerful spirits.

What we first saw

Me and my brothers are standing on the chairs to look out the loungeroom window. Late 1960s, Wudjari Country. Lort River Station. I'm not going to school yet. A special day. We are dressed up, in our good shorts. Maybe we are going to church.

Outside the loungeroom window is another world. Thousands of head of cattle are being moved in from the top paddocks to the main stockyards. Poll Herefords. Big red-brown mounds with pale patches along their spines. Charging around, stirring up the dust. Tomorrow morning we'll be woken by the sound of semitrailers slowing down to turn up the road to the stockyards.

And then charging across our loungeroom window screen comes Wangkathaa man, Bart Billon, at full gallop, right to left, standing in his stirrups, arms and legs flailing wildly, yelling out in Language. Bart's hat is on the back of his head, dust and sweat on his skin, riding like he's got no fear. Reckless abandon and cool control rolled into one.

Over the other side of the river of cattle we can see two of Bart's cousins. Them Wongi stockmen always seem to be laughing.

They can swear at the cattle in their own language, says my eldest brother.

Us other three, our jaws drop. He can ride flat out like that, all arms and legs flying, and he can swear in another language. His own language.

Was he swearin then?

Bet he was!

He was!

Told ya!

Bloody hell.

(And 'bloody hell' is a term reserved for maximum respect.)

On the school bus there was one kid who knew 'shit' in German. Someone else knew 'up your arse' in Gaelic. Another Mick knew 'meet me at the sunrise on the last day'. But no-one had his own Language.

We watch them Wongi fullas rounding up the cattle for twenty minutes or so before they're gone. We could still see them yelling out in Language but couldn't hear their voices over the noise from the livestock. But we just knew they were swearing.

Bundi-sticks and tears on the freeway

I come to driving on the freeway. South through Boonwurrung Country. The Melbourne traffic is heavy. I start to slow down. Check my mirrors as we slow to a crawl. Check the face of every driver of every car. The lanes either side of me. I go from car to car. Scrutinising faces, haircuts, clothes. Car types. Just knowing who they all are. Don't want any surprises. I'm in Henry's car. I drop my right hand from the wheel and feel down beside my seat. My fingers find the hard wood of a nulla-nulla. Henry's bundi-stick.

Henry's voice rings in my ears, his laughter breaking over the car like surf. His naughty laugh. Nothin to talk about here. Except that I can't help wondering how many men of peace need to carry a weapon to defend themselves? How many gubbahs (who aren't crims) fear the police like this? Traffic almost comes to a halt. I've got the night off. Going down bush to visit my Boonwurrung sister and niece. My hand caresses the bundi-stick.

I think of Henry parked at a set of traffic lights. The noise of the Royal Commission clanging in his head like the sound of prison doors closing. He jumps out of his car and snatches up the bundi-stick. Three cars back is a new grey Commodore. Full of big no-necked gubbahs in shirts and ties. Boofheads, big feet. Henry is sick of them following him. Everyone is nervous to have a Koori investigating Koori deaths in custody. He might find something he's not supposed to. Everyone's madly sweeping shit under the carpet and here's this Gunditjmara fulla lifting up the carpet and asking, What have we here?

Henry strides back to the Commodore full of detectives. The bundi swings back and — crack! Smashes right into the car! The lights change. Other drivers hit their horns. Henry smacks the cop car again and again and again. The boofheads jump out and are all screaming at Henry. Henry ignores them. Smacks into the car. Smashing something with every swing. Side mirrors, panels, headlights. The bundi-stick holds up. Fire-treated.

One of the boofheads draws his service revolver. Aims it at Henry. Henry laughs and continues his demolition job on their car. Now they're all getting out their pistols. Yelling. Getting real nervous. Henry screams back at them. Daring them to fire. They can't. It's public. They can't hide this. The War in this Country is a secret war. Not to be carried out in public. Against an enemy standing up. A secret war against helpless young men in cells and the backrooms of country police stations. Helpless from drugs and alcohol and diabetes and poverty and weakened by being denied Culture, Heritage, Land.

Henry screams at them. They're all pointing their weapons at him. He takes a step towards them. The Gunditjmara challenge. They step back. Henry laughs. Turns, goes back to his car. Drives calmly off. His car. This car.

Stupid fat jungais standing next to their wrecked car with

their pistols out and their ties waving in the gentle breeze.

I have to blink hard to see the traffic in front. I know Henry felt terrible about this. There is no violence in his heart. He remembers too well what that old uncle said to him, 'You gotta fight hate with love.' But sometimes you gotta make a stand, or they bury you. Bury you up to your neck in your own sacred soil. I'm still blinking. The waking dream all around me. Blink away the tears. But great sobs are wracking my body. Working up from my toes and swirling through my heart like a willy-willy. The gubbah dilemma that I couldn't articulate to Mum in that windy alleyway. The dilemma of the gubbahs who cross over. My body convulses. Contractions like I'm giving birth. Like every fibre of every muscle is trying to shed my skin like that old snake does. Have I outgrown this skin? Am I weeping because I'm reaching out to those children buried up to their necks in the beach sand, or because I know I am the wearer of the thick leather boots striding in to kick at their beautiful child faces? To kick and kick until their little heads come off.

Gubbahs make me nervous. I know what they're capable of. What we're capable of. What I'm capable of. I fight the urge to pull over. If it wasn't for the peak-hour traffic slowing me to a crawl, I'd probably be dead. I won't pull over. Not on this path. I'll tread it. I'll drive it. Fast as I can.

In an hour or so I'm in sanctuary. The sanctuary of Family. I sit on the verandah and smoke. I eat and sleep and talk quietly about matters close to our hearts. I'm truly thankful for my family. For the path we choose.

Naming names

We've done our performance. The audience are clapping. Mostly polite gubbahs who think the performers will leave the stage if they keep clapping. Of course, the Mob will never leave the stage as long as there is clapping.

Eventually Henry gets up and makes a speech. Then the Attorney General for the state gets up. The play has been sponsored by the Justice Department which is about to begin a review of the implementation of the findings from the Royal Commission. So the Attorney General is pretty pleased with himself. A former head of the Koori Legal Service, he feels pretty close to the Mob.

The Attorney General launches into a death-in-custody case which he worked on where the law failed. A young fulla in a remote community is so down he attempts to hang himself with a length of garden hose. The hose doesn't work. He gets caught by police and thrown in the lock-up. He is dead twenty minutes later. And then the AG is quoting Henry.

I wrote this down, he says.

We can change. By planting a seed …

Henry, my djaambi, gives me a glance. The AG is an

intelligent man. In this instance he seems happy — or perhaps he doesn't realise — to be Henry's puppet. This is why I do this job. Ya might change one.

Ya might change one, says Henry.

But the AG started his oration with the lad's name and the name of the community. I'm being tugged away and down. Under the rolling surf. This is why some Mobs have taboos to do with this subject. I can't breathe. I don't know which way is up. I tumble over and over. The walls melt away. I see him there. Hanging in his cell. I see rooms full of People weeping. Mum and Dad identifying the body. My hands are shaking. I'm sweating hard. My eyes cloud over.

I look over to Djaambi who seems to say, Yeah, with his eyes.

I've crossed a line somewhere. Ya can't go back.

Was it, Yeah, this is what it's like for us?

Or was it, Yeah, come with us, Stevey Boy?

I look into the audience and see the same look in the eyes of uncles and aunties. This is what Uncle Kumanjai Presto was talking about.

Grab you by the back of the head and run you through my life. Our lives.

Once you've seen that journey … was the unsaid bit.

Finish-up

After the last show. Djaambi arranges for all the cast to come on to the little stage in the foyer of the old grog factory. We each get presented with a poster of the production, signed by everyone. Uncle Paulie says a few words.

As he is speaking I feel the taut strings of my heart give way with a loud twang. Everyone around me jumps. I begin to weep. I couldn't tell you why. And, you know, shame job in front of everyone. Lance and Mary and Serena cuddle me. Hide my teary face from the Mob crowding the little stage.

Uncle Paulie presents something to his countryman, Djaambi. Djaambi has a few words. Actually, none of us can ever remember him only saying a *few* words …

We amble away. I'm wiping away tears and snot with my sleeve as I reach the doors to the alleyway outside. Desperate for a cigarette to compose myself. I take a big slug of VB, and hear Djaambi say into the mic:

And, welcome now to the stage Mr Stephen Motor who will sing us a beautiful song!

There is some applause. I look back to Djaambi. He's smiling his naughty smile. Always a soldier. Gotta be ready to go at any moment. I turn and mock-trudge back to the stage.

In my Country, in WA, they still have mandatory sentencing.

I step back from the mic to sing:

Well, they're calling time for exercise
Round her majesty's hotel

And when I get to the chorus, the whole room sings with me.

Four walls
Wash basin
Prison bed

I go outside and have a nyandi with Ned, that Pitjantjatjara man. We talk long time about the nature of loss. A cool breeze blows down that alley in Boonwurrung Country. Just enough to tickle our hair.

We get the whole Mob up to the stage again to sing the songs from the show. We really celebrate them this time. All of us get swept away. I sing 'Warinor' with Djaambi and Uncle Paulie. I'm ten foot tall and bulletproof. I'm riding a wave. Feel strange. Elated. Like I'm coming out of the closet — I'm not gunna act like a gubbah in public any longer. No pretending. Like I'm not me at all, and, at the exact same moment, the most me I've ever been.

I see my gubbah brother, Keith, afterwards for a beer.

Never seen you like this before, Brother, he comments.

I smile at him and his woman. I suddenly catch my

reflection in the glass doors near the end of the bar. I'm shocked to see that I look like a gubbah. Shocked.

Is this what Elizabeth, that Palawa sister, means when she says I have the soul of an Old Fulla? She sees this happen to me?

I drag on my cigarette. Finish my VB with one big slug. It's cold and tangy in my throat.

We go around the back of the theatre to the carpark to do our finish-up Smoking Ceremony. All the cast and crew and everyone else involved. We stand around this big fire that Little Big Man gets goin in a ten-gallon drum.

After the Smoking proper, we burn pages of the script. Everyone says what they've got to say. I've got a lot to say but am struck dumb in the moment. Burn some Sorry Scar script. Look the Rat in the eye over the flames. Then Djaambi. Then everyone. The circle is tight. Bound by love in this moment. Whatever happens in our life between us, we'll always have this moment right now. This circle. Where People from over a dozen Countries and different histories can stand here. Stand tall for each other. Bound by love.

Later on I will confess my subterfuge to the Rat. Strip to show him my purple and blue rib cage. Now turning yellow at the bottom. Show like a soldier. I got Sorry Scar on the inside, now. Where the bones are knitting back together. They can identify me by this at my autopsy. I'm deeply sorry for my deception. But proud too.

The Rat probably thinks I'm a crazy wadjula. Yeah, well. This war makes us all a bit crazy in the head.

You know, carpeta rroor-ta! Makes gesture of flicking fingers from open hand at the side of head, with a twist to finish! (Crazy in the head.)

Tomorrow night I'll be sleeping in WA. Nyungar Country. With my family.

Don't ever drink with them

I'm soon back in Melbourne to work with Henry on a mainstream TV drama.

I go to St Kilda to see my man. You know. Afterwards I'm standing in the street. Roll a cigarette to wait for a cab. A street guy sees me roll and comes over for the bite. I've gotta expect this. I cadged a cigarette off a bald Pommy backpacker waiting for the skybus at the airport.

This street fulla, I met him in the POW pool bar ten years ago — he was a coke dealer then. Arrogant. Flash Jack. Jack got into smack and now he walks the streets of St Kilda and hangs with the Parkies.

Can I get a rolly? he asks out the corner of his mouth.

Yep. Ya wanna filter?

Nah. What's the point? he laughs.

Less tar.

What's the point? he repeats, convinced it's a really funny joke.

Gotta light?

Want any drugs? I can get good drugs, he suddenly asks.

Good drugs?

I ponder this question. The question of *good* drugs.

Good smack. Smoke. Speed, he continues as though he didn't hear my question.

Nah, thanks.

Really good smack?

He won't let it go. Can he see the addict in my eyes? I decide to spell it out.

There's such a thing? I ask.

What about a smoke? he asks without hesitation.

Got some.

And then I don't know how it comes up. I always get the feeling I've got a big sign on me.

Libby owes me a taste, he says from nowhere, looking away to the McDonald's across the road.

What?

She says to me, I'll knock you out, you gubbah cunt! Jeez. Fuck. Don't ever drink with em. And as he finishes this little tirade he finishes rolling his cigarette.

He asks me what I'm doing.

An ep for a TV show.

I went to the Jimmy Patterson memorial in Fitzroy, he says. It was scary. I was the only gub there. Eventually, this Koori fulla turns around and says: Are you a pig, or what?

I was just there, he confesses, like I'm Father Murphy.

Did you know Jimmy? I ask.

No.

What *were* you doing there?

He doesn't hesitate. His mouth seems to have a life of its own. Off he goes.

Ya can't drink with em. Don't ever drink with the cunts. It's just a thing. Ya can't drink with em. Libby owes me a taste.

Libby is my family, I say evenly.

They don't give a fuck, Mate. They're hard.

I gotta go, I say.

You wanna roll a joint in the park?

Na, thanks.

Cuppa tea at my place?

Thanks for the offer, I lie.

My hand flicks up and away. Narcoo (no).

Can ya sling's a bud? He asks again.

Lloyd is like a son to me, I say, wondering why I'm bothering.

They might be in the park.

They're not. I checked, I say.

What was your name again?

Steve.

Jack.

We shake again. Flash Jack wanders off and I get into a taxi with a Sikh driver.

I can't say no

I go down to the park to look for Lloyd. I see Auntie Wyn.
Auntie calls me over with a lift of her chin and two flick-curls
of her left hand.

You got a smoke, my boy?

Yes, Auntie. Rollie.

Roll me a nice thin one, can you, my boy?

I start to roll.

Where you from?

From WA. Born Narrogin. Wiilman Country. Lived in St
Kilda for a long time, though. Long time. Park Street.

Auntie suddenly jumps up and hugs me to her expansive
bosom.

Steve! Stevey! My nephew! I'm sorry! Sorry. Didn't know
you. Steve. My nephew.

Even if I wanted to get out of the embrace I wouldn't be able
to. Auntie is as strong as an ox. She grasps me by my cheeks
and holds my face.

Ah. Steve. The St Kilda gubbahs!

She hugs me in tight again and holds me for a long time.

How is your family? I used to have cups of tea with Liz. All the time. How old is your daughter?

Charlotte? Three. Charlotte is three now.

Three? True? Aaaaah.

We sit down and smoke. I get introduced to this old Wiradjuri fulla. Colin. I roll him a smoke.

Lloyd isn't here. Just left.

Know where he went, Auntie?

Town.

We smoke in silence. The Luna Park roller-coaster, the oldest one still in operating in the world, clanks away behind us.

My nephew, can you buy me a beer? Big bottle. I can't drink wine.

Auntie indicates the brown-bagged bottle at Colin's feet.

Two.

Auntie's son, Big Connor, comes back. He shakes my hand. Proper way. Without a word Big Connor slips two redbacks into his mum's hand. Auntie stashes the two bills in her bra in one fluid movement. Auntie winks at me.

For tucker. Later.

Winks at me again.

You workin with Henry?

Yeah.

You tell him I want twenty dollar.

I look at her.

Yaaaaaah!

Auntie and Big Connor laugh. Me too. She had me goin alright.

He's my nephew. Good strong fulla. Good for twenty! Yaaaah!

I laugh. Auntie is infectious.

What about two big bottles, Steve?

So now I'm the government. The government man doling out flour, tea, sugar, blankets. Doling out the fucken dole. The gubment man. The gubmeh. Gubma. Gubbah. Gubbah cunt. Killing the People with grog. But Auntie is my son's mother's mother's sister. Great aunt to me. My Auntie. I can't say no.

Yes, Aunt. Then I'm goin to look for Lloyd.

He's in the pinny joint.

Big Connor shakes my hand again.

He got out the tram at the pinnies, anyway.

Okay.

I kiss Auntie. Hug her. Shake with the men. Buy two big bottles of VB. Kiss and hug Auntie again. Shake with the men. I tram it to the pinny parlour. Lloyd has moved on.

The loop

When Lloyd's money for the film came through I opened an account for him.

Sometimes, when I was angry and frustrated in Broken Hill during the filming, I'd promise myself that I'd recoup all my personal funds expended on Lloyd and Freddy. Shit thinking. Takes a long time to become conscious of these thoughts as not my own, let alone to banish them completely.

Libby and I are both signatories on Lloyd's account. I naively thought I could keep the money for Lloyd alone. Why I wanted this seems stupid now. Lloyd doesn't share my ability or desire to see himself as separate from his mum. And I still love her. It's just the disease, the addictions, and all that goes with it that I don't love.

Once everyone saw the balance of the account there was a steady stream of people coming to the front door in St Kilda.

Lloyd was with his mum in the park. BJ turned up with a withdrawal form in his hand, already signed by Lib. No amount. I knew the money was for drugs and piss, but what can I do? Suddenly I'm the Department of Social Security — doling out cash bit at a time as if Libby and Lloyd are children who can't think for themselves as far as money is concerned. I felt stupid.

True, they don't know about money and don't care about it. I know Lloyd wouldn't know the difference between twenty and two hundred bucks, let alone three grand.

But I didn't know what to do. I started off arguing. Telling BJ I needed to discuss it with Lib. This tactic didn't work. Nothing works. It took three weeks for the money to be all gone.

Lloyd did get a ride on a Harley. I came out the front of the house after a flurry of beeping to find Libby and Lloyd and an uncle with a huge beard stuffed into the back seat of a three-wheeler. One of those city tours. Driven around by a large bearded gubbah. Lloyd was beaming.

Another time they hired a car to drive to a funeral in the country instead of having to catch the train. Libby knew all the church places where they could stop on the way and get free fuel and food. Libby always knew how to travel in style.

When the money was gone I felt stupider. Lloyd still had nothin. In the end I detached myself from it. Stupid fucken gubbah. Wha'd I think was gunna happen?

So I put in a tax-return form for Lloyd. It took a lot of jigging around with the Tax Department. And took two months to get a birth certificate for Lloyd. Like he doesn't exist to the system. In the too-hard basket. In the end I wore them down with sheer persistence and the help of my accountant, and Lloyd got twelve hundred bucks back.

I took the money and opened another account. In Lloyd's name, but with me as the only signatory.

Sometimes it feels wrong. Sometimes right. Keeping the

dosh for a rainy day. Hard to pick when that lad lives in a storm. Henry's words again. We live in a storm. All around us. In us.

So I wake up one morning. It's raining. Wurundjeri Country, Melbourne. Staying with the Rat; doing the TV gig with Henry. I don't want to be here. Missing my family. Need the money.

I have a big yarn to the Rat. I wanna take Lloyd shopping. Anything of substance I buy will be hocked for cash. Cash for piss and drugs. Anything not too sturdy will be smashed. I've been down that street. The Rat knows this world too. He gives me good advice. Get him clothes, shoes, footy gear and a bag to put it all in, so he can keep it all together. Give him a fighting chance, anyway.

So I go down to the park near Luna Park in St Kilda. Can't see em anywhere. Big Connor directs me to the army, navy, airforce club across the road. Lib, Lisa and Auntie Pringhael Esmae are playing pokies. I say g'day to them all. Lib and Auntie give me a big hug. Lisa puts the bite on me.

Lloyd is shy. I haven't seen him for two years. Last time I saw him he was a boy. Now he is Little Big Man.

We all go back over to the park. It's early on so everyone is still pretty sober. I go down the street with Lloyd and buy a big mob of fish'n'chips for everyone.

As we walk down Acland Street there is a ladder. Some bloke working on the sign above his shop. Lloyd is very careful not to walk under the ladder. I don't care. We eat fish'n'chips and drink coke. The adults are all into VB now. I don't have one. Lloyd notices that I drink coke. I take Lloyd shopping. He asks if he can bring his lil mate Sammy-Boy. I hug him.

Yeah, he can come.

We grab a cab to the city. The boys love the cab ride.

You from up north? the driver asks me.

The boys giggle in the back.

Swan Hill is north, I say.

The boys giggle some more. We want to go and see *Spiderman* but it hasn't opened yet. We buy some tickets for *Star Wars III* or whatever it is and then go shopping.

We walk around the middle of the city. I have to walk quickly to keep up with them. Lloyd and Sammy-Boy negotiate the heavy traffic on the footpath and the road with consummate ease. I occasionally struggle.

I've never felt right at home in a city. Too much of a station boy at heart. When I see the city skyline, I always think it looks foreign somehow. As if humans couldn't have built such a thing. Shouldn't have.

We go to the Nike shop. Buy a jacket. Some pants. The staff are wankers who follow us around but don't seem to want to help. Whatever Lloyd wants, they don't have it in his size. They don't seem like they're looking very hard.

We go down the road to the MSD. Get runners. Some for Sammy-Boy too. I know what it's like to have two sons. Let them choose. Get footy boots, shorts, socks.

Lloyd won't try anything on. It takes me ten minutes to convince him to try on the footy boots. Won't get a Collingwood jumper, they don't have a long-sleeved one. And we get a footy. Get the shop kids to pump it up hard for us. Get a big bag to put it all in.

The Rat knew what he was talking about.

We walk back to the movies, carrying our packages. We buy ice-creams, huge drinks, a tub of popcorn that Lloyd and Sammy-Boy could take a bath in. The boys love the film. I find it slow. The young Darth Vader is boring.

Back on the street. We only go a block before we run into Lloyd's cousin. He's standing on the corner where Freddy and I got pulled over by that young cop. We remember each other from him coming to our place in St Kilda.

I remember the first time I saw this fulla. We were at home and watching TV.

I feel like some popcorn, says Lloyd suddenly out of the blue.

Well, a few minutes go by, no-one thinks anything of it. Then our doorbell goes. We go down there and it's Lloyd's cousin.

Ah, this Lloyd's house?

Yep. How ya goin?

Good. Look, I was just going by and wondered if Lloyd wanted this popcorn?

And he held out an opened bag of popcorn, not much had been eaten.

Eh. Thanks. Ya wanna come in?

Nah. Gotta keep movin. Check ya.

And goes. And Lloyd has his popcorn. We laughed. Not because we were surprised.

Anyway, now we meet his cousin on the street corner.

What's in the bag?

Nothin.

Got ten, Cuz?

Lloyd's cousin is older. I'd given Lloyd fifty earlier on for himself. I gave it to him sneaky way, so no-one would see. Leaned in close to speak.

This is for you, Lloyd. Not everyone. Just your own money.

Lloyd smiles up at me and the banana disappears.

Now Lloyd is looking away.

Got nothin, Cuz.

Cousin Roy playfully punches Lloyd's upper arm.

Carn, lil Cuz.

Got nothin.

We shake hands goodbye and go to Flinders Street. Lloyd's uncle and Uncle Elton are there. The two Uncles are both drinking. I get introduced. They all remember me from before and stand to hug me. All around the commuters scurry past in their rent and mortgage hazes. Uncle Elton shakes my hand. Then he lifts his hand high and brings it back down quickly to hover just above mine. Uncle stares me hard in the eye.

Don't hate your father.

I don't.

You don't understand.

No.

You don't need to.

And Uncle releases me and grabs Lloyd in a hug. Everyone loves Lloyd. The flower of the Wemba Wemba.

We go and jump in a cab. The cabby looks nervous. I 'accidentally' flash money in my wallet as I put it into my pocket. Pre-emptive strike. Like announcing to any available women you're working with that you're married-up, just to avoid confusion later on. The cabby settles down.

As we go around the corner the boys wave to their Uncles. The Uncles wave back.

There is a young kid who has broken his skateboard clean in half and is doing tricks on the two halves like unicycle rollerskates. Lloyd and Sammy-Boy know this kid. He is a famous graffiti artist. They yell out to him, then give him the finger, then all crack up. And we're back in St Kilda in the park and it's dark and cold. When Lib and Lisa see all Lloyd's loot they want me to come back tomorrow and take them shopping.

Workin tomorrow, I say.

I have a beer with Big Connor. Lisa gets picked up by the co-op bus to get taken to the dentist. There are two bodies passed out on the ground. Gubs. Everyone politely steps over them. Auntie Pringhael Esmae and BJ leave. Lloyd and Sammy-Boy kick the footy under the lights in the park. Lib goes to the pokies. I kiss and hug Lloyd and go. Tell him he's welcome to stay with us in WA anytime.

Family, I say.

Lloyd nods. I go home and tell the Rat all about my day. He's happy for me.

I'd planned to spend Lloyd's money on him. But in the end I used mostly my own. Save some for Lloyd in case it rains a bit harder. Gets a bit colder. I'm happy. I know why I had to stay an extra week in Melbourne doing this TV gig.

After all these years

So Henry and I have this gig in mainstream TV. It's an old story. The sausage factory constantly needs new blood. It's a tough ep to shoot — multi-layered set-ups and interlacing action aplenty. So they get Henry. He's probably the best film director in the country not yet poached by H. Wood.

We're on set. Cold day in Wathaurong Country. Near the borders with Boonwurrung and Woiwurung Country. The crew seem a little afraid of Henry. Not sure how to take him.

Then the first assistant director turns off his radio at a crucial moment and stops listening to his director. All the action is taking place inside this big workshop and Henry's only means of communication from where he sits at the video-split is the radio.

This is a precarious time for the guest director. The regular crew will take over if they get half a chance. Maybe Henry's got this ep because he is an uppity Koori. Certainly at rehearsal we suddenly had all these extra producers looking in. I've done guest roles on this show eight times before and I've never seen these producers at rehearsal previously.

Anyway, Henry gives his instructions to the first AD and

nothing happens. Henry is staring at the video-split. The crew not involved in the immediate shot are close by. Everyone is looking very casual and relaxed. Henry suddenly explodes.

Fuck me dead! He's turned off his fucken radio! Fuck me! Fuck me!

Jesus, the crew sit up like they've had a hot poker shoved up their collective moom. People fall over each other running to fix up the problem. The menace in his voice unmistakable. After they've all scattered, Henry flicks me the tiniest of smiles: That put the wind up these lazy gubbah cunts, eh?

I turn away so no-one sees me laughing to myself. We're the crazy underground bulls and they've let us in here. The china shop.

Later, I'm holding this old double-barrelled shotgun I have to point at the jungais. This beautiful young actress drifts over to have a look.

Pretty safe with me shooting, I quip. Couldn't hit a dunny wall from the inside.

The actress laughs. Moves away.

Only good for shooting Kooris.

I turn to the voice. The gun-man, Jeff. I remember his smile that day when I had to shoot Freddy. Out in Wiljali Country. His quiet remark.

Good shot.

Why don't you say that a bit louder? You'll be catching spears with your chest.

Jeff looks at me. The beginnings of a smile. Not sure if I'm joking or not. My voice is light. I'm not joking. If eyes were weapons I'd be noticing a huge bloody hole in the centre of Jeff's forehead right now.

Ya gotta fight hate with love, that Old Uncle always says. (From Henry's play.)

Later, I'm eating lunch with two security guards. Henry moves past, his restless energy draws the eyes of the bull-necked gubs.

Is he still angry?

Nah. Reckon he's a friendly native now.

Even though Henry is thirty metres away, they speak overly quietly. I finish my lunch. Walk down to the set to smoke with Henry. I've finished all my tobacco. Botting off Henry.

Anyone say anything?

Henry is my brother. My djaambi. He's asking me. I have to tell him. So I repeat what I've overheard. Why can't I learn to keep my fucken gubbah mouth shut? I see that sad come into his eyes.

After all these years, still hurts.

I look down. Light the cigarette he's just given me.

Later I see Henry talking quietly with the gun-man. Teaching. This is what Henry does. We feel strange working with all these gubs. We laugh about it. Makes me feel weird. I don't get them. Can't work em out. They don't make sense. That taunt from my childhood haunts me at these moments.

You gotta work out whose side you on!

But I already knew. Henry and I concentrate on doing what we do best in the china shop.

Smash!

Smash!

Ooops.

Adult conversations

Wudjari Country, Coomalbidgup. I'm about five years old. I often find myself tuning in to adult conversations whenever they talk of the Wongi stockmen, like what they said about Bart.

… he has to get initiated.

… it's barbaric. They cut them.

… he's gotta do it.

… someone should stop them.

… ya can't. It's their way.

… they cut their private parts.

Or the stories about Bart, always imitating his way of talking English.

How many cattle go through, Bart?

Aaaah … bout … aaaah … porty-seven somethin.

English wasn't Bart's first or second language.

Does your raindance work, Bart?

Dis raindance always work! … Sometimes take pew days … Sometimes week … Sometimes month … Once took three year (laughs)! … Always work (laughs) … Dis rain dance always work (laughs)!

And the station manager, a moleskins-Range-Rover-lives-in-town station man, would get pissed and, as a party piece, do the raindance Bart taught him.

Saw him once, through the legs of stockmen, at a party up at the shearers' quarters. I didn't get it. I thought, if everyone likes the dance so much and, you know, the way they talk is so funny and that, why aren't Bart and his Mob invited to the piss-up barbecue?

Once, my brother and I saw the Wongi stockmen marking the young steers. They'd cut out those bullock testicles, chuck them straight onto a hot plate and then gobble them down still-hot. Even the wadjula fullas were eating them. We thought it was yuk. Just the immediacy of it all was somehow shocking to our young eyes.

I always knew that Bart had seen me looking. I thought him old and wise at the time — but I realise now that he musta been a young fulla — if he was just going through Law around about then.

On the couch with Family

My last night in Boonwurrung Country for a while. I'm sitting on the couch at Henry's place. Flight home in the morning. Henry's stuff all around me. Henry's uncle on the wall with his Gubbah djaambi. Smiling down. In uniform. Squinting a little bit under the Palestinian sun. I toast them both with my beer. And my vodka.

Henry had to go to work. Left me all alone with my moorroops. Bin drinkin. Listening to CDs. Playing guitar. I'm worse when I'm drunk. Which is saying something, cause I'm terribly average when I'm sober. Drinking some more. Really wounded.

I blink and there is a big mob here. Gunditj and other Kooris all around. Smokin. Drinkin. Yarnin up big. I'm slurring my words. Slurping my worms. Henry is cackling at me slouched in a puddle on the couch here. Henry's niece gets her bloke to cook up some spaghetti. I resist. Well, I try. You ever try to resist them Gunditjmara women? Henry tried to get me to eat earlier on. I think I told him to fuck off. He laughed like he just heard Little Johnny Sorry-Sorry say Sorry. So now his niece makes me eat. I protest but end up eating a heap.

The room stops spinning enough for my drunken eyes to notice how beautiful these Gunditjmara girls are. I think Henry's niece goes to flirt with me. I call her Uncle. Claim my unity with her Old Man. Claim family. Henry is still laughing. I reach down the couch and hold hands with Lance, my Tharawal brother.

I blink and I'm all alone. Everyone else has gone to bed. Alone with my ghosts. My moorroops. I look up to Djaambi and Gubbah Djaambi smiling down at me from Palestine, 1943. I share my last cigarette with them. Then lie down on the couch and fall fast asleep.

Right where Jesus got the nail

Kaurna Country, Adelaide. I'm working on this play about Artists vs Governments. It's my day off and I'm walkin down the street. This fulla is crossing my path. Him and his Mob leaving the shade near the wall to the governor's residence. Hittin out up town.

Hey.

His voice low deep down there.

Hey, Coorda, I say.

His eyes fairly light up.

You got smoke, Bro?

Rollies.

Can you roll him?

I'm taking out my pouch. I offer it to him.

Me roll, or you roll?

This fulla opens his hand to show me. There is an old wound there. Not that old. Still hasn't healed. Right where Jesus got the nail.

Can't roll. Think, maybe stab wound?

It's almost like he's asking me to confirm what made this wound. I roll a cigarette. No filter. Fat as I can make it.

I'm not from here.

I look up suddenly. I know for sure I was forming that question in my head.

I'm Heath.

Steve.

Pete, ya say?

Steve.

Steve.

What Mob you? Arrernte?

Warlpiri.

Heath really lights up now. I hand him the cigarette. Suddenly his brow grows dark and his eyes seem to be madly searching for a weapon.

But we Northern Warlpiri! Not those fucken Southern Warlpiri!

I smile. Heath definitely don't want to be mistaken for no Southern Warlpiri Mob. Staunch.

You don't look nothin like them, Bro.

Heath laughs at my parting shot.

Nukunya (take care), Brother.

Yeah, nukunya, Brother, I say.

We shake hands. Heath is gone. Borne away by some crazy wind up a concrete street.

Later on, I confess this encounter to Henry on the phone.

Yeah, us mob've got friends all round Australia!

And laughs. Laughs like a steam-train with all boilers firing. I laugh too.

The Bro

Just get home from work. Still in Kaurna Country. My family are in Perth, Wajuk Country. There are at least twelve Countries between us. You work away when you have to. Tired. I switch on the TV. Seinfeld. Old ep. The Man Bra. The Bro.

As I watch my skin starts to crawl and I catch myself sliding down this embankment. Rocks. Covered in thin moss. Moss is wet by rain. Or mist from the sea. Or tears from the People. I don't know. All I know is I can't get a grip. No purchase and down I slide into the darkness below. I think of Djaambi. Pray he's not watching. With the time difference between here and Boonwurrung Country, it has already screened there. I phone Henry. Engaged.

This ep of Seinfeld was a sound cue in Djaambi's play. The main character played by the Rat watches TV with his mates, me and my Charcoal Club mate, Arthur. Sitting on his couch, sipping his beer, he can't stop his mind wandering back to the cold metal in the morgue. The cold body lying on the metal.

Jack: Another death. Another fucken eulogy.

His mates try in vain to keep him in the room with them.

They don't know where he's goin. Where he's been.

My phone rings. Family. I need to speak to my family. Lonely this week. Biggest chat. Put down the phone. Feelin good. It rings again. Little Big Man. My Wiradjuri little brother. We yarn up. One of his kids has been sick but apart from that his mob are good.

I share with my brother my own feeling of dread when we had to call a doctor out to three-year-old Charlotte in the middle of the night. She's alright, too. Little Big Man has bought a mountain-top block which he wants to move to. I think Woiwurung or Taungurong Country. Get the bush growing again. Fruit and vegies as well. Get out of town. Listen to the birds.

By the time I finally ring Djaambi back it is too late to talk. He has passed out. I wake him.

You right, Djaambi?

His words are slow, slurred.

Oh, I got fucken pissed.

I let him go back to sleep. I can't stop it happening to him. Just wanted to let him know I was here and him on my mind.

Speak to him the next morning. He never even watched fucken Seinfeld. There ya go, eh? There ya fucken go.

Welcome to Country

I ring up Mum in Gunditjmara Country, Portland, Victoria. Seeing as how I'm so close, just in Adelaide, Mum invites me down for the weekend. I can fly straight to Mount Gambier.

I get in late Friday night. Drive down to Portland from Mount Gambier in my hire car. Pick up Mum. Out to Darling Downs. We light the fires and open a bottle of red. There is something so basic about chopping wood and lighting a fire. Something so good. Yarn-up time now.

Mum welcomes me to her Country. This is my first time. And I feel welcome. It's a feeling I can't really explain here. It just is. Maybe it's strange for Mum, too. To have this skinny gubbah calling her Mum. Asking questions like a child. Hungry for knowledge. Mum is different in her own Country.

When the ships first come, them Old People knew they were coming. Felt it coming.

This force of destruction. Force of blood and poison.

The dogs were crazy for days. Old People were all dyin. Young fullas sharpening axes.

Knew they couldn't stop this force of strange pale men.

They knew, Mum says again into the crackling fire.

Hours later Henry arrives. He has three car-loads with him. Elizabeth, a Palawa woman and her three kids, his ex, his son and his step-daughter. Don't get too caught up in these labels. We yarn up and finally go to bed at 4.00 am. Time is relative.

Next morning I sleep in. When I get up my Palawa sister cooks me bacon'n'eggs. Makes me a cigarette and a coffee. As we smoke together in the morning sun two Waa fly across our front, south to north.

One for sorrow, two for joy, Elizabeth says.

We watch them fly until they disappear.

That's my totem, Crow, Elizabeth says.

I nod. The crow tattoo on my back, the Great Mother Goddess in her final powerful phase of life, the Morrigan, seems to itch or tickle me under my shirt, as if she ruffled her feathers. I say nothing of this.

Elizabeth tells me I have the soul of an Old Fulla. One of the People.

I'm flattered but also feel strange about this. Confused. My people are from Ireland and Cornwall. Liz's people from Ireland and Scotland. I'm proud of my heritage. If I have the soul of one of them Old People — then my journey would be one of coming home. But this is not how this path feels. Not coming home. Seeking home would be a better description.

Even though that Wudjari Country (Esperance, Coomalbidgup) calls to me in my dreams — when my body goes back to dust and water I will fly there — this doesn't mean I can say it is my Country. Those are words for a traditional owner. A Wudjari man. I am of that place. I can hear its song even though I can't sing it. See? Confusing.

And I mean no disrespect to my Palawa sister by saying this.

She is an extraordinary woman. Bringing up three kids on her own. Holding down three jobs in between mothering. Every morning she meditates on making the best of this day. Taking this day for what it is and living it to the hilt. Every night checking herself that she had the best day she could have. You know, she's got nothin. Her children are her wealth. Her joy.

Mum and Henry arrive back from town. We yarn. Laugh. This place rings with laughter. Since time immemorial. The wave-crash of the sea ever-present.

You wanna go for a cruise, Steve? See Country?

Mum touches me on the arm and points with her lips back along the coast.

Djaambi is busy with kids and that. I stand and stretch. Finish my cigarette.

We jump in the hire car. A few minutes down the road we see a hawk fly off to the north. Waa sits on a fence-post to the south. My eyes go past him to the strip of land between us and the sea. Mum only glances out that way. Then eyes ahead.

Convincing Ground.

I nod. Mum is heavily involved in the fight for all this Country. Her Country. A hundred and sixty years ago, when the gun and spear and rope and axe and rape and poison war was in full swing, this is the place where the Gunditjmara POWs and non-combatants were brought to 'convince' them to come in, stop fighting and abandon Country. A secret and bloody war. None of the POWs ever returned after being 'convinced'. Like the Native Police 'dispersing' Murri and Gurrie Mobs further north. This killing field is now up for freehold sale. The gubbah owners get wind that the People are interested in the land and overnight the price doubles.

This hotel chain is interested in it, too.

Wouldn't want to stay there, Mum. Pretty hard to sleep.

Mum smiles at my hard little joke.

We talk constantly as the car hums along the bitumen. We drive out to the high ground behind the Alcoa monstrosity and park the car. Get out. Look out to sea. Past the Gannet Rocks I can make out Denmaar low and flat in the ocean. Spirits of Gunditjmara Mob journey to the Dreaming through this island. Its song hums in Mum's veins.

We go west along the coast. We stop for fruit juice. We sit on the bonnet looking at this beautiful expanse of beach. Mum is telling me about how her People hunted whales here.

And we're back in the car driving around to the petrified forest.

As the road goes up the first hill it cuts right through a huge midden. For tens of thousands of years, hundreds and hundreds of generations, Mum's Mob gathered in this spot to eat their day's catch of seafood. Shells are clearly visible where the earth has been cut for the road. Obviously it must have been very difficult to make the road go around such a site.

When will Australians realise that this is the heritage of all of us? This is part of all our culture now. Not the just-built-the-day-before-yesterday temples and churches and museums of Europe. That place of alcohol and blood is just where we gubbahs came from.

As we drive we see two more birds of prey. As if I didn't already know this was a Spirit Journey.

As I drove down from the Mount last night there were signs along the highway telling me to watch out for roos. But I see none until I cross into Gunditjmara Country. Then one by the side of the road. She is waiting for me. Mum's totem is kangaroo. I was going to ring to say I'm running late because of the late plane but know I don't have to. A few clicks down the road I see another on the other side of the road. Same thing. Calmly stands to watch me pass. No thought for moving. Mum. I switch off the radio and sing 'Warinor' at the top of my lungs to announce my presence. This is a Wiradjuri song that travelled south-west thousands of years ago. Cultures that trade in songs, not futures, stocks and bonds.

The hire car flies through the heavy mist — like I'm sitting on a horse that knows the way home. If I wanted to I could climb into the back seat for a sleep. Ha! I don't. Not for me to test these boundaries.

As we pull down into the carpark above the cliffs and the petrified forest, I think I see a little brown bird flutter out from the side of the road. I think we clipped him with the car.

Fuck.

I back up.

Did we hit him? I wonder.

No.

But I'm still not sure. I feel a little shaken up.

No, Mum says again.

I get out of the car to check. A single fluffy brownish feather drifts in the breeze. I check under the car. Nothing. The low coastal scrub. No. I get back in.

Just rubbish, says Mum.

I look at the road and see a rolled-up brown paper bag right on the spot where I thought the car hit him. Didn't notice it before.

Maybe moorroop, I'm thinking.

We walk down to the cliff edge. This is the cliff edge from

Henry's play. Where our man Jack confronts his demons. Challenges the spirits from the core of his being.

Two or three hundred metres below us the heavy seas from Bass Strait smash into the edge of the continent.

When The War was raging in this Country, this is where they tracked that Old Fulla to. That old warrior. They hunted him for twenty years and couldn't catch him.

He'd creep past shepherds at night and break the legs of hundreds of sheep. Not kill them. Just break their front legs. The shepherds would get a flogging and the overseer would have to shoot all the sheep. That old warrior knew to hit them in the hip pocket. And the next morning he was gone. Vanished like mist as the sun comes up.

So they reckon they had him cornered here. Country is pretty open. No place to hide. He just disappeared. I'm sure plenty of Gunditjmara Men know where he went. Not a question for me to ask. Not today.

I get that feeling and sneak a look over my left shoulder. Nothing. No-one. Mum sees me. A tiny nod. We know.

We walk around the forest. Trees that were alive tens of thousands of years ago. A huge thick forest of moonah trees. Mum's People were here then. The whole place is literally littered with artefacts. Trees are turned to stone now. They'll be here for tens of thousands of years to come. Same as Mum's Mob. Always been here. Always will be. I get that feeling again. Mum nods at me.

Moorroops, she says quietly.

We turn as one and move back to the car. Pass two Japanese tourists taking photos. A couple of other blokes who look like professionals.

Magazines shoot this area all the time, says Mum.

We drive off.

You wanna see the mish?

I nod. I do. We head out there. It's a lovely drive. Back the way I drove in last night.

Just before we get to Heywood, where Mum was born, we come across this Waa on the road. But this fulla, he's not eating roadkill, he's just strutting back and forth, his feathers glinting all metallic in the sun. Our car is bearing down on him at one hundred kilometres an hour — he just looks up at us and puffs out his chest. Staring us down. That same look that Mum or Djaambi gives me when we both know exactly what is going down and no words are necessary. This fulla knows me too well. I brake heavily and swerve around him. In my mirrors I see that he is still there once we pass. Mum and I laugh.

How bout that fulla?

Djaambi is Crow totem. Me too. Bart Billon put the Crow on me. Painted now on my back with thousands of needle pricks.

We drive through Mum's birthplace. Mum wishes she'd been born by the coast. Not this one-horse town full of miserable rednecks. None of us know the why of these things.

We pull into Three Waterholes Road. There is a lump in my throat. The road is bituminised now. Not how I remember it. But then, I've never been here before. There is a huge echidna on the road. I slow. I stop. Back the car up to look at him. He is a beauty. Big fat fulla. Never seen one in the wild before. Mum tells me he is big one. Been asleep most of the winter.

Good eating, too.

We take off again. I'm keen to get there. It's a fair way out.

The mission. Away from prying eyes. Just like Convincing Ground. Mum is quiet now. She doesn't like coming out to the mish.

I starved out here, she says matter-of-factly.

The mission rations would be sold off by the administrators, then nothin for the People.

We pull in to the mish. We cruise slowly down the hill. There is a little transportable office there. We see some fullas there. Mum's eyesight is poor at this distance now.

Who are they, Son? Gubbah?

No, Mum. Mob.

I indicate with my lips. (You know. Proper.)

One of the fullas waves. Mum waves back.

We'll say g'day, Son.

I turn the car around and we cruise up. Two of Mum's brothers and one nephew. We get out and say g'day. Hugs. Handshakes. I get introduced to the uncles and the nephew. We get invited to the house. Mum and Uncle William have a beer. The older uncle leaves. The woman of the house makes me a cup of tea. It's a welcome.

Mum and Uncle William have business to talk. Land-claim business. Gas pipeline royalties for traditional owners. I drink my tea. I have a smoke outside on the balcony. This is not talk for me to contribute to.

In response to Uncle's glance in my direction, Mum nods to him that it's all right to talk in front of me. Gunditjmara politics is personal and passionate. All Mob politics is this way. At one point, in response to something Uncle William says, Mum comes out with:

Oh, same old fucken story! A little mob of gubbahs trying to ride on our backs — keep all the money for themselves!

Mum looks over at me.

No offence, Son.

None taken, Mum.

We share a secret smile. Tiny and fleeting. The conversation moves on.

Uncle William is a hard man. Tough man of the old school. No school. A warrior.

When Uncle and Mum have talked long time, Uncle tells me we are going for a drive. Him and me.

Uncle has the same name as my father. Coonbana — same name. I warm to him. We sit in the car. We talk. Well, I'm listening now. The place of the nephew.

Uncle refers to Mum's conversation about starving out here, in her childhood. Uncle tells me the president of the United States, not the current one, but his father, once described Australia as the most corrupt country in the developed world. When the government has tried to starve you, destroy you, it isn't easy to forget. Looking at the old mission buildings brings it all flooding back. Corrupt at every level of government. The Rum Corps never really went away. Just changed currency. Changed names. Changed hats.

Uncle is telling me he read an excerpt from the Captain's Log of a ship that sailed from Adelaide to Melbourne in the early 1830s. The ship's captain thought that the entire shoreline was on fire when night came. All he could see was one continual line of glowing red and orange for hundreds and hundreds of kilometres, from Kaurna Country, past Ngarrindjeri, Gunditjmara, Giraiwurung, Gadubanud and into the entrance to Port Phillip between the twin points of

Wathaurong and Boonwurrung Land. This captain decided to sail in closer to the land to observe this massive bushfire for himself. Of course, as the ship sailed in closer to the shore, the captain realised that it wasn't a bushfire but many, many, individual cooking fires.

Uncle takes a sip of beer. For a moment, I don't get what Uncle means. Then it dawns on me. The sheer numbers of the People.

Fuck. I'm starting to feel funny about calling what happened the Land Wars. I mean, it flows better than the Land Holocaust — but maybe isn't as accurate. Would we call what happened in Cambodia a war? Fuck. We are a bloody lot. The truth about those temples and churches and museums in Europe is that they're all built on foundations of congealed blood.

Uncle directs me to drive down to the mission proper. We park the car on the hill overlooking the river. The old tumble-down bluestone buildings look like they were in use five hundred years ago, not the place where Mum and Uncle William grew up, cold and hungry in their own Country.

You see them rocks …

Uncle points with his chin and lips. Across the river to the thick scrub where the ground is strewn with piles of volcanic rock, like huge piles of large dark bricks, left behind by the cosmic builders. Put there for a purpose.

They stretch for long way. Up to the mountain.

We look north-east in the direction of the Grampians.

Way down.

We look back towards the coast.

Those rocks are the reason the People are here today.

Uncle sips his beer. Drags on his cigarette. I take out my rollies as I wait for it. I'm controlling my breathing too. Not sure what is coming. I finish my cigarette and put it in my mouth. Light it up. My eyes are on the sparkling water. I know that eels from the river are what kept Mum and Uncle alive when they were being starved.

See, they couldn't get their horses in there because of the rocks. Come in after us on foot in close country …

Uncle chuckles to himself as if remembering some past battle. I wouldn't go in there after Uncle on foot if I had a repeating rifle and Uncle had a spear and an axe. You should hear that little chuckle. No fucken way.

Couldn't poison the river because it comes up from underground and flows too much for them. One time they blocked it off.

Uncle gives another little chuckle.

It just went underground.

Like the People?

Like the People.

Uncle nods his approval of me understanding the lesson. Them Uncles always teaching. Always testing.

After a long while, these killers just gave up and went away. Another gubbah got this Land. He started to cross the river to talk to us. To trade. Got friendships going. Then he built a massive church. Oh. The biggest church you ever saw. And he starts encouraging People to come. He was Church of England, now. Then gradually they get everyone out of the bush and start up the mish.

Out of the stones?

Out of the stones. The same stones. Our life stones.

Uncle talks more about the river now. Of course, the meaning of the river and the stones to the People goes far beyond the last five minutes of history, since gubbahs came. Uncle tells me these things because of Mum. Treats me as a Man. As Family. I don't take this privilege lightly.

After a while Uncle stops talking. We look until our cigarettes are finished. Third one while sitting here.

I turn the car around and we head back. Over near the new buildings we see this other fulla. Uncle inclines his head slightly in this fulla's direction so I swing the car down and park under a huge tree. We get out. I wait while he and Uncle greet each other.

Alex is a big fulla. Warm eyes. Soft voice. Hands and body covered in prison tatts. Swallow on his right hand. The mark of the solitary survivor. Uncle introduces me.

Alex, this is Pete.

Steve.

Eh?

Steve.

I laugh. Doesn't matter here. Alex shakes my hand. He is a veteran of The War. His handshake is light and cool. Crisp as new linen. We yarn little bit, then go back up to the house to Mum.

We all say our goodbyes, and then we drive back down Three Waterholes Road, along the coast and back to Mum's place in town.

Later, we head out to see Henry do his gig. He is singing with Arthur at The Lighthouse. Henry calls them The Charcoal Club — for burnt-out Kooris and singed gubbahs. Then laughs, of course. I've never known anyone to laugh as much as Henry. My djaambi.

He gets me up to sing. I expect it now. I love it.

We go back to Darling Downs, the little farm Henry has bought in the Country of his Ancestors. Sit up late. Telling moorroop stories. They're funny and scary. But after a while we have to stop. Talking about them will definitely get them interested.

They'll come to have a look, Mum says matter-of-factly, looking out into the dark Gunditj night as if expecting them Old People to be standing there, watching us. Maybe they are.

I go to bed. Sharing a room with Arthur, my Charcoal Club brother, and Jed, my Palawa nephew.

The lad is whimpering in his sleep. He's at that age where soon he will leave boyhood behind. I project my spirit through my back to give him that Uncle-love. Father-love he's never known. After a little while his breathing is back to normal. I am exhausted by the effort. Strange that being on Mum and Djaambi's Land is reawakening my spirit.

Next morning is Father's Day. My Palawa tidda (sister) makes me bacon'n'eggs and coffee. I ring my dad on my mobile phone, then I drive Mum back to town. She has to visit her nephew. We have lunch. I drop Mum off.

We both hate goodbyes. I head back to Adelaide. Back to work.

We take off from Mount Gambier. Flying north-west over Buandig Country. The coastline just to the south. The sun is still in the sky so I can see the Country clearly. I'm seeing a line of fires. Cooking fires. Fires for warmth. Unbroken to Adelaide. They aren't there now. But I see them anyway. My heart is heavy for leaving Gunditjmara Country. This is the nature of Family.

In the system

I'm back in WA, Wajuk Country. Libby rings me. Lloyd played footy on the weekend in Geelong. Wathaurong Country. He was seen by Kevin Sheedy, the coach of Essendon, and Mick Malthouse, the coach of Collingwood. Kevin wanted to sign Lloyd up to the under-fifteens. Mick too. Kevin was comparing Lloyd to Jimmy Krakouer. I felt great. Libby had a house and was out of the park. A doorway was materialising for Lloyd.

Only bad thing, BJ has been locked up for warrants, Libby says.

So I decide to ring the Rat to tell him my news about Lloyd. I can't believe it. Maybe our shopping spree started something, or rekindled something. Maybe I'm gunna impose on him to visit BJ. I want people to visit. BJ isn't a bad lad. Not violent. Shouldn't be in the system. In prison, casual violence is a way of life. A currency.

BJ just hangs on the street to be with his mum. Same way Lloyd.

Lloyd dutifully told me that he was goin back to school when I took him shopping. I just smiled at him. Where Libby goes, he's gotta go. Culture. Deeper than Culture. Like he already knows about the Big Nothing. There is nothing else. Even drugs can't erode that. Not that Lloyd is doing drugs. The odd cone. He's too smart. He's seen what King and Robby can do sober.

I don't wanna see BJ lost.

The Rat answers the phone. His voice is low and flat.

Yeah.

It's Stevey, Bruz.

Hey, Bruz.

You right, Bruz?

You read the papers?

Nu.

Oh, shit. I was gunna ring ya last night but it was too late.

And he tells me. One of our circle has gone down. Suicide. In Eora Country, Sydney. A talented man. A strong man. A good man. Another good one lost (from Henry's play). I didn't know this fulla. Met him once. He was one of us. Standing in the light. Gone now.

Coulda been me, says the Rat suddenly.

Silence.

Or you, Bruz.

The Rat apologises for telling me. Fuck. I put down the phone.

The sad takes a while to come. I'm empty. Then angry. Before the sad hits me I listen to Ned on CD. To Henry. Mary. I need their voices swirling all around me. Pitjantjatjara, Gunditjmara and Yorta Yorta. I think on the terrible grief and loss of my early adulthood. Wonder if this is why I needed to be around people who understand grief. For those who live in The War Zone, and with the ghosts of war zones. Grief is a constant companion, walking hand in hand with his sister, Joy.

I hate this fucken country, I hear myself saying to Liz on the phone.

Same country giving Lloyd a chance, she says back.

She's up north, in Fitzroy Crossing, interviewing some Gooniyandi women for the ABC show she works for. The women are taking her through baby-smoking ceremonies. Near the border of Nyikina and Gooniyandi Country, just south of Punuba Country.

I ring Robby, my Yorta Yorta brother. Maybe he could visit BJ. By now Robby is in a car on the way north for the funeral. I tell Robby about Lloyd. Robby has been a good Uncle to that lad. A role model. Robby is cautiously pleased. He's in a car with the Rat.

Liz rings me. Tells me to ring Dylan. Feels like he's got the story wrong. I ring Dylan. Tell him I spoke with the Rat who told me.

You spoke to the Rat today?

Yeah. He told me about this other fulla.

Oh, Jesus. I'm at work here. Trying to get my bottom lip off the ground. I thought it was the Rat.

Nah.

Oh, thank fuck. Oh, shit, sorry, Bruz, didn't mean it like that, it's just, I thought, well, fuck, it's still fucked. I better go and get ready for the show. It wasn't him?

He's got too much to do.

I'll tell everyone here.

Alright, Bruz.

You spoke to him today?

Today.

The same conversation my whole life

Night. Wajuk Country. I'm in uniform again. Another show. Another costume. Paying respect to those Old Diggers. I'm having a pre-show cigarette. The security guard sees me and wanders over. Her uniform is dark. Like a cop from LA. I'm in khaki. She stays overnight on our site to watch our gear.

We're doing this show in a huge tent. The play is set in an army camp in 1944 at Mataranka in the Northern Territory, just south of Nitmiluk (Katherine), near where Jarwoyn Wardaman and Yangman Countries meet. They've trucked in red soil from Wangkathaa Country, Kalgoorlie way, for authenticity.

After our first night in the big tent we get burgled. What do they take? Blankets and pillows. It's obviously the Parkie Mob. One of the actors sees the blankets and stuff over under a tree the next day. The designer of the show is keen to get them back. We've got a low budget. Anyway, I was thinking that we could do without the blankets and pillows and it wouldn't make any difference to the drama. But big difference to the Parkie Mob. It's still cold out, this time of year.

So this security guard ambles over.

Having a good night? I ask.

Yeah, better than last night.

I should just let it go. Do I want to know?

Why, what happened? I hear myself dutifully ask. As if I couldn't take an edumacated guess.

These drunken Nyungars attacked me. I got punched a few times. Hit with something.

Shit.

They were hopped-up on drugs or something. Off their faces. Got such a big chip on their shoulders.

Yeah, they've had it tough.

You know, it's like they think it's *their country*!'

And she makes inverted comma signs in the air with her fingers.

It *is* their country.

It's our country, too.

I know.

Yeah, but, you know, they've got such a chip. Like, you know, the world owes them a living.

Yeah, they've been treated badly.

Jeez, I've been treated badly and I'm not like that.

And you can see the real pain that this woman has survived, shining in her eyes like a beacon fire on a distant hill on a clear cool night. I smoke my ciggie. She is looking at me now. Suddenly wondering what my angle is. Her head cocked at a tiny angle. Aren't we all on the same team?

I want us to be. I really do.

I've been having this same conversation my whole fucken life.

Tonight I'll be doing my play. Pretending to sleep on blankets. That Park Mob will be sleeping out. In the same Country that their great-great-great-great-great-great-great-great-great-grandmothers camped in. They've got no blankets. They're dying of third-world diseases. I've got my house that I've worked hard to pay for.

We gotta stop thinkin it's either-or, us wadjulas. No people want what is ours. Just what is theirs.

As Aussie as you are

Late night in Wajuk Country. Just done the army show. Catching a bus home. Long wait. City is deserted. The bus comes. When I get on there are two pissed rednecks sitting up the back. I wander down and sit a few seats away.

Owyagoin?

The bigger redneck with the goatee calls out to me. I nod politely and sit. They're not sure where to place my 1940s army haircut. I take out my book to read. A little Asian girl gets on after me. Sits a few seats in front. The rednecks start up straightaway. You know, shit under their breath. The girl is about four foot nothing, wearing glasses. Her body language contracts like a sea anemone as she hears them start. I guess she's heard it all before. Finally, one of these brave men speaks up.

Why don't ya go back to ya own fucken country?

All I can think is, this is not Australia. This is not what we stand for. What we want. Is it? Is this really us?

I try to read my book. A biography about a great writer. It comes again from behind me. This time a real nasty snarl in the voice.

Why don't ya fuck off back to ya own fucken country?

Why don't you?

I hate it when my mouth just takes off without waiting for my brain. What made these bastards so angry? The under-the-breath muttering stops. There is a silence.

What, Mate?

I close my book and turn around to face them.

I'm not your fucken mate. And I said, why don't *you* fuck off back to *your* fucken country?

They look pretty confused. This isn't in the script.

This is my fucken country.

I look right through this lad. I was worried. But now I see these blokes are as weak as piss. My voice is from another time and place.

I fucken doubt it.

I'm as Aussie as you are, Mate.

Exactly.

The little Asian girl quietly gets up and gets off the bus. Won't be another one for another hour. I turn and watch her go. I open my book. There are a few mutterings from behind me. But quieter than before. Half of me is really hoping they'll say something to me. They don't. The bus moves off. I'm sick of all these wankers giving the rest of us a bad name. Fucken sick of it.

Blind leading the blind

Hot day in Perth. Wajuk Country. Been working in the city. Going home. Catching the train from Perth back to Freo.

A hundred and fifty years ago, when my great-great-grandfather got off the boat, it cost more to travel from Freo to Perth than the entire fare for the passage from England or Ireland. Not that my great-great-grandfather had to pay a fare.

It's a crowded train. I walk on and sit down. Lot of standers. At the last minute about five Nyungars, uncles and aunties get on. They sit this one auntie down and everyone is hugging and kissing her. Telling her they love her. Tell her they'll see her again in a few days. Only that one auntie stays. The others all go to step back onto the platform. But the last auntie, she stops at the door — spins on her heel and goes back for one last hug. Sisters. Right then the doors close and the train starts to move off. The leaving auntie runs to the doors and physically tries to open them. Can't. She gets little bit upset. Yells out.

Hey! Open the doors! I wanna git off!

The train starts to pick up speed. Lotta wadjula mooms suddenly tighten up when this middle-aged Nyungar woman yells out.

I wanna git off! I wanna git off!

Auntie gives up. Laughs it off to herself. Goes back to kiss her sis. The love between them strong. All they got. There is nothin else. My eyes tear up. I look away. Shame job.

We get to the first stop. Auntie squeezes her sis's hand, turns and dances off the train.

That big silver slug pulls out and clatters down the coast to Freo. The carriage empties out a bit. No standers now but still plenty of sitters.

I'm looking west. Out to sea. It's a clear day. You can see Rotto and Gage Roads. Those invaders crash-landed out here. Them old wadjulas got stuck out there on Garden Island for a while too. And later they used Rottnest as a prison for the Nyungar POWs. Took them warriors out there to die. Wajuk Men. Pinjarup. Wiilman. Bibbulmun. Wardandi. Nyaki-Nyaki. Except for Pringhael Yagan. And the others like him. Couldn't catch them fullas. Couldn't beat them. Never will.

Auntie hasn't moved during the journey. There are two Nyungar lads sitting near her. Footy socks and basketball shirts and beanies in this heat. They lean forward to talk to each other. Still kids, but with the definite stamp of worldliness on them.

Auntie's security, I catch myself thinking.

A moment after I've thought this, the train stops. Last stop before Freo. The lads amble off the train. Not a look or a word to that Auntie. Don't even know her. What am I? Mr Gub-gub sitting here thinking all Nyungars know each other or they're all related or what? Mr Wadjula Assumption? Mr Fucken Know-all?

As I'm coping with my own shallowness, Auntie opens up a

small leather case and takes out a folded-up plastic stick. She methodically opens the stick section by section until it is fully extended. It's not until this moment that I comprehend that Auntie is blind. Mr Fucken Observation.

The train pulls in to Fremantle station and comes to a stop. A woman in a suit opens the door and steps out. Everyone else in the carriage follows her. Everyone except blind Auntie. And me.

Auntie gets up and, with the stick out in front of her, she feels for the doorway. Finds it. Walks steadily out. I get up and follow. I look up and down the platform. No-one waiting for Auntie. I look to her. She is wandering up to a closed office door. Her walk has slowed. Uncertain. Steps shorter. I ease up next to her. Keep my voice low and soft.

You right, Aunt? Where you tryin to get to?

Oh, my boy. Gotta catch a bus.

Oh. This way, Aunt. Little bit right. Yeah. Straight ahead now.

Auntie takes my arm and we go toward the exit.

What number, Aunt?

Gotta look at pamphlet. Leeming.

I see the stand with the bus timetables. Kind of behind the door.

Left, Aunt. Yeah, straight now.

I grab out the Leeming bus timetable.

Got it, Aunt. Straight out the front.

Thank you, my boy.

We turn. She loops her arm into mine now. I'm not giving instructions. We're just walking. We go out the front exit and make a left. It's the bus stop right down the end. We head on down. We get plenty of stares from wadjulas and Nyungars alike. We could be mother and son. Apart from the obvious. Even then — still could be. I'm remembering walking down the street in Portland with Mum. The looks we got.

Where you from, my boy? What Mob you?

Oh, Lord. My heart races. It's the second time this Auntie has made me tear up in half an hour and I don't even know her. I take a deep breath through my constricted throat.

I'm born Narrogin, Aunt. Grew up Coomalbidgup, near Esperance.

Mmm. Mmm.

We arrive at the stop. As we do, so does the bus.

This is it, Aunt. This your bus.

Thank you, my boy.

Auntie touches me with her fingers on the upper arm. She turns and steps up the stairs of the bus. I turn and walk. I'm torn between pride and shame. Pride because this blind Nyungar auntie took me for one of the Mob. Shame because I was unable to reveal my true identity. This is another feeling I have come to know well.

Can you understand this gubbah? I have strong feeling for Country. For Family. Skin and Blood. Even though I can never really understand these concepts. Just journey towards them. Can I ever escape the fact that my ancestors came across the sea and took this land by force? Destroyed everything held so dear by this blind auntie and all her Mob. Turned Country into prison.

When Auntie asked me 'what Mob', my heart was torn open. Like most Celts, I am pale and sharp-featured. Only a blind Nyungar woman could mistake me for one of her People.

Of course, she asked me because I'd helped her. Not standard wadjula behaviour.

I walk down to the Roundhouse on the shoreline and then almost due east, back up the high street. This is my great-great-grandfather's walk. His first walk in Wajuk Country.

I stop near the mall to give this Old Goreng Fulla a smoke. I roll it for him. He has no teeth. His hands too shaky to roll.

By the time I get home my feet are sore in my nice work shoes, which I'm not really used to, and I'm sweating like a bastard. I get myself a cold beer and smoke a cigarette and watch the sunset.

Greater love hath no man ...

I'm standing in the umpires' race at Subiaco Oval. Wajuk Country. I'm in uniform again. Khaki. I'm on the phone to Mum. Her machine answers.

Hello. You've rung Gunditjmara Country. Please leave a message.

I've gotta talk over the drums and didj. A navy drummer is marching from one end of the oval, while from the other the Nyungar Elder comes out playing didj. The stadium rings out like a giant concrete and steel speaker, with the grass at its core.

Hello, Mum. It's Stephen. I'm in Wajuk Country. Me and Freddy are about to do this thing at the footy. A ceremony to pay tribute to the Nyungar, Yamatji and Wongi returned servicemen. Freddy and I are gunna do a scene from the film, while they're playing it on the big video scoreboard. They've got all these old Diggers. Uncles with their medals on. Have a look on the telly if ya get home. Love to all the Mob.

Freddy is looking up at the scoreboard. The crowd is cheering. I follow his gaze. Shit. There we are. Up there. We're meant to be on the ground at this point. Our crew guy with the walkie-talkie is still waiting for the signal to go.

Freddy just takes off at a full run. I follow. He runs to the centre of the red part of the huge red, black and gold flag, and dies a spectacular death. I go down too and hold him close, my dying mate. A cheer goes up from thirty thousand throats. The hair on our bodies prickles.

The ceremony moves on to the next section. The senior Uncle goes to light the flame of remembrance, his medals reflecting the light from the flame as it catches. Freddy and I stand and move to the edge of the flag.

We look across to Dylan standing with them Old Men. Dylan is the compere for the event. Three Old Fullas to stand for the thousands of others who fought. From World War Two, Korea and Vietnam, and a young fulla who was with INTERFET in East Timor. Medals and ribbons on their proud chests.

The oldest three of these Nyungar Diggers were fighting for a nation in which they were not considered citizens.

The Diggers stand for the Last Post. A great cheer goes up from the stadium as these fullas stand. All around the ground, the other Diggers in the stands rise with them. We've all got lumps in our throats and tears in our eyes.

If we can fight together, maybe we can do anything together, we Australians. These Uncles and that young fulla stand proud. These fullas who fought. Fought for someone else's country. Only the young fulla there fought for his own country. These Old Fullas believed in this country long before this country believed in them.

Later on, when I'm watching the footy from my seats in the members' stand, Djaambi rings me. He is honoured his film was used. I describe the scene of the ceremony to him, the old Nyungar Diggers in the jeeps, taking the salute from the brigadier.

It's good to start something. Something overdue. To be part of it. To fight a good fight. A drop in the ocean that sends out waves across the water in every direction.

Acknowledgements

The author would like to thank the People from the following Nations (in alphabetical order) who, through their generosity, allowed his journey to unfold: Arrernte, Bibbulman, Boonwurrung, Bundjalung, Danggali, Eora, Gooniyandi, Goreng, Gunditjmara, Indinji/Komet, Jarwoyn, Koori, Kurnai (Gunai), Ku-Ku/Merman, Muralag, Murri, Ngan'giwumirra, Ngarrindjeri, Noonuccal, Ngatumay, Nunga, Nyawaygi, Nyikina, Nyungar, Palawa, Pinjarup, Pitjantjatjara, Tharawal, Waka Waka, Warlpiri, Wemba Wemba, Wiilman, Wiljali, Wiradjuri, Wongi (Wangkathaa), Wudjari, Wurundjeri, Yamatji (Watjarri), Yorta Yorta.

All boundaries and spelling of Countries are taken from the *Encyclopedia of Aboriginal Australia* (D Horton, general editor) published in 1994 by Aboriginal Studies Press, except where superseded by local oral history and knowledge (as told to the author).

Copies of *The Aboriginal Australia Wall Map* can be ordered through the Aboriginal Studies Press website:
www.aiatsis.gov.au/asp